became rarer and rarer in the decades following Tanner's remarkable research, the bird was feared to have become extinct. Since 2005, reports of sightings in Arkansas and Florida made headlines and have given new hope to ornithologists and bird lovers, although extensive subsequent investigations have yet to produce definitive confirmation.

Before he died in 1991, Jim Tanner himself had come to believe that the majestic woodpeckers were probably gone forever, but he remained hopeful that someone would prove him wrong. This book fully captures Tanner's determined spirit as he tracked down what was then, as now, one of ornithology's true Holy Grails.

Y0-BDX-146

Ghost Birds

Ghost Birds

Jim Tanner and the Quest for the Ivory-billed Woodpecker, 1935–1941

Stephen Lyn Bales

Foreword by Nancy Tanner

The University of Tennessee Press • Knoxville

Copyright © 2010 by The University of Tennessee Press / Knoxville.
All Rights Reserved. Manufactured in the United States of America.
First Edition.

The paper in this book meets the requirements of American National Standards Institute / National Information Standards Organization specification Z39.48-1992 (Permanence of Paper). It contains 30 percent post-consumer waste and is certified by the Forest Stewardship Council.

All maps are by the author.

Library of Congress Cataloging-in-Publication Data

Bales, Stephen Lyn.
Ghost birds: Jim Tanner and the quest for the ivory-billed woodpecker, 1935–1941 / Stephen Lyn Bales; foreword by Nancy Tanner.
— 1st ed.
p. cm.
Includes bibliographical references and index.

ISBN-13: 978-1-57233-717-6 (hardcover)
ISBN-10: 1-57233-717-6 (hardcover)

1. Tanner, James T. (James Taylor)
2. Ornithologists—United States—Biography.
3. Naturalists—United States—Biography.
4. Ivory-billed woodpecker.
I. Title.

QL31.T346B35 2010
598.092—dc22
[B]
2010024333

To Nancy

This book would simply not exist without her help, encouragement, wise counsel, and dogged determination to keep us moving forward one paragraph at a time.

And she did it all for her husband, Jim Tanner.

Looking for an ivory-bill . . . takes the mediating nature of birdwatching to an even higher level, because in this case the quarry is a kind of ghost bird, a creature that does and does not exist.

—Jonathan Rosen,
The Life of the Skies

Contents

Foreword ix
Nancy Tanner

Prologue: "Someone Needs to Write a Book . . ." 1

1. Sabbatical 5
2. The Journey Begins 15
3. The Swampy South 21
4. The Ghost Bird 33
5. Hot Sauce and Bird City 51
6. Days of Wind and Dust 55
7. Has Anyone Seen a Young Ivory-bill? 61
8. Westward Ho 67
9. Swansong 79
10. On His Own 89
11. Back at Singer 105
12. A Need to Move On 123
13. On the Road Again 129
14. A Second Nesting Season at Singer 135
15. On the Road Again, Again 165
16. From the Santee to the Sunshine State 175
17. Finding Sonny Boy 197
18. I Go Pogo 211
19. The Fellowship Concludes 219
20. At Home in Tennessee 225
21. Our Lives Changed Forever 231
22. Aftermath 243

Epilogue 247

Appendix: Jim Tanner's Itinerary, 1937–1939 255

Author's Note and Acknowledgments 257

Bibliography 259

Index 263

Illustrations

PHOTOGRAPHS

Cornell Students with Peter Paul Kellogg, circa 1934 9
Kellogg, Allen, and Tanner before Leaving on the 1935 Expedition 16
Tanner Using a Parabolic Mirror to Record a Limpkin in Florida 23
A Wagonload of Supplies in Tallulah 37
A Male Ivory-bill, John's Bayou, Singer Tract, 1935 46
Teenager Jim Tanner with a Rescued Golden Eagle 71
Tanner in Front of a Sweet Gum, May 1937 121
Alexander Sprunt Jr. and Jim Tanner in the Santee, Late 1937 130
Site of 1938 Ivory-bill Nest in the Top of a Red Maple 137
Recently Banded Ivory-bill Perching on J. J. Kuhn 143
Charlie the Horse and Jim's 1931 Model a Ford 147
Logging Operations in the Santee Swamp 216
Nancy Burnham Sheedy and Jim Tanner Wedding Picture 235
Tanner in His U.S. Navy Uniform 248

MAPS

1935 Ornithological Expedition 87
Tensas Region 116
Florida Search Sites, 1935–39 193

Foreword

Ghost Birds by Stephen Lyn Bales brought back many wonderful memories of my husband, Jim Tanner, and the magnificent ivory-billed woodpecker. Many of the places Jim visited in the 1930s, he and I revisited on long canoe trips years later. Several of the people Jim met in the course of his research, we kept in touch with afterwards. I still get letters from Edith Whitehead, the daughter of J. J. Kuhn. Lyn's book brought back a flood of memories of those rivers and swamps, people and places.

Ghost Birds also reminded me of the amazing work done in an era without today's technology, such as zoom lenses, GPS units, camcorders, audio-recording devices, and other things we now take for granted. Lyn writes that in 1935 it took 1,500 pounds of equipment to record bird songs, and it was very difficult. You had to get the equipment close to the bird. He describes how Arthur Allen and the team from the Cornell Lab of Ornithology recorded the songs of many endangered species of birds; their recording of the ivory-bill is the only one ever made. The cameras of those days also were inferior to today's digital cameras. Even so, Jim and Doc Allen got excellent pictures. When Jim wanted to take a picture, he had to get close to a bird because he had no zoom lens. Then he had to use a separate light meter, estimate the distance, set the f-stop and the shutter speed, all before he could compose the picture, and most birds did not pose and patiently wait for their portrait! Sonny Boy, the ivory-bill nestling, climbed all over J.J. while Jim matter-of-factly operated his camera. Also, back then there were no safety devices or mechanized slings to help one climb up to a nest hole, so Jim had to hammer in spikes to step on as he inched his way up the trunk of a tree, and Sonny Boy's nest was fifty-five feet above the ground!

Lyn shows that field work, which is always unpredictable, was certainly more difficult in the 1930s. Jim had to cover eight states, and he used horses, mules, canoes, rowboats, a Model A Ford, and his own two legs to get about. If something broke, he had to fix it. And, as Lyn retells it, when Charlie the horse turned up lame deep in the swamp, Jim made sure he got out to a vet. What an adventure! But the entire book is an adventure.

Ghost Birds details life in a bottomland swamp, Jim's notes on the ivory-billed woodpecker, and many amusing events and humorous problems. And he also relates the historical events in the world that coincided with and affected the ivory-bill studies. He does all this because Lyn is not only an excellent naturalist with the soul of a poet, but also a historian, a tireless researcher, a skillful writer, and a man who reads widely. So I am delighted with his book, *Ghost Birds*, which is very interesting, accurate, informative, and easy to read.

Thank you, dear friend Lyn, for writing about my husband Jim Tanner and the quest for the ivory-billed woodpecker, 1935–1941.

NANCY TANNER
KNOXVILLE, TENNESSEE

Prologue

"Someone Needs to Write a Book . . ."

Epiphanies happen. Ideas spark. Journeys begin. Sometimes it's just a matter of providence. Call it kismet. But this book's existence is based on being in the right place at the right time, both for the story and the storyteller.

It has been my good fortune to know Nancy Tanner for many years, and over that time we have become close friends. We met through the Knoxville chapter of Tennessee's ornithological society; and indeed, Nancy enjoys birds, but her real forte is witty conversation. A former on-stage performer at the University of Tennessee's Clarence Brown Theatre (she played opposite John Cullum in *Sabrina*) and former tennis player at Harvard (making it to the finals in mixed doubles), Nancy loves a spirited repartee, a good serve and volley, a give and take, a lively turn of phrase. She has lived on this planet for over nine decades because she keeps herself engaged, stays curious. An avid reader, she always has something on her mind.

Nancy and I live only a few miles apart and generally speak by phone or in person weekly, often over lunch at the home she shared with her late husband, Jim. The modest structure is a flat roofed, three-level eyrie fit for a falcon and perched on the side of an East Tennessee ridge top. It's also where they raised their three children: David, Betsy, and Jane.

In the fall of 2005, over one of these lunches, Nancy was voicing her concern that Jim's legacy, his fieldwork, his long hours researching the ivory-billed woodpecker might not be remembered as it should be; and although his 1942 book about the species is still in print, still considered the bible on the subject, still often quoted, she worried that his hard work of more than seventy years ago might somehow be forgotten.

"Oh," I said. "Someone needs to write a book about Jim." And almost as soon as I said the words, I knew the obvious truth. "And that someone should be me!"

At the time, I was finishing the manuscript for my first book, *Natural Histories*, for the University of Tennessee Press and pondering whether I would or should or could begin a new project. Writing a book is like putting socks on an octopus: if you ever complete the task once, you're not so eager to dive into the ordeal again. But the obvious truth is the obvious truth, and Nancy and I entered a pact to begin as soon as possible.

In his wonderful book *Life of the Skies,* Jonathan Rosen writes, "The swamp is a stirring place. It was easy to see how both birds and myths about birds could survive there." He was referring to no other bird than the ivory-bill, the species Jim Tanner spent so much time pursuing. Since the early 1900s, one question and one question alone has swirled around the largest woodpecker to live in our part of the world. Is it dead or alive? And by dead, we mean dead in the most emphatic sense—that is, extinct. Gone. Lost to this world.

Ivory-bills have attained mythical status because they represent all that is wild and unobtainable and resilient in our natural world. It is a bird, Rosen adds, "flying between the world of the living and the world of the dead, between the American wilderness and the modern wasteland, between faith and doubt, survival and extinction. No wonder the bird has taken on a sort of mystical character."

And there the magnificent bird teeters, one zygodactyl foot in the here and now, the other in the hereafter. For more than one hundred years, the grave has been dug, but no one can confidently fill it in. Dressed in black, we stand around the gravesite with no final corpse to bury.

Over the past decade, authors Cokinos, Weidensaul, Jackson, Hoose, Gallagher, Steinberg, Snyder, and Rosen have all written about the ivory-bill, adding to its mythos: a feathered Lazarus that has risen from the dead more than once. In her 1969 work, *The Inland Island,* Pulitzer Prize–winning author Josephine Johnson suggests that its presence embodied the divine that one might experience in the forest, "If I sit here long enough, God will come / . . . If not the deer / Then a great bird, / The Lord-God bird, / The woodpecker with a flaming crest, / And the bill that could make a cavity, / Out of your chest if he willed to." And in his 1985 *Galápagos,* postmodern novelist and satirist Kurt Vonnegut wrote of them as being emblematic of a ruined world, "These big beautiful inhabitants of primeval forests really were extinct, since human beings had destroyed all their natural habitats. No longer was there enough rotten wood and peace and quiet for them." The ravages of war—a world gone mad—had influenced both Johnson and Vonnegut, and war plays a role in this story.

In 2005, when researchers from Cornell University announced that several people had sighted a lone ivory-bill on several occasions in Arkansas, the revelation stopped the presses, making national news. The quintessential *rara avis* had been spotted yet again. People cheered; they applauded; they openly wept. They slapped each other on the back and bought T-shirts to commemorate the joyous rediscovery. Why? Because the ivory-bill is a victim of our excesses, our gluttony. We logged and hunted it to oblivion, or did we? To survive, it would have had to become the most wary of the wary.

My friend Chris Cokinos took the title of one of his books from an Emily Dickinson poem whose opening lines are especially appropriate here: "Hope is the thing with feathers / That perches in the soul / And sings the tune without the words / And never stops—at all." Never stops at all. That's our hope. For if a bird as plentiful as the passenger pigeon and one as leery and lost as an ivory-bill can both go extinct, then there is no hope.

Historically, despite their reclusiveness and the remote, swampy environs they call home, the ivory-billed woodpecker has always drawn attention to itself. In 1731 the English naturalist Mark Catesby provided the world with the first published description, giving the bird the cumbersome name "Largest White-Bill Wood-Pecker," adding that the bill was "white as ivory." Catesby was also the first to record something of their perceived value: certain Native Americans paid three deerskins each for one of those ivory bills. Half a century later, the American naturalist William Bartram added to the mystique, describing the bird as "*Picus principalis;* the great crested woodpecker, having a white back." Hoping to sketch the species, the father of American ornithology, Alexander Wilson, tried to spend the night with a wounded ivory-bill in a hotel room in Wilmington, North Carolina. But such confining spaces are made of wood, and the feathered captive darn near drilled its way out. In 1831, also noting their economic value, John James Audubon wrote in his journal that steamboat travelers paid twenty-five cents for two or three ivory-bill heads. Yes, twenty-five cents, one quarter of a dollar.

A self-made frontiersman, Audubon did everything with panache. In addition to painting the species, he left behind the earliest and perhaps most lyric description of the watery, forested solitude the ivory-bill haunts, the "deep morasses, overshadowed by millions of gigantic dark cypresses, spreading their sturdy moss-covered branches, as if to admonish intruding man to pause and reflect on the many difficulties which he must encounter, should he persist in venturing farther into their almost inaccessible recesses, extending for miles before him."

But soon after the Civil War, these inaccessible recesses in the vanquished South began to fall to opportunistic lumbermen, who did indeed venture farther; and as their old-tree habitat disappeared, so did the ivory-bill. Tanner writes, "By

1885 the birds had disappeared from North Carolina and northern South Carolina and from all the region west of the Mississippi Delta excepting the very southeastern part of Texas. By 1900 they were gone from almost all of Alabama and Mississippi." Tanner believed that by 1915 they only remained hidden in the largest of swamps. And by then a new descriptor began to appear. In *Birds of America,* first published in 1917, T. Gilbert Pearson writes that the ivory-bill is a bird of astonishing strength and vigor, "nearly extinct." And, indeed, none were seen for years until Arthur Allen, the founder of the Cornell Lab of Ornithology, rediscovered the species, perhaps the last nesting pair in Florida in 1924, but a local collector soon brought them down.

By the 1930s most believed the species was lost. One prominent ornithologist wrote, in effect, that enough is enough: they are gone, and it's time to accept the fact.

This is where *our* story begins. Where I enter the fray. And my guide? None other than James T. Tanner himself, through the four-hundred-plus-page travel journal he left behind. All I had to do was climb into the seat beside him. At first, we shared the journey with Cornell's Arthur Allen and Peter Paul Kellogg; and then for the last three years, it was Jim and I alone in a 1931 Model A Ford. As a silent stowaway, I let the adventurous, dedicated bird chasers lead the way, day by day, swamp by swamp, muddy mile after muddy mile, on the hunt of a lifetime, a search for the historic ivory-bills: the ones first photographed, first recorded, first caught on motion-picture film, first banded, first studied by trained ornithologists, and for most of us, the only ones we have ever known, the Cornell ivory-bills of the 1930s—the ghost birds.

Chapter 1

Sabbatical

The idea grew, and soon we had a hunting expedition well in mind—an expedition which would leave guns at home and would "shoot" the birds with cameras, microphones, and binoculars.

—Arthur A. Allen

Bluster. The man had bluster. As with any good Southern lawyer in the 1930s, it was as much a part of his persona as his penchant for white linen suits and straw hats. But on this one point, Mason Spencer knew what he was talking about: ivory-billed woodpeckers were not ghost birds. No sir! Although the last documented sighting of the species in Louisiana had been in 1899, they were still alive in the state and he could prove it. Damn right! And armed with a gun and a hunting permit he obtained from the State Conservation Department, Spencer ventured into the misty bayous along the Tensas River near Tallulah, and when the smoke cleared, he had his proof: a fresh, bloodied specimen he had just shot himself. Until his gunshot brought it down, this one ghost bird had been very much alive.

It's a strange thing—slaughtering a bird to prove it wasn't extinct—but that's what he did. Spencer was well educated, an attorney, and a state representative. He was a big man, both in physique and influence, reportedly fond of bars and gambling. It was said at the time that he was the only man capable of beating Huey Long at his own game—populist politics—but he didn't seem to have the inclination. Among naturalists of his day, Spencer was no villain or pariah for having shot an ivory-bill. Many tenured professors of zoology at the time would have done the same thing just to get a special specimen for their collections—though today this does represent an antiquated, shoot-first-ask-questions-later attitude toward the sanctity of a species. Spencer's ivory-bill shooting did cause a stir. It happened on April 15, 1932, and the killing set into motion a chain of events that would resonate all the way to the Cornell Lab of Ornithology over thirteen hundred miles away.

Almost three years later, three men of science busied themselves on the Cornell campus for a journey. Their plans had been made, itinerary set, maps secured, equipment bought and checked, rechecked, and packed into two recently purchased trucks. Spirits were high.

Wednesday, February 13, 1935, was a cold, overcast day in Ithaca, New York. The temperatures the day before had barely inched into the low thirties. The weather forecast was for warmer conditions with rain or snow developing, but that mattered little. The men were headed to sunny Florida and points beyond, a long way beyond.

Across the nation, all eyes and ears were tuned to news from the Hunterdon County Courthouse in Flemington, New Jersey. The prosecution's case against Bruno Richard Hauptmann, accused kidnapper and killer of Charles Lindbergh's young son, was going to the jury. The group of eight men and four women spent only eleven hours and six minutes before finding the German-born carpenter guilty. "He's a low animal," declared Attorney General David Wilentz in a scathing closing statement. Labeled the "Crime of the Century," the darkness of the deed had cast a malaise over the entire country, which only eight years before had celebrated Lindbergh's history-making solo flight across the Atlantic.

But at Cornell University, in the Finger Lakes region of western New York, the three men were focused on the task at hand. Theirs was an exciting undertaking; some would even call it the adventure of a lifetime, in its own humble way as unique as Lindbergh's flight from Roosevelt Field on Long Island, New York, to Paris in 1927. In the history of ornithological science, no one had ever attempted an endeavor such as the Cornell men envisioned. Their plan: to travel across the country and make sound recordings of birds in their natural habitat. Sound recording was still a relatively primitive technology; and to take the bulky, cumbersome equipment into marshes, mountains, swamps, and prairies in unknown weather conditions seemed extraordinarily difficult, if not impossible. The group's goal was to seek out species rumored to be vanishing and to find, photograph, and record them before they were lost to the world.

Ornithology, as a specialized, named field of study, had only been around since the mid-1800s. The first half-century of the science was the province of men with guns who shot birds and had them stuffed, collecting not just their bodies but also their eggs and skeletons. The specimens were labeled; the birds were affixed to their proper places in the natural order; and museum drawers were filled up with the dead and lifeless "study skins." To make matters worse, some species were disappearing. North America had already lost five: great auk, Labrador duck, passenger pigeon, hearth hen, and Carolina parakeet. Others were believed to be close to extinction. Couldn't men of science do more than just shoot and collect, label and file? Wasn't there a way of gathering information without killing the bird?

Field research was a relatively new branch of ornithology. Rooted in the growing popularity of bird-watching, it was discounted at first by the old guard, those shoot-and-stuff museum men. Edmund Selous coined the term bird-watching in his 1901 book, simply titled *Bird Watching.* A pioneer, Selous wanted to change ornithology, to move it into the light of day, away from the museums and gunpowder and outside to where the birds actually lived. "The zoologist of the future should be a different kind of man altogether: the present one is not worthy of the name," Selous wrote. "He should go out with glasses [binoculars] and notebook, prepared to see and think."

Thus, ornithology was divided into two camps. Historian and ornithologist William Mullens describes the traditional shoot-and-stuff men as "united in a common hatred and contempt for the field-naturalist." They viewed the field guys as amateurs, but that was soon to change, writes Tim Birkhead, biologist and professor at the University of Sheffield: "It all finally came together in the 1920s as a result of a particularly remarkable, young German ornithologist named Erwin Stresemann. By expanding the boundaries of traditional museum-based ornithology to embrace the study of wild birds, Stresemann drew the two disparate strands of bird study together to create a new ornithology."

Dr. Arthur A. Allen, founder of the Cornell Laboratory of Ornithology, was just that kind of an ornithologist, and in late 1934 he was contemplating a half-year sabbatical. One evening he and his good friend Albert Brand began to hash out plans for going out into the field with cameras and microphones to document as many birds as possible. Guns would not be needed.

Arthur Augustus Allen was a product of Buffalo, New York. He had a genuine curiosity about natural history. A tireless visionary, he entered Cornell University in 1904, progressed through his studies, and completed his master's thesis on the mammals of the Cayuga Lake Basin, the watershed where Ithaca and Cornell are located. At this point he could have focused his attention in any direction. He chose ornithology. His doctoral thesis, completed in 1911 at Cornell, was titled "The Red-winged Blackbird: A Study in the Ecology of a Cattail Marsh." It won instant acclaim. Frank Chapman, chairman of the Department of Birds at the American Museum of Natural History, declared it "the best, most significant biography which has thus far been prepared of any American bird." It was groundbreaking, setting a pattern for future studies based on careful field observations of the bird's relationship to the environment and its life history. After Allen received his PhD, Chapman arranged for him to spend a year in Colombia, South America, collecting specimens for the museum. His first discovery there—the ant thrush—was a species unknown to science. After a bout of malaria, Allen returned to the Cornell campus to teach the study of birds. He would spend the rest of his career on the picturesque campus. In 1915 Cornell created a graduate-level program in ornithology and named Allen as its head. Known affectionately and simply as "Doc," he ultimately taught and mentored over ten thousand students, the young ornithologists who would change the science.

In the early days, Allen's "Grad Lab" was located in old "decrepit, creaky and drafty" McGraw Hall. "Its setting contradicted its youthful *esprit* and the activity which was practically round the clock," writes former student Olin Pettingill. Opened in 1872, McGraw Hall was the second building at Cornell. (Morrill Hall had opened in 1868.) Like many of the early buildings at the university, it was built from native Cayuga bluestone quarried from the base of Libe Slope, the very bedrock under Cornell itself. Jennie McGraw Tower, Cornell's most iconic building, sits in the center of the campus atop the rock formation.

During the 1930s, even as the Great Depression caused declines in college enrollment across the country, Allen's graduate program thrived. It continued to grow, so much so that the Grad Lab had to be relocated to the roomy top floor of Fernow Hall. The department's success and vitality were due to Allen's unwavering enthusiasm for ornithology. For him it was an all-consuming passion—from early in the morning to late at night, seven days a week. Although he could be lured into a few games of table tennis with one of his students, Allen was rarely distracted by sports, religion, politics, or music for any length of time. There was too much to learn about birds. As a leader, Doc Allen was an unswerving optimist, his enthusiasm infectious. He always saw the bright side in any given situation. Noted for his personal warmth and humanity, he gave his students his undivided attention. "He provided advice and criticism only when requested," recalled Pettingill, "he did not impose his own ideas on his students, and yet gave generously of them and of his knowledge when sought." His gentle guidance encouraged his young charges to develop independence and self-reliance.

Doc Allen also had a lively sense of humor. He loved puns, limericks, and telling amusing stories of his own experiences. In the field he was unruffled and even-tempered. If something went terribly wrong, he was noted for saying, "We must remember not to do it that way again." In short, he was precisely the type of man to lead a trip across the country's back roads with unproven equipment, a journey just oozing with potential problems, headaches, and setbacks. In Allen's own words, it was a project that would prove "as fascinating as it was difficult, and as time-consuming as it was productive."

Before we leave on the 1935 expedition, a little background is needed. Early in 1929 Peter Paul Kellogg, instructor of ornithology at Cornell, had become

Ornithology students at Cornell, circa 1934. Jim Tanner and Peter Paul Kellogg are at the far left holding a songbird. (Photo courtesy of Nancy Tanner.)

interested in sound equipment. Late that spring, the Fox-Case Movietone Corporation approached Doc Allen about recording birdsong. Talking pictures, or "talkies," were just beginning to appear. The Movietone system was a sound-on-film method that recorded both the picture and sound on the same strip of film, with the audio track running along the side. Theodore Case and his assistant, Earl Sponable, perfected this system in 1925 at the Case Research Labs in Auburn, New York. The following July, William Fox bought the company and its patents and formed the Fox-Case Movietone Corporation. Perhaps the most famous use of the system was in the Fox Movietone Newsreels produced from the late 1920s to the 1960s. Shown in movie theaters across the country, such newsreels were the way the nation "saw" the news and current events in the days before television. Fox's first reporting was Lindbergh's takeoff from Roosevelt Field on May 20, 1927. The early morning departure was filmed and shown in a New York theater that same night, much to the delight of the audience.

A couple of years later, Fox-Case sought to record singing birds on location to demonstrate the quality of its sound-recording cameras. For close to two weeks, two of their best operators, equipped with a sound truck, wrestled with the problem, but every time they got their cameras and microphones near the birds, the songsters flew away. The bulkiness of the equipment made it impossible for the cameramen to chase after them. These failures led Fox-Case to contact the ornithologists at Cornell. "Finally, patience exhausted, they came to our Laboratory of Ornithology for help," wrote Doc Allen, "thinking that our knowledge of birds might supplement their knowledge of sound recording with desirable results." Allen, Kellogg, and the Movietone crew spent one morning in an Ithaca park taping a song sparrow, a house wren, and a rose-breasted grosbeak. With the recording complete, the Movietone people had what they needed and were ready to move on, but the germ of a project was beginning to form. "We conceived the idea of making a permanent record of the songs of all North American birds," wrote Allen. The revelation initiated a new stream of research for his lab. Today, Cornell's Macaulay Library's collection of natural sounds includes more than 160,000 recordings, constituting 67 percent of the world's birds.

In addition to the scientific and educational value of the recordings, Allen appreciated their more transporting aspects. Listening to them lifted you out of your favorite chair and took you to faraway places. "There may be some who object to reducing the ethereal music of wild birds to the prosaic acetate disk of a phonograph," wrote Allen poetically. "Those who do not mind the march of progress into the woods and fields . . . can close their eyes and recall the fragrance of jasmine in Georgia, the odor of balsam in the Adirondacks, the scent of new-mown hay in Connecticut, or the tang of salt air on Barnegat Bay."

The bedrock for this world-renowned collection of recordings began with the cross-country expedition that Allen and Brand were contemplating in the fall of 1934. But such an adventure would cost money, and during the depression that was in short supply. That is why Brand's participation in that early planning session was so important.

Albert Rich Brand was a self-made man who grew into his middle name. Born in New York City on October 22, 1889, he was forced to drop out of City College for financial reasons. He soon found a job as a runner for E. D. Levison & Company and within six years was made a member of the firm, representing them on the New York Stock Exchange as a bond broker and arbitrager. He spent time as a partner of the E. H. Stern & Company before he opened his own business as an arbitrager on the exchange. Brand was so successful that he was able to sell his seat on Wall Street after only four months and retire. He was only thirty-nine years old, ready to start a second career. At the advice of Frank Chapman at the Museum of Natural History, he decided to return to school at Cornell to nurture his growing interest in ornithology. After completing his undergraduate studies, Brand was appointed an associate in ornithology at the museum, working under Chapman. Three years later he returned to Cornell as a research associate. He then turned his attention to making sound recordings of bird songs, a field so new it had no experts. Brand was at the right place at the right time, and he had money. He began buying, testing, and modifying equipment, but initial results were weak.

Recording outdoors presented a range of problems that were not present in soundproof studios. Ambient noise often drowned out the soft-toned birdsong. Three men from Cornell's College of Engineering—True McLean, W. C. Ballard, and Arthur Stallman—began rethinking the equipment. The high-pitched sounds of birds required special amplifiers and other technical adaptations. A breakthrough came when a Cornell undergraduate, Peter Keane, suggested using a parabolic reflector—a device shaped like a portion of a parabolic curve and used to collect sound, radio waves, or light—to intensify the signal picked up by the microphone. The Cornell Physics Department had some old parabola molds left over from experiments conducted during World War I to create an enemy-aircraft detection system. All of the departments pulled together, and the parabolic microphone was created. (Basically, the same setup can be seen along the sidelines of pro football games today, as TV crews are able to capture the distinct sounds of the players even as cheering fans roar in the background.) The Cornell parabola, a large circular disc three feet in diameter, was mounted on a tripod that enabled it to be moved noiselessly, either vertically or horizontally. A gun sight was fixed to the outer rim of the reflector to enable the operator to zero in on the target. When the microphone and singing sparrow were in perfect alignment, the birdsong was significantly amplified while the unwanted ambient sounds were reduced.

Early in 1932, Allen and Kellogg used the greatly improved sound equipment to conduct a behavioral investigation of the drumming noise made by a male ruffed grouse as he stood on a log. The series of muffled, accelerating thumps sounds like a distant motor starting: *thump . . . thump . . . thump . . . thump . . . thumpthumppumppumppump.* No one knew exactly how the grouse produced the sound. You could watch him beat his wings, but it happened so fast: did the bird drum the log or his sides, or did he merely beat the air itself? Spending the night in a blind, Allen filmed a male grouse early one morning while Kellogg and Keane made a sound recording. By studying the film frame by frame, they proved the bird beat the air and the air alone. Their findings, presented at the American Ornithologists' Union annual meeting later in 1932, proved the importance of recording and filming birds, marking a significant leap forward in ornithological research.

Two years later Albert Brand published his own book, *Songs of Wild Birds*, which included two small 78-rpm phonograph disks containing thirty-five songs. They were crude, but the work paved the way for a sequel. Brand's 1936 book,

More Songs of Wild Birds, contained three disks and forty-three birdsongs and, as a bonus, the calls of two species of frogs. Besides the three records, the 116-page book contained black-and-white illustrations and extensive commentary on the attributes of the songs, information on the species' range, field characteristics, and song habits of the birds. It sold for $2.50. Work on the books put Brand on the cutting edge of the serious study of birdsong. He was now ready and able to do more. Most important, he offered to help finance Allen's 1935 sabbatical trip and make available whatever equipment would be necessary.

With the core team in place—Allen, Kellogg, and Brand—the trio focused on their transportation. Two dark Ford panel trucks were purchased. The smaller one became a rolling sound studio, housing special amplifiers, the parabolic reflector, and 250 feet of microphone cable. If they could get the truck within eighty-four yards of a singing bird, they could record it. There was also room in the back for one bunk that would allow Kellogg to sleep on location so that he was ready to record at the break of day. The other panel truck was larger. It carried the various cameras and camping gear plus sleeping room for two men. The big innovation it sported on its roof was a collapsible platform that could be raised eight feet above the truck. When fully extended, it allowed for photography twenty feet above ground. The platform would prove to be invaluable in "securing intimate close-ups" of nesting birds.

The American Museum of Natural History and the National Association of Audubon Societies both approved the cross-country expedition. Because of Albert Brand's financial contribution, Doc Allen called it the "Brand–Cornell University–American Museum of Natural History Ornithological Expedition."

Into this arena stepped the youngest member of the 1935 expedition, and for him it was the opportunity of a lifetime. James Taylor Tanner, a graduate student of Doc Allen's, was only twenty years old. He was chosen as a "handy man to act in any necessary capacity." Affectionately known as "Jimmy" by the group, Tanner was born on March 6, 1914, in Homer, New York, at 69 North Main Street. The Victorian-style house, built around 1890, still stands, restored and as invitingly homey as it looked when the Tanner family lived there a century ago.

Jim Tanner's father, Clifford, owned the C. J. Tanner Dry Goods Store at 5 South Main in downtown Homer. The forerunner of the modern department store, a "dry goods" carried items not traditionally found in either hardware stores or food markets, mostly things for the home: rugs, wallpaper, draperies, linoleum, fabric, yarns, and some apparel, including gloves, hosiery, and underwear. If the local hardware store was the domain of the male shopper, the hometown dry goods served the same role for women. In 1919 the Tanners moved a few miles south to Cortland into a larger home at 67 Greenbush Street, and C.J.

moved his dry goods business to a large brick building on the corner of Main Street and Groton. (While researching this book in 2007, I bought a short-sleeved plaid shirt from the same location.)

In many ways, Jim had spent his entire life preparing for the 1935 Brand-Cornell expedition. He and his older brother Edward were outdoorsy: they roamed the countryside around their Cortland home and slept outside on a screened-in porch even on the frostiest of winter nights. They shivered but rarely fell ill. Jim became known for his mechanical ability, taking things apart, repairing the broken pieces, and putting the lot back together. It was a skill that would come in handy time and time again. Perhaps, knowing that all things were fixable made him unflappable. Remaining cool, calm, and collected were all a part of his makeup. He also developed an interest in birds as a young boy, owing to the influence of his local minister and scout leader. He became quite good at identifying birds by their songs and calls, realizing that habitat—where one saw or heard the bird—was also vital in knowing the species. He also enjoyed photography and often carried a camera with him on long hikes, developing the film in the darkened family bathroom.

"Jim learned a lot from school," writes author Phillip Hoose, "but his most valuable lessons came on those long hikes. He kept a journal, starting with the date and time of day and noting the weather and direction of the wind. He made himself go a long time between meals. He learned to sit still against a tree even if the bark was digging into his shoulder blades and itching like mad. Most important, he learned that while you can't meet wildlife by appointment, if you study wild creatures carefully enough, you can predict where they will be."

Yes, as the late winter days of 1934 faded into 1935, the resourceful twenty-year-old Jim Tanner was fully prepared for an expedition that would utilize all of his skills. Destiny had already seen to that.

Chapter 2

The Journey Begins

Right here in the United States there are treasures to be sought; treasures that in a few years may be past obtaining.

—Albert R. Brand

What did Confucius say? "A journey of a thousand miles begins with a single step." In this case, it was a step up into the cab of a dark-paneled Ford. At 9:30 AM on Wednesday, February 13, the Cornell expedition left old McGraw Hall. Allen and Tanner were in the big truck, Kellogg in the smaller one. Having developed unexpected health problems, Albert Brand was not present. The financier planned to meet them in Florida, where he was convalescing. It was a good day for driving, and a nice sunset greeted the Cornell trio as they approached Washington, D.C. They arrived at the Ambassador Hotel roughly twelve hours after leaving Ithaca. Allen had scheduled several speaking engagements during their cross-country sojourn; for him it was a working vacation with the emphasis on working. After they visited the buildings on the Mall, including the U.S. Capital, Allen gave a public lecture sponsored by the National Geographic Society. In a testament to Allen's growing reputation, some three thousand people attended the talk on the evening of February 15. The next morning they left Washington, driving southward through Virginia. Tanner described the countryside as "rolling hills covered with pines and oaks, red earth showing in the road cuts and stream banks." He was seeing his first glimpses of the South.

They drove straight through and arrived in Raleigh at 4:00 PM, going to the home of Ralph Waldo Green, an economics professor at North Carolina State College and a fellow Cornellian. Green's avocation was ornithology and conservation. His wife, Charlotte Hilton, had just published *Birds of the South* with the University of North Carolina Press. She was an early champion of the Tar Heel State's environment and for forty-two years wrote a popular newspaper column, "Out-of-Doors in Carolina," for the *Raleigh News and Observer.* Green had arranged for Allen to speak at his college that evening to an audience estimated at three hundred people. The Greens were "dandy people," wrote Tanner, and they

Peter Paul Kellogg, Arthur Allen, and Jim Tanner at Cornell before they left on the 1935 expedition. (Photo by Arthur Allen. Copyright © Cornell Lab of Ornithology.)

served as the group's hosts in the state. They lived in a small home surrounded by trees and bird-feeding stations. The next morning, Sunday, February 17, the Cornellians got up early to record the first bird of the trip—a Carolina wren, appropriately enough—and made additional recordings of scolding jays, titmice, and cardinals. They lunched at the Greens, where Tanner noted having his first taste of Southern cuisine: collard greens. The expedition left for Georgia at 3:30 in the afternoon. In his journal, Jim wrote, "Beautiful sunset, more beautiful moonlight. In the soft dusk, the road went straight, curving, up and down. The west was crimson, the east blue gray with the yellow moon. Pine trees were black, sharply cut against the sky." That evening the moon was almost full, a beautiful night for a drive: "The moon lit up the road ahead, the land around, the river beneath and the sky above." The trio finally settled in for the night at Strait's Tourist Camp on US Highway 1 in Columbia, South Carolina.

The next day they drove from Columbia to Milledgeville, Georgia. Ever the student along the way, Tanner recorded that the country was flatter and that black vultures were seen in greater numbers than turkey vultures, "flapping more and flying higher as a rule." He wrote that loggerhead shrikes were common along the telephone wires. Milledgeville is located roughly eighty miles southeast of the Piedmont National Wildlife Refuge. That night they stayed at Westover Plantation. To a group destined to spend many nights outdoors over the next few months in all kinds of conditions, Westover offered a lavish counterpoint, a lingering hint of the old Antebellum South. Built by the Jordan family in about 1822 when Milledgeville was still the state capital—Atlanta became Georgia's capital in 1868—the spacious old Federal-style mansion boasted tall white pillars in the front, a grand spiral staircase inside, and large square rooms with fireplaces. That night Doc Allen gave another public talk at Georgia State College for Women, where writer Flannery O'Conner would graduate ten years later.

The next morning, February 19, Tanner got yet another taste of Southern cooking, learning that if you put grease into the waffle batter, it made them crisper. The group went to historic Fort Wilkinson on the Oconee River to record birdsong. The area was openly wooded with oaks, sweet gum, pines, and a few beeches. They saw several common birds, including fifty black vultures feeding on a dead cow, and recorded a second Carolina wren. In the evening they were treated to a traditional southern barbecue. The main course was a roasted pig basted with hot sauce and served with, as if the basting alone wasn't enough, more hot sauce, plus potato salad, stew, bread, and cake. Jim noted that he needed a "brass stomach" to handle the meal, but he liked it nevertheless.

The Piedmont Hotel in Atlanta was their next stop. Doc had several engagements the following day in the city, including lunch in Rich's Department Store with members of the local bird club and some newspaper people. Afterward, he spoke to students at Bass High School. Tanner described Atlanta as "active, nice, smoky, and hard to find your way around." The Atlanta stop included putting up the truck's platform tower to pose for newspaper photographers.

Saturday, February 23: The group left Atlanta in the afternoon, driving 227 miles to Thomasville, Georgia, just north of the Florida state line. Tanner wrote that south of Albany County the landscape "really began to look Southern, much flatter." Doc thought he saw their first common ground dove, a bird only found in the extreme part of the South. At Beachton, Georgia, they met Herbert Stoddard, an authority on bobwhite quail, at his home, Sherwood Plantation. Stoddard had arranged for a flock of wild turkeys to be baited with corn and peanuts in a clearing on the estate of Colonel L. S. Thompson. By the 1930s wild turkeys were all but gone. Over-hunting had made the bird extinct in many states; now they could only be found in the wildest and most inaccessible regions. Hidden behind a preconstructed blind, the Cornell group hoped to obtain movies and sound recordings of the wild birds "uncontaminated by any domestic blood." They got good pictures but only mediocre sound. Ever wary, the birds were reluctant to gobble, even though, as Allen wrote, "On one occasion two old gobblers approached within thirty yards of Stoddard and me as we crouched immovable behind the sound mirror in full view."

Stoddard was a respected naturalist with interests in all aspects of the environment. "Tied to no particular academic school of discipline, his keen and inquiring mind was free to roam the whole gamut of the interrelationships of all living things, but his special emphasis was on ornithology," wrote his longtime friend and wildlife artist Owen Gromme. Stoddard's 1931 book, *The Bobwhite Quail: Its Habits, Preservation and Increase,* was regarded at the time as the premier document on wildlife management of any species in any given region. Although Aldo Leopold is considered the founder of game management, Leopold felt the distinction should go to Stoddard. Curt Meine, Leopold's biographer, writes that Stoddard was "the first to examine a game species in detail and to utilize that information in a restoration effort." Bobwhite quail were on the decline, and Stoddard had been hired to figure out why. It was he who posited the importance of fire in sustaining the bird's habitat, but fire had become a dirty word to foresters of the day.

From 1928 to 1931, the American Forestry Association sent its "Dixie Crusaders," young uniformed foresters, throughout the South to spread the word about the importance of fire prevention. The two-member Crusader teams traveled to every small town possible in trucks specially fitted with an electric generator, a motion picture projector, and exhibits. They held movie screenings and lectures in over eight thousand schools, churches, sawmill settlements, and turpentine camps. Their public relations campaign was one of the most intensive and innovative ever conducted. It is estimated they ultimately reached three million people in the South with the message that wildfires were bad for the environment, including the traditional controlled burns used in the agricultural practices of the day. Such burns actually dated back to the Native Americans, who employed similar methods of keeping areas open.

In the 1930s there were over two hundred game-hunting plantations, averaging about ten thousand acres each, scattered across the Southeast. The plantation owners formed the Cooperative Quail Study Association and hired Stoddard to conduct his bobwhite research, which ultimately included findings about the value of fire in wildlife management.

The first evening at Sherwood Plantation, under a sky "crowded with stars" and with spring peepers calling outside, Allen, Kellogg, and Tanner sat around a fireplace talking to Stoddard and his assistant, Ed Komarek, about the benefits of controlled burns. A biology student at the University of Illinois, Komarek went to work for Stoddard in 1934, helping the respected wildlife manager study the declining quail population. In time, the two would create the Tall Timbers Research Station to study the new science of fire ecology. Their findings were groundbreaking: fire was necessary to rejuvenate the open, grassy habitat needed by bobwhite quail. (In 1938 Komarek would purchase a plantation bordering Stoddard's near Thomasville in southern Georgia. The 565-acre parcel later became Birdsong Nature Center, a model of biodiversity and environmental stewardship, showcasing fire-dependent ecology with viable stands of longleaf pine, wiregrass, and their associated flora and fauna.)

The morning after their fireside chat, the Cornell group toured Stoddard's Sherwood Plantation. Tanner got his first good look at a habitat type he would later know very well. "Pine forests, interspersed with clearings, loblolly, slash, short and long leaf pine, occupy the higher ground," he jotted down. "In the lower hammocks are magnolia, beech, live and water oak, Smilax, cane, palmettos, yuccas, making up a climax forest." And for the first time on the trip, they encountered ticks. Yet, as they would soon discover, those blood-sucking arachnids were just minor inconveniences compared to other challenges that lay ahead.

Chapter 3

The Swampy South

At night the loud, wailing cries of the birds reverberate up and down the river, sending shivers down one's back.

—Arthur A. Allen

Florida is another world, its terrain, flora, and fauna exotic. Swampy wetlands—ideal ivory-bill habitat—can be found anywhere in the state. Long before improved roads and automobiles, northern tourists came to the state for sunshine and sightseeing. During the late 1800s, railroads punched into Florida, making it a popular tourist destination. Henry Flagler constructed the Florida East Coast Railway from Jacksonville to Key West and built numerous luxury hotels along the route, including accommodations in St. Augustine and West Palm Beach. The prosperous 1920s saw large areas opening to development, spurring the Florida land boom. The Great Depression slowed the growth, but nevertheless, Florida's first theme parks soon opened: Cypress Gardens in 1936 near Winter Haven and Marineland in 1938 near St. Augustine.

At Herb Stoddard's suggestion, the Cornell trio drove to Wakulla Springs, fourteen miles south of Tallahassee. The spring itself is an artesian well, a portal to the deepest underwater cave system in the world, noted for the clear blue water that bubbles up from 185 feet below ground. The pristine water forms the Wakulla River that flows south to the Gulf of Mexico. Scenes from the 1954 movie *Creature from the Black Lagoon* would be filmed there because it looked like the Amazonian jungle where Hollywood's "Gillman" was supposed to live. The Cornell trio saw no monsters, but as Tanner noted, they did see "monstrous fish" in magnificent numbers.

Monday, February 25: The Cornellians recorded a northern mockingbird and made the first sound recordings of a limpkin, a wading bird with a slow, strolling gait that for some resembles a limp—thus the name. Long-necked and lanky, limpkins are secretive birds related to and resembling small cranes; they are found in brushy swamps and marshes in extreme southern Georgia, Florida, and the American tropics. For the Cornell trio this was cause to celebrate:

getting a microphone close enough to record the limpkin was a coup, an inkling of good fortune to come.

Limpkins are not backyard or city park passerines. Brownish and streaked with white, the *Gruiformes* are exotic, secretive creatures, hard to find and thus even harder to approach closely with a microphone. Allen had hunted for limpkins before. On an earlier trip to Florida, he had reported, "Yesterday I was fighting my way through the saw-grass marshes of the St. Johns River, hunting for limpkins; I was struggling through the tangled willow roots, waist deep, where the egrets and ibis chose to nest until I could barely put one foot in front of the other." Needless to say, the leggy birds nest in isolated locations, primarily eating large aquatic snails that are generally nocturnal, as are the limpkins. Also known as "crying birds," they emit a call described as an anguished, wild-sounding wail: *kwEEEeeeer, kwEEEEeeeeer.* "It would not be difficult even for the most prosaic person to imagine that some lost soul had come back to earth, or at least that some luckless black brother was losing his leg to an alligator," wrote Doc Allen.

After recording the otherworldly wetland bird and enjoying a quick campsite supper, Tanner took a boat and paddled upstream, listening to limpkins and barred owls in the dark. The waning, last-quarter moon rose late. Absorbing the exotic sounds of the Florida night, Jim then drifted quietly downstream through the alien world and back to camp, where he slept in the truck, noting for the first time the presence of bothersome mosquitoes. Ticks, mosquitoes, and late-night paddles on dark, languid water: for young Tanner, his five-year adventure in the swampy South had truly begun.

The next morning Stoddard joined them. He and Doc Allen went upstream to construct a blind, hoping to get close-up photographs of a limpkin. "Here, enthralled by the magical scenery which was rendered even more eerie by the hooting and laughing of the barred owls, we spent several days," recorded Allen. Blending into the background, the group had no problem photographing and recording the limpkin again, as well as ospreys, snakebirds, and Ward's herons, a southern subspecies of the great blue heron. "When conditions were inauspicious for recording, we spent long hours and covered many miles hunting for ivory-bills," wrote Allen. Although the Cornell trio intended to record as many species as could be found, locating an ivory-billed woodpecker was first and foremost in their minds, and Allen knew that the entire state of Florida held promise. Speaking to local residents, the trio found one man who said he had seen ivory-bills around Wakulla in the past.

On Thursday, February 28, Allen, Kellogg, and Tanner said goodbye to Stoddard and drove farther south through "much wild land," mixed stands of longleaf pine and scrub palmetto. Tanner noted that the central part of the

Tanner using a parabolic mirror microphone to record a limpkin in Florida. (Photo courtesy of Nancy Tanner. Copyright © Cornell Lab of Ornithology.)

state had more towns and lakes. The next day, in Winter Park, the group met up with their benefactor, Albert Brand, who was living with his wife in the Lincoln Apartments on Morse Boulevard. The reunion was poignant. Brand, who had helped plan and finance their trip, was gravely ill, having learned only recently that he had a mortal kidney disease and was expected to live no longer than ten more years. (He actually died five years later in Ithaca on March 28, 1940.)

Using Winter Park as their central location, the Cornellians spent the next three weeks exploring the middle of the state, making many side trips to photograph and record Florida birds. In those days, central Florida was largely undeveloped. Roads were few, and the spaces between towns and cities were vast.

On the morning of Saturday, March 2, Doc Allen and Tanner scouted a swamp a few miles east of Sanford. Lakes Monroe, Jesup, and Harney and the St. Johns River punctuate the flat environs. "The swamp was bordered by scrub palmetto and a few pines," wrote Tanner, "swamp maple in full leaf stood sometimes in or out of a few inches of water."

Joe Howell, a young birder from Orlando, joined them. He became quite taken by the group. Tall and wiry, with a bushy head of hair, Howell had been a member of the American Ornithologists' Union since he was fifteen years old. An avid egg collector with an athletic build, he was very comfortable climbing trees. (Ultimately, Howell donated his entire collection—3,690 eggs, representing 134 species—to the American Museum of Natural History.) He graduated from Rollins College in Winter Park the same year as the Cornell trip and soon became one of Doc Allen's grad students, completing his PhD in 1940. Howell went on to teach at the University of Tennessee in Knoxville from 1946 until his retirement in 1978.

Allen, Tanner, and Howell located an active osprey's nest, and Doc photographed a "black buzzard's" nest with two eggs. That evening Allen gave a lecture to the Florida Audubon Society and met John Bonner Semple, a retired businessman turned amateur ornithologist. Three years before, Semple had published an article on the "Glossy Ibis in Florida" in *The Auk* and knew the region well. The next day Semple joined the group as they went to Fort Christmas near Orlando and south into a prairie along Jim and Taylor creeks. No one they encountered knew of any ivory-bills in that part of the state.

Monday, March 3, was a big day. A caravan formed and headed toward the Kissimmee Prairie. Howell led the way in his roadster, followed by Semple in his Franklin touring car. Next came Kellogg, driving one of the Fords, with Tanner bringing up the rear. Allen took turns riding with Howell and Semple, asking them questions about the local birdlife.

The Greater Kissimmee Prairie was once vast. Before the Europeans came, it covered perhaps 2.8 million acres, stretching from the Atlantic Ocean westward to the Lake Wales Ridge, the state's central backbone, and from Cape Canaveral south to the Everglades at Lake Okeechobee. In addition to its scattered lakes and rivers, the region had dry prairies—very flat expanses dominated by grasses, saw palmettos, low shrubs, and other broad-leafed plants—as well as marshy wetlands intermittently covered with shallow water. The prairies were called dry because during the spring, when little rain fell, the hardpan, sandy, nutrient-poor soils became desert-like.

In 1936 Albert Brand described the core of the expanse as being "eighty miles long by forty wide" and "practically uninhabited. The only signs of civilization are occasional herds of scrawny cattle that eke out a meager existence on the sparse prairie grasses." It was Florida's cattle country—to many locals, a bit of the Old West transported to the east. Ranchers lived throughout the region, while cowboys wearing big hats and boots drove herds of cattle to market along the few roads that pierced the prairie.

The four-vehicle caravan drove down a sandy one-lane road that passed from prairie flatwoods to marsh. The men saw snowy and American egrets, as well as various heron species—Louisiana, little blue, and great blue—scattered throughout the sawgrass marsh. Tanner noted a white cloud of ibises that took to the air far away like "a puff of snow flakes." The flock formed a large spiral overhead and drifted toward the Cornell group only to dive abruptly toward the ground and disappear into the marsh. That night the men camped along the side of the road. Under a starry sky, they heard cricket frogs around them, and a few limpkins cried in the distance. Mosquitoes bit and buzzed.

The next day was spent exploring the area and taking photographs of herons and ibises. Sandhill cranes occasionally called and caracaras flew over. Late in the day Kellogg left the group to spend the night in the sound truck. He hoped to record the sandhills early the next morning but had no luck. Semple and Tanner visited a burrowing owl's nest and looked for crane nests. The group broke camp soon after lunch to move deeper into the prairie, and Semple left to return to his home in Coconut Grove. That night the Cornellians built a campfire after supper; it was Wednesday, March 6, Jim Tanner's twenty-first birthday, a time to celebrate. Afterward, Kellogg and Howell positioned the sound truck closer to some sandhill cranes, hoping again to record their early morning bugling.

"Toward evening and at dawn these mighty birds fly over, trumpeting as they go," wrote Brand, who visited the group. "There is something awesome about their loud voices ringing over the otherwise hushed prairie; the peculiar light, the unending, flat, rolling seas of grass and palmetto, give one a feeling of reverence in the presence of powers far greater than those of insignificant man."

Sandhill cranes are tall and vigilant. Photographing and recording them took extreme skill and Herculean patience—long hours of sitting and waiting, hoping to be in the right place at the right time. The group found two cranes that "trumpeted some, then flew the wrong way."

The Cornell team had two objectives in this part of the state: to photograph and record as many Florida birds as possible and seek out information on ivory-billed woodpeckers. Allen had planned to spend most of March in central Florida searching for any possible surviving ivory-bill. The men had reason to be eager: Doc Allen had some firsthand information that gave them hope. Eleven years earlier, while on another university sabbatical seeking rare birds in Florida and Texas, he and his wife, Elsa, had traveled through this same area. Historically, ivory-billed woodpeckers had lived in the cypress swamps of central Florida, but by 1924 most knowledgeable birders felt they were no longer there. Yet, one account surfaced. W. H. Mann reported seeing four ivory-bills along Taylor Creek in Osceola County. In April, after a month of searching, Doc Allen, Elsa, and their guide, Morgan P. Tindall, found a pair. Allen wrote, "The birds I observed in Florida, although nesting in a cypress swamp, did most of their feeding along its borders on recently killed young pines that were infested with beetle larvae. They even got down on the ground like flickers to feed among palmetto roots on a recent burn." Allen photographed the birds and reported the find in *Bird-Lore* magazine. His rediscovery of the lost bird would have been cause for great celebration, but Allen learned the day he was to leave Florida that taxidermists had shot and collected two ivory-bills. Later, he was told that the two living ghost birds he had found so joyfully along Taylor Creek, perhaps the last in the state, were never seen again—a bitter pill for him to swallow.

Early in the morning on Sunday, March 10, Kellogg and Tanner recorded some Carolina wrens and a catbird. Later in the day they drove to Fort Christmas and spoke to several cattlemen in the region about ivory-bills. A man named Jim Mitchell reported that Boat Hammock, near the mouth of Taylor Creek, was the best place to look for them. In his field notes, Tanner sketched out the series of creeks—Tosohatchee, Second, Jim, Newberry, and Taylor, all south of Fort Christmas—which flowed into the St. Johns River. On the map he circled an area on Taylor Creek he labeled Boat Hammock.

On Monday, March 11, the Cornell team drove to Merritt Island due east of Winter Park and Orlando. Part of the Canaveral Peninsula, Merritt Island is divided into two parts separated by the Banana Creek: North Merritt is eight to nine miles wide and roughly ten miles in length; South Merritt is much longer and more narrow. The two together are shaped something like a tadpole with its tail pointed toward Key West. North Merritt is bordered by Mosquito Lagoon to the east, while the Banana River separates South Merritt from Cape Canaveral, an area later made famous as the home of NASA and the Kennedy Space Center. Indian River is west of the location; the Atlantic Ocean is due east. In the 1930s, the site was rich in wildlife, in part because it is an ever-shifting mix of habitats, geographically active, a place where ocean, river, marsh, lagoon, pool, beach, and dune mingle. The ever-present trade winds and coastal tides are constantly reshuffling the deck.

Tanner noted numerous ponds near Indian River where he found "shovelers, skimmers and some shore birds. Several unidentified sparrows popped in and out of the grass." It is possible that one of the unidentified birds was a dusky seaside sparrow, a subspecies once found in this small region of Florida but now extinct because of habitat loss and other factors. Historically, the dusky was never widespread; in fact, it had the most limited distribution of any bird in North America: Merritt Island and along the St. Johns River were the only places they were found. In the 1930s before development and NASA tamed the peninsula, this region was a wonderment of wildlife: sea turtles, manatees, Florida panthers, alligators, snakes, and in the spring, wave after wave of migrating birds. Tanner encountered a sizable diamondback rattlesnake that the group was forced to kill. Later that evening he skinned the dead reptile. The specimen measured six feet nine inches long, with eleven rattles. (Today the mounted skin is on display at Ijams Nature Center in Knoxville, Tennessee.)

Tanner described a large part of the landscape as a prairie much like Kissimmee except for the trees: cabbage palms and a few pines were more scattered. It was open and wild with not many places to hide. The Cornell group built a blind near an eagle's nest and spent two days on Merritt Island photographing the aerie and other birds before pulling up stakes at sunset. After eating in Titusville, they drove inland and set up camp on Second Creek south of Fort Christmas. They had ivory-bills on their minds.

Thursday, March 14, dawned bright and cool. Chuck-wills-widows, whip-poor-wills, and barred owls had called during the night. Kellogg made an excellent recording of a pine-woods sparrow. Known today as Bachman's sparrow, it is a species found in grassy and brushy patches within open pinewoods. After ward, Allen and Tanner went with guide Jim Mitchell to Boat Hammock at the mouth of Taylor Creek to look for ivory-bill sign: nest holes, peeled bark, any evidence that an active bird or birds might still be there. The area was fairly large with many big cypresses. Tanner described some parts of the region as being "beautiful" with deer, raccoon, turkey, and cat tracks. Ospreys were common, and there was a sizable heron rookery. The hammock was just a few miles east of where Doc Allen had located the pair of ivory-bills in 1924. They found some possible evidence of an ivory-bill but nothing definitive. Tanner also noted that the woods in the area were starting to be cut for the turpentine industry.

On Friday, March 11, after a trip with Brand to Lake Eola near Orlando to photograph gulls, the group returned to Taylor Creek, hoping to take pictures of an osprey's nest. It was a calm, quiet evening. A three-quarter moon hung over the forest, its soft light making the old cypresses look "fresh and young." The next morning, Allen, Kellogg, Tanner, and Howell returned to Kissimmee Prairie and their old camp at Long White Slough. Kellogg and Tanner went to a nearby rookery to take photographs. Jim estimated that there were about a hundred great egret's nests, forty to eighty feet from the ground. The loose assemblages were made of sticks and built close to the trunks for support. The egrets were in nuptial plumage. Some nests had eggs, while others had nestlings ready to fledge. Tanner described it as "a noisy place with squawking and fighting herons, loud wing beats of buzzards."

Early the following morning, Kellogg and Tanner tried again to get the sound truck close enough to sandhill cranes to record them. They were setting up when the group of fourteen flushed and flew away. Frustrated, they moved on to a caracara's nest in a cabbage palm for some pictures. They drove the trucks out through the pathless prairie to a hammock with a few hardwoods and cabbage palms. In one of the palms, twenty feet above the ground, was a caracara's bulky nest with two young close to fledging. Albert Brand and Sam Grimes joined them. Grimes was a local photographer whose color photos of the state's avifauna would later appear in an updated edition of *Florida Birds: Biographies of Selected Species Occurring in Florida.* At the nest site, he donned climbing irons and shinnied up the tree, but one of the nestlings bolted and flapped to the ground. Crested caracaras (in 1935 known as Audubon's caracara) are members of the falcon family; they are strikingly patterned birds with white heads, red faces with thick bills, and black caps that look like poor-fitting toupees. They are a tropical bird found in Central and South America, but the northern edge of their distribution stretches into south Texas and Florida. Frequenting open woodlands and prairies, they are not fast-flying hunters like other falcons but are instead rather sluggish, often scavenging on carrion or preying on slow-moving small animals.

The young caracara that flew to the ground caused quite a stir. Almost full-grown, but yet to fledge, the nestling looked duller then its parents. Tanner described it as active and intelligent looking. It led the group on a merry chase through the saw palmettos until they caught it and returned it to the nest—but not before taking several photos. One that shows Brand holding the squawking nestling appeared in the *National Geographic* two years later. Doc Allen observed, "When uttering its hoarse, rasping call, the bird throws its head back like an opera singer."

The following day, Jim set up movie equipment to film a red-shouldered hawk's nest in the top of a cabbage palm located in a dense hammock. His camera was a 35mm Bell & Howell "Eyemo," which he operated with a string to capture the action in the nest. In its day the Eyemo was a real workhorse. First produced in 1925, it could hold one hundred feet of film and was for years the most compact camera of its type. Favored by newsreel and combat cameramen for its ruggedness and portability, it was ideal for the 1935 Cornell expedition. That same morning, Doc and the group finally succeeded in recording the voices of sandhill cranes. Later, with Brand and a local man named Bob Wine, they also obtained action photos at the caracara's nest. It was a productive day. That evening they broke camp and returned to Winter Park.

On Saturday, March 23, the Cornell team traveled north to Interlachen and on to Grandin and "Manywings," the private bird sanctuary of local businessman W. E. Browne. At the heart of Manywings was Browne's home, a rambling one-story house near a lake surrounded by orchards, landscaping, and flower gardens. Sweet gums, live oaks, and various fruit trees shaded the house. Browne had been working with his birds for many years, and nine or ten backyard species were trained to swoop down and catch peanut pieces he tossed into the air. Doc Allen was impressed that blue jays, "which are particularly wary in most places, are especially adept at darting from the trees like flycatchers to snatch the tidbits in mid-air." Titmice and cardinals fed from Browne's hand. A sandhill crane was so comfortable with Browne that it would come to the back door to accept chunks of cornbread. The Cornell team photographed and recorded several species. One, an overly friendly Florida wren (at the time, but no longer, considered a subspecies of the Carolina wren), began to build a nest inside the sound truck as Kellogg worked there.

The next morning they rose early, recording a pine warbler, ground dove, and several other species before leaving Manywings for Tallahassee, where Dr. George Miksch Sutton joined the group. Sutton was an artist-author-ornithologist who spent much of his time traveling to paint birds from life and writing accounts of what he saw. He "was to accompany the expedition as bird artist until we should find the ivory-billed woodpecker—a rather indefinite commission," Doc Allen wrote.

Born in Nebraska in 1898, Sutton later became one of the most accomplished writers and bird illustrators of his generation. He received his PhD from Cornell in 1932, serving as the university's bird curator before holding academic posts at the Universities of Michigan and Oklahoma. Before his death in 1982, he wrote 13 books, 18 monographs and museum publications, 201 journal articles, and 18 articles for the general public.

The next morning, the Cornellians returned to Wakulla Springs, with Doc Allen and Sutton making the final leg of the trip in a borrowed boat, gaining a river's-eye view of the picturesque, almost primal environ. "The Wakulla is a remarkable stream," wrote Sutton, adding,

> Rising, full formed from the ground, it emerges through a rock-girt funnel whose appearance calls to mind a vast morning glory. So clearly blue is this gigantic flower that, viewed from a rowboat, its center is as unfathomable as the sky itself. Framing the bluest, most remote depths are silvery gray ledges of coralline rock, and weeds that wave with the rising current. Some of these are long-leaved and dark; others are bunchy and grayish green; some are frosted with a coating of minute bubbles. Among and above these weeds swim scores of indolent fish—bullheads with long feelers sticking out round their mouths; and shining mullets.

The riverbanks below the spring were covered with moss-covered cypresses filled with snakebirds (anhingas), herons, ospreys, and other fish-eating birds. "The snakebirds were nesting in scattered colonies, one of which was a mile or so downstream from camp. Here we watched the females, which were brown on the head, neck, and breast, sparring with their mates," Sutton continued, noting the considerable posturing of the ardent males: "Lifting their paddle-shaped tails straight in the air, flapping their wings, and bowing so far forward and downward in their attempts to be beautiful that they came very near to falling from their perches. The Anhinga is an amazing bird—a sort of Hoactzin of subtropical North America." (The hoactzin, also known as a hoatzin or "stink-bird," is a peculiar, pheasant-sized tropical bird with a spiky, rufous crest and a disagreeable, manure-like odor.)

Tanner noted, "The place was much prettier than a month before with green cypresses, flowering dogwood." Bald cypress is a species of deciduous conifer; its tiny leaves, spirally arranged on thin branchlets, turn brown in winter. By late March they would have been greening up for spring, and their reflection in the languid water was no doubt tranquil and beautiful. Allen and Sutton arrived at camp late, reporting a limpkin nest nearby. The complete Cornell ivory-bill group—Allen, Kellogg, Tanner, and Sutton—had finally assembled, spending two days at Wakulla taking photos and making recordings. Sutton took an easy chair and set up a floating artist's studio in a flat-bottomed, square-sided punt boat. He drifted in the shallow water, making drawings. A photo taken at the time shows him, sketchpad in his lap, floating among huge cypress trunks, absorbed in his work. The group's time at Wakulla seemed idyllic, except that the "ticks were thick." The following day, Thursday, March 28, they drove back to Stoddard's place in Georgia, where they tried to record Chuck-wills-widows and screech-owls but had no luck.

Over the next three days the group spent time back at the blind at "Thompson's place" (the estate of L. S. Thompson), photographing and recording turkeys. Kellogg and Tanner also got audio of a bluebird and finally a Chuck-wills-widow. On Friday evening, Doc spoke to a group of college students after supper in Tallahassee.

Monday, April 1, was another travel day. Tanner scared up a Chuck-wills-widow in a dense clump of pines: "It had something of a nighthawk-like flight, something like a sparrow hawk." Later the group drove to May's Pond near Monticello, Florida, a location with many cypresses and nesting egrets. The Cornell team recorded several heron calls that were mostly overshadowed by the ever-present frog choruses of the season.

In planning the itinerary, Allen had allotted extra time for Florida, and the group had now spent over a month in the Sunshine State. It was time to move on. Although the Cornellians had made many remarkable recordings and taken oodles of photographs, their quest for the ivory-bill had come up short. At all stops, their query had been the same: "Have you seen an ivory-bill?" Most folks in the know seriously doubted that the bird was still in the state. Doc Allen was surely hopeful: finding an ivory-bill again would have eased any lingering pain over the lost pair eleven years before. But it wasn't to be.

On Tuesday, April 2, Allen, Kellogg, Sutton, and Tanner drove west to investigate recent reports from Louisiana. With no luck in Florida, Doc Allen perhaps felt that the Bayou State was his last best hope of finding a living ghost bird.

Chapter 4

The Ghost Bird

From the Wakulla River our expedition proceeded to northern Louisiana, which we found largely under water, with all but the improved roads impassable to our trucks.

—Arthur A. Allen

Doc Allen's road trip was inspired by the news that an ivory-billed woodpecker had been shot and killed in the Louisiana woods in 1932. And now, three years later, it was time to see if the story was true. Leaving Herb Stoddard's plantation around 9:00 AM, the Cornell group of four drove toward Selma, Alabama. In the mid-1930s a patchwork of first-class, "improved" second-class, and "unimproved" third-class state highways linked the cities and towns of the South. The so-called improved ones were graveled but not paved; the unimproved third-class roads were generally graded and earthen. It had been a wet start to spring. In Mississippi the big truck got stuck in mud near Jackson, and the group entered "a classy hotel lobby" at the end of the day wearing muddy clothes, a foreshadowing of the weeks to come: the coat-and-tie academicians were morphing into backwoodsmen.

Early the next morning, Wednesday, April 3, the foursome crossed the "sweeping, muddy" Mississippi River at Vicksburg (yet more mud) and arrived at noon in Tallulah, Louisiana, where they booked rooms at the Montgomery Hotel. Tallulah is in the northern part of the state, roughly forty miles from Arkansas and ten miles from Mississippi. Doc wasted no time, soon making contact with the supposed ivory-bill shooter, the colorful southern attorney who began this account.

When Mason Spencer spoke, people listened. On the subject of ivory-bills, he was quite adamant: he had seen them in his home parish and had shot one along the Tensas (pronounced "Tinsaw") to prove his point. The birding publications of the era were also steadfast: ivory-billed woodpeckers were listed as extinct throughout their range, except with the possible exceptions of the swamps of Florida and Louisiana. The Cornell team had failed to find them in Florida, and many doubted they were still in Louisiana. Was Spencer's account true? And if so, were there any more birds? Dr. George Beyer of Tulane University had made the last documented sighting of the species in Louisiana in 1899, a full thirty-three years before Spencer allegedly shot one—after which, Armand P. Daspit, director of Louisiana's Fur and Wildlife Division, promptly ordered a ban on all such hunting permits. If any ghost birds remained in Madison Parish, he was going to protect them and ordered J. J. Kuhn, game warden for the region, to look after whatever population might be left. Kuhn took his edict very seriously.

Joseph Jenkins Kuhn (his friends called him Jack) was an expert woodsman born in central Louisiana, the oldest of nine children. As the firstborn, he helped on the family farm and attended a one-room school on land donated by his father. Edith Kuhn Whitehead, J.J.'s daughter, recalls that his free time "was spent hunting, fishing, trapping, and learning everything he could about nature. It became his passion. His curiosity was limitless. He was an avid reader, especially history, and always believed that Mother Nature was the greatest teacher of mankind. This was the foundation for his great faith in God." Whitehead remembered her father saying, "Any man who sees the incredible interdependence of everything on earth and did not believe in a higher power was unbelievably stupid." As the game warden assigned to the wildlife preserve along the Tensas River, Kuhn soon became an expert on all of its inhabitants.

Spencer's ivory-bill kill in 1932 had not gone unnoticed. The word had spread in the birding community to a young student named George Lowery. In the future, Lowery would become Boyd Professor of Zoology, director of the Louisiana State University (LSU) Museum of Natural History, and president of the American Ornithologists' Union (AOU) from 1959 to 1961. His book *Louisiana Birds* would first appear in 1955. At the time, it was acclaimed "not only for its ornithological value but also for its engaging and readable style" and would win the Louisiana Literary Award the year it was published. But in 1933 those career achievements were still ahead. Lowery was working on his B.S. degree at LSU. Born in Monroe, Louisiana, in 1913, he was five months older than Jim Tanner, and like Tanner he was one of the country's rising young ornithologists.

A year after Spencer shot the ivory-bill near the Tensas River, Lowery and John S. Campbell spent a week in June searching the same area for ivory-bills but to no avail. They covered fifteen to twenty miles every day, listening for their calls. After such an intensive search, not finding one was disheartening, to say the least. Then, on December 24, 1933, they returned with Lowery's father and J. J. Kuhn to count birds as part of the national Audubon Christmas Bird Count, an annual census within designated circles that was first organized by the National Audubon Society in 1900. But more specifically, they were there to look once again for ivory-bills. Had Spencer indeed killed the last one?

"My companions and I were out at daybreak, quietly stalking through the magnificent hardwood forest," wrote Lowery. "After walking about in the rain for several hours our hopes were severely dampened, needless to say; but when things looked most discouraging—it happened. Through the woods came a loud, clear, high-pitched *yaamp-yaamp,* unmistakably the call notes of an ivory-billed woodpecker. With utmost caution we approached the spot from whence the sounds were coming and in the next minute gazed upon two males and two females feeding energetically on a dead tree." After a week in June and a long wet day in December, Lowery and his group had found their grail.

"To stand there in the midst of one of Nature's last strongholds and look at four birds that might possibly be the last surviving individuals of a vanishing species was thrilling to the extreme," Lowery concluded. "We watched the birds at fifty feet for some fifteen minutes until they finally retreated into the taller timbers, ceased calling and were lost from view. Hunting for a dozen birds—if there are a dozen—in a 100,000 acre primeval forest is much like looking for the proverbial needle in a haystack." But in this case, the needle had wings and kept shifting its location.

At the next AOU annual meeting in Chicago on October 23, 1934, Lowery presented a paper on the rediscovery. He didn't have slides or motion pictures, only his eyewitness account, but that was enough to excite the audience. Doc Allen, Peter Paul Kellogg, George Miksch Sutton, and Jim Tanner were all present; now, six months later they arrived in Tallulah to investigate the story. If the Cornell expedition could be compared to the fabled quest of Jason and the Argonauts, then the ivory-bill was the Golden Fleece. Finding it and bringing back motion pictures and audio recordings of the lost bird would be no less epic.

Their meeting with Mason Spencer in Tallulah was congenial. "The talk," wrote Sutton, "kept us on the edge of our chairs. There could be no doubt that we were in a fearful and wonderful country. We were amazed to learn that mammalogists considered wolves more common in this section of Louisiana than any other part of the United States." Spencer warned them about mosquitoes and the dangers of getting lost in the pathless, sodden woods. Fearing that Spencer was confusing the ivory-bill with the similar-looking pileated woodpecker, Sutton queried him for more details.

"Man alive!" answered Spencer hotly. "These birds I'm telling you about is Kints! Why, the pileated woodpecker's just a little bird about as big as that," gesturing with his fingers a size somewhat smaller than true to life. "Why, man, I've known Kints all my life. My pappy showed 'em to me when I was just a kid," barked the colorful attorney. "They're big birds, I tell you, big and black and white; and they fly through the woods like pintail ducks!" His description of their straight-as-an-arrow, pintail-like flight convinced the Cornell team that the bellicose attorney knew his woodpeckers. His name for ivory-bills—"Kints" (sometimes spelled "kents" or "kients")—derived from their distinctive call.

The group needed permission to enter the refuge, and that took a few long-distance telephone calls and telegraphs. "Sentiment was a bit against us at the start," wrote Tanner. "But we soon obtained permission to enter the refuge." After all, they were not there to collect specimens for Cornell but to capture the species for the first time on film.

The State Department of Conservation notified J. J. Kuhn to aid the Cornell team in finding the ivory-bill and to protect the college men, keeping them from harm's way in the Louisiana wilderness. "Dad didn't quite know what to think of the team's ability in the woods," recalled Kuhn's daughter, Edith Whitehead, "but he quickly began to respect Dr. Allen's woodsman skills. My father wasn't sure if they would drown, get snake bitten, or fall in a gator hole or quicksand. But he was delighted they could function." Indeed, the Cornellians proved highly adaptable in what Sutton described as "a land of timber wolves, panthers, razor-back hawgs, and deer."

The refuge was flooded, and the sole dirt road into it was impassable. "The stickiness of this Louisiana mud, or 'gumbo' as it is called, is exceeded only by its hardness when it is thoroughly dried out," Doc Allen wrote. "Let a little water fall upon it and one sinks in it almost literally up to the knees." It wasn't a place you could take a truck. The group had to find another way to get their necessary belongings to the base camp being established at J. J. Kuhn's cabin.

Ike Page, a local farmer, was hired to help out, and the next day, April 4, he met the group along the highway south of town, transferring their basic gear and luggage into the back of his wagon. With help from two mules, Ike moved the load the necessary five miles into the swamp, becoming an unsung hero of the expedition. Ike's son Albert came along to serve as camp cook. Doc had arranged with Tallulah's mayor and town marshal to park the trucks and valuable sound equipment in the courtyard beside the local jail.

"The road was fairly straight and wide," recorded Tanner. "The mud was slippery yet stiff." And the weather was beautiful: white spider lilies bloomed everywhere, while hooded and prothonotary warblers sang along the five-mile route of Sharkey Road. And since it was early April, the mosquitoes did not show themselves. The group reached Kuhn's cabin—a three-room house with a big screened-in front porch—on Methiglum Bayou about noon. Inside, they got a sense of the capriciousness of the wetland: waist high on the walls were water

A wagonload of supplies in Tallulah. From left to right are Tanner, J. J. Kuhn (foreground), Peter Paul Kellogg (on horseback), and Grover and Ike Page. (Photo courtesy of Nancy Tanner. Copyright © Cornell Lab of Ornithology.)

stains. The mud they had slogged through was nothing compared to the Great Flood of 1927, which had inundated Tallulah and put the entire refuge under several feet of water. During the early months of 1927, the Mississippi River broke through its levee system at 145 places, ultimately flooding 27,000 square miles up to depths of thirty feet. The flood caused over $400 million in damage and killed 246 people in seven states. Evidence of its devastation was still apparent eight years later.

With their sleeping bags unrolled on Kuhn's front porch and provisions stacked in the kitchen, that afternoon and all the next day the Cornell men looked for ivory-bills but only found pileated woodpeckers. "Two days we hunted Kints," Sutton wrote. "Walking, as we did, through water ankle-deep and deeper, we gradually became accustomed to this amphibious existence." And Tanner noted, "Wading the hip-deep 'boughs' eventually gave us no especial thrill. Wading was easier, anyway, than creeping over the slippery logs that bridged the streams." Though discouraged and waterlogged, Jim still figured they would find the birds soon.

Perhaps sensing their frustration, Kuhn said, "Now, men, by this time I guess you all must be thinkin' that this is a put-up job. But I want to tell you that the ivory-bills are here. I know it because I've seen 'em myself and I know the man who saw 'em last. He saw 'em right here, right in that very tree, not more than three weeks ago!" Yet, despite Kuhn's confidence, still no ghost birds showed themselves.

Saturday, April 6, was dark and overcast, the undergrowth damp from an overnight rain. The group decided to push deeper into the swamp. Kuhn and Sutton took one side of John's Bayou, while Doc Allen and Tanner took the other, working their way north. Several spring warblers sang. During the low-water season, bayous run clear, but it was spring, the season of rain and mud. Rivers and streams test their boundaries; water seeps into every available low spot. A few miles north of Kuhn's cabin, John's Bayou takes a hard turn to the east. The foursome reunited at the bend but promptly split up again to follow the waterway to the east. They marched abreast, several yards apart—Tanner on the extreme left, then Sutton, then Kuhn, and finally Doc Allen on the far right. Progress was slow as they pushed through "the gigantic trees, poison ivy and invisible pools," Sutton noted. The four men shouted loudly so that they would not lose one another. "The tangle was so dense we gave up trying to avoid the ivy," wrote Sutton. "We had gone about a quarter mile when, emerging from a tangle of cat's claw, I thought I heard Kuhn shouting something to me. His voice was way off somewhere, ahead and to the right."

The swamp played tricks on them, ringing with echoes. Tanner heard the "hooting," as Sutton beckoned him in his direction. Kuhn had heard a "kint" south of their location, toward Sharkey Road. Both pileated and red-bellied woodpeckers were calling, keeping the searchers on their toes, nerves on edge. J.J. suggested they walk slower, so as to hear any unfamiliar sound. "We had walked a hundred steps or so when we came upon a big cypress log," Sutton remembered. "In order to move forward more rapidly and to see the woodland more clearly we climbed upon this log and started for its farther end." Kuhn led the way, soon whispering hoarsely, "There it goes Doc! Did you see it?" The woodsman turned and noted Sutton's bewilderment, grabbing his shoulder and turning him. He pointed into the forest. His excitement almost toppled them from the log. "It flew from its nest," he proclaimed. "What do you think of that! A nest! See it! There it is right there!"

The attuned game warden had spotted a hole in a large stub straight in front of them. Tanner noted, "When he [Kuhn] got beneath the stub, he glanced up and saw a big, white bill sticking out of the hole. Then a female bird slipped out and flew to a nearby tree." J.J. yelled and Sutton "ran like a hound." By the time

Tanner arrived, Kuhn and Sutton "were shaking hands, patting each other on the back, and acting like best friends, slightly oiled, reunited." Doc Allen soon joined their merriment, crashing through the undergrowth like a bear.

"We stood there marveling that at the very moment of discovering our bird we should discover the nest also," wrote Sutton. Indeed, the discovery of the nest was most fortunate. "The cry was strange, bleatlike, not quite sharp enough for a woodpecker's cry. It was slightly nasal in quality and it sounded to me like 'Gip!,' with a hard *g*. The moment I heard the sound I knew I had never heard it before." They watched the bird work its way up the tree. To Tanner, the back shield created by the folded wings looked like a white pillowslip going up the trunk.

The nest hole was in a dead tree. It appeared to be newly dug, about five inches across. Chips around the base of the tree also seemed to be recent but not fresh. The four men moved back away from the tree, sat down, and waited. Imagine their heightened state, their prize at hand. "It wasn't long before the female suddenly slipped into a nearby tree and started to call, sometimes slow, sometimes fast," wrote Tanner. "Then the male suddenly appeared, called, and flew to the nest hole. He clamped on to the lower part of the hole with his feet. He looked around." For the Cornellians, it was a long-imagined, career-defining moment, an experience they would tell and retell for years.

"His big white bill and white eye were in strong contrast with the dark hole and black face," Tanner continued. "His crest was long and scarlet. The white on his wings was prominently covering half his back and was met by the curving white lines down from the neck." The Argonauts had found their Golden Fleece, except that this one came in black, white, and fire-engine red. The fleece of Greek mythology hung from an oak tree near the Black Sea. The Cornell team had found their prize in a swamp maple near John's Bayou, but the mud beneath their feet was indeed black.

"Everyone of us had his eyes glued on the bird," Tanner continued. "A moment later he disappeared head first into the hole. The female all this time stayed nearby, calling occasionally." Suspended in time, Allen, Sutton, Tanner, and Kuhn watched from the shadows, hidden among logs and bushes. For them, it was the chance of a lifetime; for Kuhn, just another day in his alluvial paradise.

"Something disturbed the birds and the male came out of the hole in a hurry and went to a nearby tree, almost over George, who said he looked mad and angry as a big bull seeing scarlet," Tanner wrote. As Sutton remembered,

> The whole experience was like a dream. There we sat in the wild swamp, miles and miles from any highway, with two ivory-billed

> woodpeckers so close to us that we could see their eyes, their long toes, even their strongly curved claws with our binoculars. The male bird sighted me, called more rapidly, and then, instead of flying off in alarm, swung to a tree above me, looked at me first with one eye then with the other, and stationed himself not more than thirty feet away. What a splendid creature he was! He called loudly, preened himself, shook out his plumage, rapped defiantly, then hitched down the trunk to look at me more closely. As I beheld his scarlet crest and white shoulder straps I felt that I had never seen a more strikingly handsome bird. His crest was gorgeous. But somehow what struck me most was the rich whiteness of his beak and the staring whiteness of his eye.

And Tanner added, "The female came nearer for a moment and both birds scolded. We watched for a while and then left quietly blazing a trail. We were a hilarious bunch on the way back, not believing our good fortune, pitying Paul who had stayed behind." The approaching evening looked stormy but even more rain could not dampen their enthusiasm.

The next morning they hoped to capture the ivory-bill pair on film, and they had a special camera to do it. An expedition supporter, Duncan Read, had loaned Allen an Akeley 35mm ciné camera for the trip. It was state-of-the-art. It was also heavy.

Carl Louis Gregory Akeley, a true renaissance man, had created the camera in 1918. In addition to designing motion-picture cameras, Akeley was an explorer, sculptor, taxidermist, and curator of the American Museum of Natural History. His camera had a distinctive drum-shaped body with an ingenious optic system that kept the eyepiece in level position regardless of the tilt of the camera. It used 35mm roll film, producing an 18mm by 24mm image. The problem with it was its weight and bulk: it required a substantial tripod for support. It also had taken up considerable room in the back of Ike's wagon, and now they had to transport it by hand for two miles from Kuhn's cabin to the ivory-bill nest.

The next day the group set out at 7:00 AM, struggling through the bayou with the large camera in its black case and the equally unwieldy tripod. At the site, the team put up a blind almost directly below the nest, about fifteen feet from the tree, to conceal the Akeley with its seventeen-inch lens. Sutton built himself a brush blind about twenty-five yards away, a safe place to sketch. Kellogg, Kuhn, and Tanner explored upstream along the bayou, leaving Doc Allen behind to film. While the trio was away, the ivory-bills behaved beautifully: Doc cranked out 350 feet of film, and Sutton filled a pad with sketches.

Noting his place in history, Sutton wrote, "For hours I sat there quietly, thrilling at every new posture, bearing in mind as I worked that even Audubon could not have had a better chance than this to draw an ivory-bill from a living model."

Now that they had located ivory-bills, how could they record their vocalizations? They would need to transport the recording equipment the five muddy miles to Kuhn's cabin and then two more miles to the nest. That was seven sloppy miles, and the sound truck weighed roughly a ton. That evening in the cabin, the Cornell team and Kuhn discussed various options. Cutting a road and finding a team of workmen and their mules to pull the truck through the muck and mud to the remote and tangled location seemed overwhelmingly impractical. Finally, they came up with the plan of transferring the gear in toto into the back of Ike Page's wagon.

Monday morning, April 8, was bright and cool with a slight breeze. Having finished his sketches, Sutton moved on to Texas to look for other rare birds. Allen and Kellogg went into Tallulah to make the transfer of sound gear, while Kuhn guided Tanner back to the blind at the nest tree. Almost as soon as Kuhn left, the female ivory-bill landed on the tree. For the first time, Tanner found himself alone with the birds he would later come to know so well. With the morning's progression, the pair exchanged places roughly every half hour. As the sun rose higher and noon approached, the interval grew longer. Tanner took several photos with his Graflex, a medium-format camera that used sheet film. Unlike modern-day 35mm SLRs, this camera required the operator to be above the camera and look down into the viewfinder to compose the image. It was a manual camera; there was nothing automatic. Tanner used a variety of settings, making careful notes of his exposures (shutter speeds and f-stops) and the images: five of the female, six of the male, and one he wasn't sure about—though he thought it was the female—plus two shots that had the pair in the same frame, female above, male below. All of the photos centered on the nest hole where the birds paused just before flying away. Tanner wrote that he got "no good pictures of the birds arriving or together."

The nest hole was about forty-three feet above the ground in a swamp maple stub about fifty feet tall and two feet in diameter at the base. The area was wet: water from two to five inches deep covered half the ground. Most of the trees in the area were second-growth ash and rock and red elm, plus oaks, gums, and maples. There were a few very big oaks and gums. Several large trunks in various stages of decay were scattered about. The undergrowth was thick and tangled, jungle-like. Tanner noted a *Smilax* he called catbrier, plus "buckvine" and poison ivy. In addition to taking photographs, as any good field ornithologist would, he watched the birds, recording his first long notation of ivory-bill behavior—in this case, the interaction of the mated pair:

> Soon after the female had gone in the first time, the male called and pounded nearby and then flew to the tree, landing below the nest. The female stuck her head from the hole, looked around, then came from the hole to the outside of the tree. The two talked together in low tones, much softer and more pleasing than their alarm notes. The female climbed a stub of the tree and soon flew; the male looked around, approached the hole, and upended into the nest. Both birds, when entering the nest, go in head first, and their tails rub against the top of the hole.
>
> The birds often signaled each other by pounding. A ways behind the nest was a dead tree with a long slanting stub near the top. The male bird frequently would climb up that, and "wham" he would give a simple resounding blow. Sometimes there were two whams done together—*wham, wham,* the first louder. This drumming was much like a pileated's, irregular but louder. They often drummed or pounded on the nest stub.
>
> From what I determine, sitting in the blind, the birds in early morning fed not far from the nest, for I could frequently hear their calls and what sounded like feeding nearby.
>
> Later in the morning the change was made more irregularly. One would fly to the tree and rap just below the hole. The other would stick its head out, look, climb partly out, look again, then fly. The first bird would then climb to the hole, glance around, then enter. The sitting bird frequently sticks its head from the hole or looked out from within the hole.
>
> About noon the male came to the tree, and the female left. He moved around and clung to the side below the nest. The bright sun caught his bill and it glinted like silver. His pale eye shone and his crimson crest gleamed. White, black, and crimson—a really beautiful sight—he stayed a moment and then went into the nest.

Tanner then noted the other birds he heard around him: warblers, cardinals, wrens, and woodpeckers. After mid-morning he heard the light footsteps near him of a hen turkey "wading diligently along." He recorded, "She calmly inspected the blind with a bright eye, clucked an alarm note, and despite my call and gobbles, walked calmly away." Tanner climbed out of the blind after noon, and despite making a lot of noise doing so, the male inside the nest did not even show itself.

While Tanner spent the morning at the nest, Allen and Kellogg went into Tallulah to unsolder all the connections and move the precious sound recording equipment—weighing roughly fifteen hundred pounds—from the small truck into the back of Ike Page's wagon. Albert Brand later wrote that the sound truck was "eviscerated." What had been so patiently assembled in Ithaca only a few months before was now just as carefully pulled apart. No one knew the setup better than Kellogg: he literally had been sleeping in the truck with the gear the past several weeks. One piece at a time, they made the transfer in the courtyard beside the local jail. Prisoners inside the jail watched the tedious proceedings and, peering through the bars, offered their help in finding more "peckerwoods," if only a leave of absence could be arranged. A photograph taken of Kellogg at the site shows a toolbox, large batteries, and the parabola sound mirror lying to one side with wires all around his feet. Moving his highly advanced sound studio and reassembling it in the back of an old wooden wagon was a challenging enterprise. There is a curious juxtaposition here: the most advanced recording equipment of the era being carried into the sloppy backcountry in a wooden wagon. A motion picture shot of the journey confirms the group's need for Ike Page. On this trip in, it took four mules to pull the heavy load.

On Tuesday, April 9, in anticipation of the sound equipment's arrival, Kuhn and Tanner left early, walking up John's Bayou and starting a crude trail to the nesting site. They heard the *kents* of another woodpecker and followed the sounds. "It called some more and once I saw it fly," Tanner wrote. "It sounded as tho two birds were talking and right near there, Mr. Kuhn found a hole high in a tree." The second nest was fifty feet above the ground in a dead oak, two miles to the south of the first nest in the swamp maple. Tanner continued, "It looked exactly like an ivory-bill hole, freshly dug. There were fresh chips at the base of the tree." (The following day, Kuhn discovered that a black squirrel had displaced this second pair of ivory-bills.)

Tanner later noted, "Without much trouble we took the wagon in." Page's caravan performed perfectly: Ike in the wagon; Allen and Kellogg aboard the two lead mules; and Tanner, Kuhn, and Albert, Ike's son, scrambling behind. They set up the sound studio on a bit of high ground roughly three hundred feet from the nest, beneath a large oak. A wide canvas tent was erected over the wagon, supported by small saplings and lashed to nearby trees. Their sleeping bags were spread out on a bed of palmetto fans, and a large pair of twenty-four-power binoculars, pointed at the nest hole, was mounted on a tripod. The sound mirror was positioned close to the nest hole to record their vocalizations. The Cornellians settled in to study the birds.

Their new home was christened "Camp Ephilus," a play on words based on the ivory-bill's generic name *Campephilus,* which comes from the Greek *kampe,* meaning "caterpillar," and *philos,* meaning "loving"—a reference to the group's fondness not for caterpillars but beetle larvae. "Gradually the birds became somewhat accustomed to our presence and we dared build a blind in the top of a rock elm level with the nest and only twenty feet away," wrote Doc Allen, while Tanner observed, "The female bird was in the tree when I started to climb, she stayed there for awhile then suddenly rushed out. The birds accepted the blind quickly."

All the effort of moving the sound studio to the swamp paid off: the first day at Camp Ephilus, Kellogg made recordings of the ivory-bills' calls, chat, and pounding. It was basic chatter in the swamp, the voice of a lost species, but back at Cornell, it would be more precious than gold. A major objective of the expedition was now "in the can." For the next four days, April 10–13, Doc Allen, Kellogg, and Tanner took turns keeping a common, detailed journal of everything the birds did.

Wednesday, April 10, was a chilly, wet day. It rained off and on. At 9:45 AM, Tanner had to leave the safety of the canvas sheltering the wagon to cover the microphone. "This alarmed the birds," the group's journal noted. "The female left and both called. As soon as Jim got back to the tent the male entered the nest with a couple of *yips* and then all was quiet. It was now raining hard." After a while, the ground around the camp became sodden and muddy. But despite the conditions, the ivory-bill pair went about their daily routine, while the Cornell trio watched and took notes. The birds' activities—the male and female exchanging places in the nest hole—began at 6:05 AM with "a few conversational clucks heard at the nest," and ended twelve hours later, at 6:05 PM, when Kellogg walked to the tree to check the microphone and the male looked out at him. After 4:00 PM the female was not seen again until the next morning.

Thursday, April 11, began with early-morning fog. The sky remained hazy all day, creating a soft, defused light for photography. There was no wind. Cardinals and wrens started singing shortly after five o'clock. (This pattern repeated itself. The team learned that roughly forty-five minutes after the cardinals and wrens began to sing, the ivory-bill activities commenced.) After recording the song of a prothonotary warbler, the Cornellians frightened the female from the nest to get more audio of her call.

At 8:45 AM Tanner climbed into the blind, taking with him a small DeVry movie camera—a precision-built, hand-cranked device manufactured by the

DeVry Corporation of Chicago. The company produced both 16-mm and 35-mm movie cameras and projectors in the late 1920s and 1930s, using the slogan "See yourself as others see you" to appeal to those with disposable incomes. While that was a small demographic in Depression-era America, Herman DeVry's company had, nevertheless, ushered in the age of amateur motion pictures. Anyone who could afford one of their cameras could make a movie. One popular model shot 35-mm film and sold for $150. Handheld and lunchbox-sized, it came with interchangeable lenses. But most important for the Cornell team, it was light enough to carry up a tree. The larger Akeley was much too heavy for use in the blind.

Hidden in the rock elm blind, perched on a narrow board, Tanner waited with the DeVry for one of the birds to appear. He was tantalizingly close, little more than two luxury-car lengths away. The male was inside the nest hole protecting the eggs. Forcing the issue, Doc Allen rubbed the tree from below; the bird quickly flew away but returned in about twenty minutes. Tanner shot thirty-five feet of film of the male ivory-bill. Like the reclusive member of a royal family, the South's ghost bird had been captured on film, an intimate and close-up portrait. But the bird seemed herky-jerky. Being so near, the rattle of the camera spooked the regal lord of the swamp; it could hear but not see its *paparazzo*.

"The camera bothered him some and he flew," Tanner recorded in his field notes. "When he returned, I took [another] 55-feet, which should be O.K., altho thin in the shadows. The misty sky reduced the shadows." Ninety minutes later, Tanner lowered the movie camera to the ground and took eight still-photos. In early afternoon, Jim took a break, and Kellogg climbed into the blind with the Graflex to take several more stills. The activity seemed to make both birds nervous, especially the female, but even so, they rarely left the eggs unattended, their sense of responsibility overriding their wariness. "The birds paid relatively little attention to us," Allen wrote, "of course, we used the utmost care to reduce any disturbance to a minimum." However, the detailed notes of the day indicate that the team's activity close to the nest perhaps had increased the birds' coming and going. They called and exchanged places more often when compared to the rest of the week.

April 12 "started out bright and sunny, but soon clouded over and stayed dark and cool all day," recorded Tanner. They learned that the foggy conditions the day before were the tail end of an Oklahoma dust storm. Perhaps mindful that their activities near the nest had been too unsettling for the nesting woodpeckers, Doc and Kellogg spent this Friday taking photos around the camp. The birds' comings and goings seemed less hectic than the day before. Tanner explored up

A male ivory-billed woodpecker, John's Bayou, Singer Tract, 1935. (Photo courtesy of Nancy Tanner.)

and down John's Bayou, finding a blue-gray gnatcatcher's nest. Myrtle warblers were in breeding plumage and indigo buntings were molting into theirs. On his way back to camp, he discovered two young barred owls "just out of the nest, wings and tails very short, plumage fluffy white with brown markings."

Ed Cochran, a local timber warden, visited the group that evening. From him they learned the history of the tract. Located Southwest of Tallulah, the great woodland surrounded the Tensas River, a slow-moving channel of the Mississippi. As early as the 1830s, pioneers began to trickle into the area, cutting the trees to plant cotton along the river. A levee was built to hold back the Mississippi during spring floods, and more families moved into the parish. Some of the homes were grand, some austere, especially the ones for the slaves who worked the fields. Even though civilization was beginning to bite into the woodland, the Tensas Swamp and its bayous, complete with big trees, remained untouched because much of these lowlands were periodically under water. During the Civil War, the North seized control of the Mississippi and its surrounding deltas, freeing the slaves and commandeering anything else of value as spoils of war. The plantation owners had little choice but to slip away into the night, leaving their fields and homes behind them. Nature began to reclaim what it had lost.

After the war, lumber companies started buying large parcels of swampland and forests across the South to harvest the timber. The old-growth trees of the Tensas would have fallen then except that, in 1913, the Singer Manufacturing Company bought part of the land for its future needs: oak for the wooden cabinets that housed its sewing machines. The price for what became known as the "Singer Tract" was nineteen dollars an acre. The strip spanned from ten to fifty miles wide, its 82,000 acres typical alluvial bottomland characterized by a subclimax forest of oak, hickory, gum and, in the wetter portions, cypress and tupelo. It was declared a refuge. Hunting was banned, and the trees could not be cut without the Singer company's approval. Wildlife was plentiful, with deer, wild turkeys, Louisiana black bears, otters, wolves, and cougars being reported. In 1920 Singer and the Louisiana Fish and Game Department entered into an agreement that provided for state management of the refuge—protection that included a warden to watch out for illegal hunters and tree poachers. Singer, headquartered in New York City, wanted to protect its assets. In 1935 the Singer warden was woodsman J. J. Kuhn.

Signs of the pre–Civil War development—levees, cisterns, and building foundations—were still visible in the Singer Tract, although catbrier and palmetto were starting to conceal their presence. Muddy Sharkey Road, which led into the abandoned Sharkey plantation, was one of those prewar artifacts. The cultivated rows of cotton were gone; the mud remained. The woodland pierced by the road was a mix of towering old-growth giants and second-growth trees reclaiming the open spaces. A swamp is essentially a flooded forest; the difference between the high ground and low ground can be only a few feet. During the spring rains, one would notice hardly any variation at all.

Allen, Kellogg, and Tanner had spent a week exploring this area after Kuhn found their red-crested prize, but it was almost time to move on to find other vanishing birds.

Saturday, April 13, "started out with all signs of a fine day, and kept its promise," wrote Tanner. There was good lighting that morning, and Doc Allen climbed the rock elm into the blind at eight o'clock. Over the next two and a half hours, he repeated the work that his graduate student had done two days before, ultimately exposing two hundred feet of movie film and taking twelve photographs. At 10:50 AM he lowered the cameras, dismantled the blind, and returned to terra firma. The group's observations widened to the surrounding area. In the afternoon, Allen left the camp moving west. He encountered the male and reported,

> I then followed him for an hour, until 3:00 PM, when he made a longer flight westward and was lost. Sometimes he fed high, sometimes within fifteen feet of the ground, and he was not very wild as I often got within forty or fifty feet of him. His flight was much more direct than a pileated's—usually sloping downward with a final swoop upward as he landed. Sometimes he chopped for ten or fifteen minutes on one tree, sometimes only two or three. Sometimes he merely chopped off the bark, but nearly as often he went to old cuttings and enlarged them for whatever was inside—perhaps carpenter ants or termites.

The observations Doc Allen was recording were a veteran ornithologist's dream. He continued, "His *kenting* varied a great deal, perhaps depending on whether he noticed me. Most of the time he was silent. His tail was always closed and pointed in flight, his head and bill straight out; his wings looked much more pointed than a pileated's, and narrower, but this might be an illusion on account of the large amount of white."

Meanwhile, Tanner explored south of the nest. Roughly a quarter-mile away from Camp Ephilus, he found the female ivory-bill feeding. "She had scaled the bark from a hackberry tree about 26 feet up and dug a hole like a pileated in the wood," he wrote in his field notes.

> She seemed to be picking something from the hole. Occasionally she called. When she left, she flew directly towards the nest. Later yet, I saw the male feeding. He tapped on a break on the bark but apparently did no eating. He then worked up a stub to the top, tapping. On leaving, he flew towards the nest but stopped once on the way and called.
>
> The male seems to spend most of the time on the nest. He has spent every night on the nest to date. When the female approaches and calls, he will signal by pounding vigorously on the inside of the nest.

What the young grad student had witnessed over the past seven days would serve him well, becoming the basis for his fieldwork to follow.

"We wanted to remain with the ivory-bills until their eggs hatched and the young were reared," wrote Doc Allen. "But we heard from our friend Verne Davidson that if we wished to study and record the lesser prairie chickens in western Oklahoma we must hasten on so as to get there before the first of May. So, torn between two desires and anxious to make the most of all opportunities, we sent for the mules and broke camp, planning to return in three weeks when the young should be nearly fledged."

After ten days in the swamp, the Cornell group returned to Tallulah. "A good bath, meal, and bed felt wonderful, but they will soon be forgotten," Tanner commented. He knew that more adventures lay ahead.

With a major goal of their expedition accomplished, the trio must have been ecstatic. They worked a full day transferring the equipment and getting the trucks ready for the next leg of their journey. Allen, Kellogg, and Tanner left Tallulah around 11:00 AM the following day, bound for Lafayette, west of Baton Rouge. Arriving late, they stayed at the Gordon Hotel on East Vermilion Street. The Renaissance-style four-story hotel was a world removed from sleeping pallets spread on the ground, but wrapped in the euphoria spawned in the Tensas swamp, the trio probably didn't even notice the difference.

Chapter 5

Hot Sauce and Bird City

This is an amazing object lesson in bird protection, showing what man can accomplish through thoughtfulness and kindness toward bird life.

—Arthur A. Allen

Stormy weather in Oklahoma forced a change in itinerary for Allen, Kellogg, and Tanner. At the invitation of businessman E. A. McIlhenny, the Cornell team made a side trip, driving south to Avery Island on Wednesday, April 17, to observe snowy egrets and a remarkable man-made sanctuary known as "Bird City." Located nine miles from New Iberia in southern Louisiana, the island owned by the McIlhenny family is not an island in the traditional sense but a monumental salt dome six miles in circumference and surrounded by marsh, swamp, and the Bayou Petit Anse—Cajun French for "Little Cove." An anomaly compared to the surrounding lowlands, the mountain is an upwelling, or massive deposit, created when an ancient body of water evaporated and left the concentration of salt behind. Today, the dome rises to 163 feet above sea level at its highest point. The 2,200-acre parcel, about three miles inland from Vermilion Bay, is host to an odd pair: Tabasco Sauce and a wildlife refuge created by a father and son.

After the Civil War, Edmund McIlhenny, believing that the diet of the South had become too bland and repetitive, decided to create a hot sauce. He started with a blend of crushed tabasco peppers and Avery Island rock salt, creating a mash that he aged for thirty days. Then he mixed it with French white vinegar and seasoned the brew for at least another thirty days. He grew his first tabasco peppers on Avery Island in 1868 and, as legend has it, was bottling his famous hot sauce in discarded cologne bottles soon thereafter. His product was a monumental success. As his market grew, McIlhenny was forced to buy thousands of *new* bottles from a glassworks in New Orleans. The cork-topped, two-ounce bottles with diamond-shaped labels looked very similar to what can still be found on supermarket shelves today. By the 1880s McIlhenny's hot sauce was being sold in most major American cities and in Europe. Although today there are many hot pepper sauces on the market and many use tabasco peppers, only one bears McIlhenny's patented name "Tabasco." He locked away the name, and the zippy concoction made his family a fortune. For decades even all the handpicked tabasco peppers used in the recipe were grown on Avery.

Edmund's son Edward Avery McIlhenny was born on the island in 1872 and served as president of the Tabasco Company from 1907 to 1947. But E.A.'s passions and creative energies flowed outside the hot sauce industry. Affectionately called Mr. Ned, he became known as a naturalist and conservationist. In the 1890s he established Avery Island as a wildlife sanctuary, began Bird City in 1892, and a few years later established a botanical wonderland known as "Jungle Gardens." He was also instrumental in the establishment of a series of wildlife refuges—principally marshes in southern Louisiana—totaling over 234,000 acres. As if that weren't ambitious enough, McIlhenny published *The Alligator's Life History* in 1935 (the wetlands around Avery Island had plenty of alligators for him to observe) and *The Autobiography of an Egret* in 1939. It was the egrets, not the alligators, that lured the traveling Cornellians.

McIlhenny's snowy egret rookery represented a conservation success story. Thirty years earlier, the species was rapidly disappearing, having become feathered gold to poachers. Much sought after for women's hats by the millinery trade, a pound of egret feathers was, at the time of highest demand, worth more than a pound of gold. The "Great Plume War" that raged in the late 1800s and early in last century saw millions of birds slaughtered for their feathers. By 1916, even though it was illegal, poachers could earn nine dollars for an egret's plume. Before McIlhenny stepped in, it was estimated that only 1,400 great egrets and 250 snowy egrets were left in the wild. The rookery on Avery Island showcased a species making a comeback.

McIlhenny created Bird City on an artificial pond. When plume hunters were killing egrets by the thousands, McIlhenny gathered up eight young chicks and raised them in captivity on the island, releasing them in the fall to migrate across the Gulf of Mexico. In the spring they returned, accompanied by others. In time, the small flock began to build nests.

"The rookery is in the trees and bushes of a small artificial pond within 200 yards of Mr. McIlhenny's house, and among the many interesting entertainments he gives his guests is to take them out to the edge of the yard of a spring evening that they may watch the Herons and Snowy Egrets coming home to roost or to relieve their mates on guard at the nests," wrote Audubon president T. Gilbert Pearson.

"Beginning 35 years ago when the snowy heron [egret] had become quite rare," Doc Allen observed, "Mr. McIlhenny has gradually built up a large colony on an artificial pond of his own creation." When the Cornell expedition visited the location, Allen estimated that the egret population numbered about ten thousand and at least that many more were expected to arrive. The Tabasco heir is credited with almost single-handedly saving the species.

At only twenty-two to twenty-seven inches in length, the snowy egret is much smaller than the great egret. The snowy is considered perhaps the most beautiful of all North American egrets because their nuptial plumage, known as "aigrettes," bellows down their backs between their wings, giving them a soft, lacy appearance. These feathers are much shorter than those of the great egret and more delicate, with a recurved end.

McIlhenny's pond covered about five acres. "Every bush is loaded with snowy egret and Louisiana heron nests, mixed indiscriminately together. Most of the bushes are buttonwood," wrote Tanner. "He has increased the number of nests by providing nesting places: brush supported by cane frames, and materials: twigs placed daily on a stand." Tanner took a boat out into the pond for a better view, drifting up to an eight-foot alligator. "In the evening more herons came into roost; then suddenly the birds dived, twisting and swooping, with all sorts of wing attitudes, to the bushes, a thrilling performance," the young grad student scribbled in his field journal.

"We recorded the froglike croakings of the snowy egrets, and, by unusual good-fortune, captured the bellow of a huge bull alligator," reported Allen. "It is a thrilling sound—like the roar of a lion, but rendered more terrifying by the sight of the churning water, and it certainly must be effective in intimidating lesser male alligators and keeping them from the chosen territory."

The next day Kellogg taped some gallinules while Allen and Tanner spent the day tucked away in a large permanent blind photographing and observing the resident snowy egrets and Louisiana herons. "The nests, platforms of sticks, averaged about four feet apart, the two species mixed," Tanner noted. "Each bird had its territory around its nest and fought off all trespassers. Most of the fighting was between individuals of the same species. They seemed to be less antagonistic towards other species. Most of the bickering was among snowys. They would grunt and squawk at each other with upraised plumes on head, back, and throat. Both birds [genders] brooded, they changed places with a little ceremony of raised plumes and bills pointing up."

Tanner further observed that "the eggs of both species are pale blue, somewhat streaked. Nests had everything from one to five eggs. Birds were continually adding to their nests, picking twigs from the water or stealing them from nearby nests. Mating often occurred on the nest."

It was Easter weekend, and the Cornell group did some general sightseeing and picture taking around the island. Allen and Tanner found a dickcissel and painted bunting, but the grad student noted the general lack of small birds in the area. On Saturday, it rained early and little could be done outdoors. Tanner toured the McIlhenny's salt plant where the 99.9-percent pure rock salt that came from the mine on the island was crushed into table salt, part of which was used in the Tabasco Sauce. Easter Sunday arrived warm and sunny with picturesque clouds. The group went to Jungle Gardens early to watch the dominant bull alligator greet the day. "Almost exactly at nine he roared," recorded Tanner. "When he finished a small female in the same pond roared too."

At the end of the day, McIlhenny gave Allen a pair of stuffed ivory-bill specimens and promised to give them a set of eggs, commenting that there once had been four or five ivory-bill pairs living in his swamp.

While at Avery Island, the Cornell team waited for the weather to clear in Oklahoma. "It was now the last of April," wrote Allen, "and another message from Davidson started us westward, through we were loath to leave our genial host and his marvelous bird sanctuary."

By Monday, April 22, the trio was on the road again but had a tire blowout before reaching Shreveport. After buying two new tires and having supper, they spent the night in a cabin near Greenwood, Louisiana. Setting out early the next morning, the group recorded a summer tanager in a mixed hardwood and pine forest along the way. Driving on through rolling woods and farmland, they passed through their first oil field in east Texas. North of Dallas came their first encounter with the flat and treeless landscape of "real prairie." They ate supper in Gainesville, Texas, and camped for the night in Ardmore, Oklahoma. Along the way, Tanner spotted two scissor-tailed flycatchers, which he had never seen before. The species is found in grass and farmland in Texas and Oklahoma during nesting season.

The next morning, Wednesday, April 24, Allen, Kellogg, and Tanner drove north from Ardmore to Oklahoma City, through the Arbuckle Mountains. Heading towards Sayre, the trio once again entered flat, largely treeless country. "Driving west gave the impression that we were losing altitude, for we would frequently go down steep pitches, over escapements; actually we had climbed to 2400 feet at the Davidson Ranch," recorded Tanner. "Turning north from Sayre, we saw really dry, dusty country. Some of it was hilly. The Canadian River was bone dry, a white snake on the land."

Fortune is a fickle mistress: what it gives to one, it takes from another. Having left the environmental bounty of Avery Island and traveling only a few hundred miles to the northwest, the Cornell trio had entered an area now infamous in American history—a land of hardship, loss, and broken dreams. They had come to the heart of the Dust Bowl.

Chapter 6

Days of Wind and Dust

Every moving thing lifted the dust into the air: a walking man lifted a thin layer as high as his waist, and a wagon lifted the dust as high as the fence tops, and an automobile boiled a cloud behind it. The dust was long in settling back again.

—John Steinbeck

"When we reached western Oklahoma a dull fog gradually obscured the landscape, and as the wind whipped over the barren fields and swirled across the road, we realized that we were in the midst of a real 'Panhandle' dust storm," remembered Doc Allen. "Furthermore, the storm continued without much abatement for seven of the eight days that we spent on the Davidson Ranch near Arnett." It was a far cry from the mud and damp of the Singer Tract in Louisiana the Cornellians had left just eight days before.

An environmental and economic disaster that ravaged the American prairie lands from 1933 to 1939, the Dust Bowl affected close to 50 million acres in parts of five states. It had multiple causes. Early settlers had removed the native grasses and plowed the region into farmland. Failure to rotate crops depleted the soil and encouraged erosion. Too many animals grazed on what grass remained. When a severe drought struck, the soil was baked to dust. At the same time, the Great Depression forced thousands of farmers, who could no longer make payments on their property, into homelessness. The region's farms, newly abandoned, lay barren. Dark clouds of Oklahoma topsoil were blown east into the Atlantic Ocean and far out into the Gulf of Mexico. The thick curtains of dust made it difficult for people to breathe when outside, forcing them to wear masks to protect their eyes, throats, and lungs. On April 14, 1935, just ten days before Allen, Kellogg, and Tanner arrived in western Oklahoma, the region experienced what became known as "Black Sunday." That was when twenty of the worst dust storms occurred, turning day into night. Witnesses reported that they could not see five feet in front of them. The "Black Blizzards" caused damage of biblical proportions. Desolate drifts of fine powdery soil lay in mounds like snow, covering empty homes and sheds. The environmental disaster ruined thousands of lives. The plight of the devastated farmers came to light in John Steinbeck's Pulitzer Prize–winning novel *The Grapes of Wrath*, published in 1939, only four years after the Cornell trio visited the region.

"It had scarcely rained for three years and from fields that had once been plowed the surface soil and the very seed were blown into neighboring counties," wrote Allen.

The Cornell trio found the ranch of Verne and Mildred Davidson, their hosts in the area, largely covered with dust and tiny oaks. The Davidsons' cattle —about eighty head—appeared in good condition despite the drought. They fed on the small oaks and whatever grass they happened to find. "The ranch is the largest in Oklahoma," wrote Tanner, "used mostly for grazing. The western part is sandhills, slightly rolling with broken ridges and mounds. The soil is sand and dust with red clay a few feet below the surface. It is almost entirely covered with shinnery, a scrub oak that is about one- to two-feet high. It is not thick enough to retard walking. On the little hills, the shinnery is three- to six-feet high."

Around dawn on Thursday, April 25, with Verne Davidson as their guide, the Cornellians set out to look for prairie chickens. However, the wind began to stir up the dust, and by the middle of the morning it was pretty thick. "The dust storm was at its worse about three o'clock," wrote Tanner.

> It made eyes smart, teeth gritty, and faces very dusty. Breathing was rather hard. We couldn't see much of the country beyond 100-yards. Most of the dust was very fine, but the wind blew up coarse sand from the ground.
>
> Several years ago this used to be good farm country, but it has been gradually getting drier. Wheat and grass grew high as the saddle. Only in the last two years have there been dust storms. Now they are pretty regular.

The lesser prairie chickens that Allen, Kellogg, and Tanner were seeking are members of the grouse family. Closely related to the now-extinct heath hen, these ground-dwelling birds are native to the plains, sandhills, and prairies in the middle of the continent. Smaller, paler, and more limited in range than the greater prairie chicken, the lesser is found in drier environments, and its population has suffered an estimated 97-percent decline since the 1800s, mainly because of the alteration of its habitat for ranching and agriculture. A major drop in range and population coincided with the Dust Bowl conditions during the time of the Cornell expedition.

Both prairie chicken species are noted for their elaborate "lekking" behavior. A lek is a gathering of males for the purpose of competitive mating displays that occur within a chosen communal territory called a "tooting ground." These displays are designed to attract females, who visit the lek to choose mates. In addition to a male's performance, location matters. Females generally pick mates that have claimed a central location within the display arena, which means that the competition to occupy the center is the most heated. After mating, the females leave to nest in some out-of-the-way place and raise their young alone. To study and record this behavior the Cornell trio needed to erect a blind. "The cattle eyed us curiously when we first erected one of our observation blinds near the home of a burrowing owl," Doc Allen wrote. "This blind was made of artificial grass mats, greener than anything in that whole country, greener than anything the heifers had ever seen. Instinctively they came lumbering in from all quarters to get a luscious meal."

During the spring, the lesser prairie chickens assemble in groups of from four to forty twice a day: in the morning and again in the evening. They choose flat-topped knolls among the shinnery and, as Allen observed, "compete with one another in a show of prowess, both in voice and body vigor." The displays last for roughly six weeks, with each male returning to the exact same spot to claim and defend its territory.

In his field notes dated Saturday, April 27, Tanner recorded,

> We reached the tooting grounds in good time, after a cool, quiet morning. The birds returned quickly after our set up and put on a real tooting show. The tooting ground was a long low ridge, and probably covered about two acres. It was covered with a thin growth of shinnery and a few flowers. Each bird has a territory about 20 feet in diameter. It toots and struts in this territory and drives all other males from it. A full performance consists of a patter, bow, and toot. With wings low and pinnae [horn-like feathers on the side of the neck] erect over the back of his head, his yellow comb erected, he stamps rapidly with his feet, producing a noticeable drum and moving forward slowly a foot or two. Then he bows and simultaneously the pink neck sacs expand, he toots and flicks his tail.
>
> When the birds are most active, there are chickens running and tooting all over the field. Sometimes they bow and toot without running; sometimes the toot is single, sometimes repeated. Occasionally two birds will get together and toot alternately in perfect rhythm, the two bobbing up and down like a seesaw—

> "toot–toot–toot–toot." They usually finish their performance by standing straight and cackling.
>
> Fights are common. Two chickens face each other, toot, then fly together; they rise up in the air, strike with their wings, bite, bark, and abide by no rules. Sometimes they will settle down to the ground, face together, and meow like a cat.
>
> Whenever they take flight, they cackle shortly and continue to cackle as they plane above the shinnery. We succeeded in getting good pictures and some good recordings.

Allen observed that "many of the combats are mere gestures or feints of anger, but others are sufficiently severe to scatter feathers over the shinnery. Sometimes when the males jump at one another and strike with their wings, a hapless bird is flipped clear over onto his back by a stronger rival." Early each morning from April 25 until May 2, the Cornell trio went to a tooting ground occupied by twenty-six males, placing their microphone in the territory of a dominant cock. For most of the week the winds and dust prevented them from recording clean audio. Luckily, one morning was quiet. "We secured a nearly perfect recording of the birds' sounds, from the pattering of their feet and the silken twitching of their tail feathers to the loud gobbling that follows," wrote Allen.

During a lull on May Day, Doc spent time photographing burrowing owls and prairie dogs. One area, covering approximately eight acres, had forty prairie dog burrows with side entrances. Young pups—half-grown to chipmunk sized—played outside near the openings to their dens. There were also two pairs of owls in the area using old prairie dog holes. Known as "howdy owls" to cowboys, burrowing owls seemed to nod a greeting at passersby. Because they are active during the day, Allen discovered the amiable long-legged owls could be found at the entrances of the abandoned burrows in prairie dog towns. Like the communal mammals, burrowing owls are common to the open sandy country of western Oklahoma. Their homes can often be distinguished from the gregarious rodents' abodes by an unusual sense of décor. Burrowing owls decorate the entrances of their holes with dried cattle or bison dung—in part to camouflage their nest sites but also to attract insects, one of their principal food sources. After spending several hours observing the area, Allen and Tanner returned to the ranch. The mid-day calm gave way to yet another dust storm in the evening.

On Thursday, May 2, the Cornellians went one last time to the display arena and had just set up to record when another dust storm came along. And that was that: the trio packed up their gear and left the Davidson Ranch before noon. They drove south to Oklahoma City, where they registered at the Bristol Hotel. They then took the evening off to see the movie *Naughty Marietta*, which featured the first on-screen pairing of Jeanette MacDonald and Nelson Eddy.

Were their minds on the movie? Perhaps not, because they knew that in the Singer Tract there should be an ivory-bill nestling waiting to be recorded, a young bird that had still been in the egg when they left almost three weeks before.

Chapter 7

Has Anyone Seen a Young Ivory-bill?

I honestly believe that there are fewer prettier places than the lakes of the big Louisiana woods, lakes of still dark water surrounded by green buttonwood bushes and straight, feathery-topped cypress. These lakes have many birds living around them, herons, anhingas, wood ducks, prothonotary warblers.

—James T. Tanner

Hoping to find the pair of ivory-bills they had already photographed feeding their young, Allen, Kellogg, and Tanner once again headed south to the Louisiana swamp. On Friday, May 3, the group left Oklahoma City. In the evening they encountered rain, buckets of rain—a stark contrast to the dusty, dry week on the prairie. For two days they drove through an almost continuous cloudburst. "We survived the trip despite water, wind, and lightning," Tanner wrote. "At times the rain was like a wall of water, looking like a gray mist, but not feeling that way. In many places the road was completely covered necessitating slow driving." The weary Cornell group arrived back in Tallulah, Louisiana, on Sunday afternoon, checking once again into the Montgomery Hotel. The next day brought more rain.

On Tuesday, May 7, the rain finally ended. Leaving the hotel at 5:30 AM, the team scouted the area for other birds to record. Driving south to a wet field, they recorded a singing dickcissel, a seed-eating, sparrow-sized bird of the Midwest. After breakfast and with improving light, they tried for photographs but had better luck with the movie camera. If the dust of western Oklahoma had impeded their work, the trio once again found the lowlands of Louisiana under too much water. The swamp had gotten swampier. Allen, Kellogg, and Tanner didn't go to the Singer Tract immediately but spent two days getting the gear ready for a return to the ivory-bill nest. They met with Dr. L. M. Dickerson, wildlife technician of the State Parks Division of the National Park Service, who was on a local inspection tour.

On May 9 Kellogg and Tanner continued to explore, looking for singing birds. Once they had located one, it was a tedious matter of positioning the microphone and hiding in the sound truck in the hope that the bird would return to the same perch and vocalize loudly enough to be recorded. It was nesting season, and the males often had favorite perches from which to sing and defend their territories. The Cornellians succeeded in locating and recording the *witchity-witchity-witch* of a common yellowthroat, a wetland-loving warbler.

Allen, J. J. Kuhn, and Dickerson borrowed horses and rode into the swamp, returning to the ivory-bill nest the team had photographed three weeks earlier, but all was quiet. Too quiet. To their chagrin, they found the nest deserted and the pair nowhere to be found. The three men spent the day waiting around, hoping the birds would return. They did not. The group also searched for a third nest Kuhn had discovered on April 29, a mile to the northwest, but had no luck relocating it and heard no ivory-bills. Had that nest been deserted as well? Curious about why the first nest had been abandoned, they cut down the tree to examine the contents of the hole. In the dim light of a rapidly fading day, they found tiny fragments of eggshells but no sign of blood, albumen, or moisture—just dry bits of wood, debris from the hole's excavation. Packaging the contents of the nest in a paper bag, they returned to town discouraged and downright bewildered.

"The next morning, however, under a desk lamp at the hotel, as the heat of the lamp warmed up the 'sawdust,' the material gradually came to life and swarmed with innumerable tiny mites," wrote Allen. They soon felt the tiny arachnids crawling all over their hands. The nest material was heavily infested. Could the mites have caused the nest to fail?

"We were reminded of the actions of the birds at the nest and how nervous they sometimes seemed after incubating for a short time and of how much time they sometimes spent preening when they came out of the hole in the maple," recalled Allen, who knew from experience that mites had killed young nestlings of other species. Mites can also irritate the parents to such an extent that they fail to brood, or incubate, properly. The shell fragments seemed to indicate the egg or eggs had hatched, but what happened after that? As there were no dead young in the nest, it remained a mystery. While Allen, Kellogg, and Tanner were in Oklahoma, Kuhn had visited the nest on April 29. The ivory-bills were still there but behaved rather strangely. The two birds took turns looking into the hole as if something was wrong. Going into the hole, they remained inside only briefly and then flew to a nearby tree, where they spent much time preening themselves. A full ten days before Doc Allen returned to the nest, the woodpeckers were apparently not feeding any young.

Allen, Kuhn, and Dickerson then rode south to look for a fourth ivory-bill nest reported by Avery Hollis, a local woodsman and game warden at Tensas. They found it forty-seven feet up a dead pin oak on the edge of a natural clearing. Hidden in a verdant tangle of poison ivy and catbrier, they watched the nest for an hour and a half, making continuous notes of the pair's comings and goings. Both birds were carrying food to the tree, indicating the presence of young. "The male came and entered with his grub," wrote Allen. "He remained inside a couple of minutes and I could hear buzzing from the young. Apparently they were too small to swallow the grub for he left with it to a tree one hundred feet away and apparently swallowed it himself." Deciding that the nestlings were very young, the men elected not to return to the nest for a few days, a decision they likely later regretted.

Meanwhile, for two days, Kellogg and Tanner continued to explore Sharkey Road and its vicinity, looking for birds to record. They succeeded with northern parula and Kentucky warblers and the *chick'-a-per-weeoo-chick'* of a white-eyed vireo. The weather was growing hotter and the mosquitoes more aggressive.

On Sunday morning, May 12, Allen and Tanner returned to the site of the original nest. Tanner noted that the road in was much wetter than it had been the month before. The tree was down, in pieces, having been cut to examine the nest's contents. Eventually, the section of trunk with the nest hole was crated and sent back to Ithaca.

Two days later, heading for the active nest they had just recently discovered, the team got an early start and drove fourteen miles south to Quimby and on to Foster's, another former plantation that was now the home of two white and four black families. Four miles of poorly maintained dirt road led into the property. As they had done the month before, the group transferred their gear into a mule-drawn wagon. This time they hoped to get color motion pictures of the birds. It would have been historic, even priceless footage, but it wasn't meant to be. They arrived at the site at 11:00 AM, but there were no ivory-bills. They waited, hopeful, but none appeared. As before, the nest seemed abandoned.

Loading their gear back on to the wagon, the group returned to the old plantation house and camped out that night. The next morning, Kellogg and Tanner staked out the nest of a painted bunting, hoping to get audio but had no luck. Allen and Kuhn returned to the new nest site and, yet again, found no ivory-bills. The pin oak the birds had chosen was huge, about ten feet in circumference at its base. "When we were thoroughly satisfied that the birds were nowhere around we secured a crosscut saw and an axe and cut the tree down," wrote Allen. "Once again the only evidence of the hole having been occupied by woodpeckers was the tiny fragments of shell similar to those in the swamp-maple nest. There was no sign of young birds having been in the nest, nor was there any evidence of blood or of spilled food or excreta, and in this nest there were no signs of mites. The young birds had just mysteriously disappeared." It was a day of disappointments. At its close, the men returned to Tallulah.

The disappearances of the two ivory-bill nests were not isolated occurrences. For Kuhn, they brought to mind a time in May 1933 when he had located a nesting pair forty-five feet up a black oak. Their activity indicated that they were feeding young, which prompted the woodsman to contact T. Gilbert Pearson of the National Association of Audubon Societies. Dr. Frank Oastler, a New York physician and active naturalist, visited in early June to verify the nest; he hoped to get motion pictures of the birds but found the hole deserted. An examination of the nest turned up only shell fragments.

The Cornellians spent two more days investigating other ivory-bill reports but to no avail. Although this second trip to Madison Parish had yielded photographs of several birds—including prothonotary warbler, Carolina wren, and orchard oriole, plus audio recordings of others—a pall hung over the group. As was their penchant, the ghost birds had once again managed to disappear. Poof!

In his notebook Tanner summarized what they had learned about the area's ivory-bills that season. There had been four nest holes in the Singer Tract while the Cornell team was there. The first on John's Bayou had been well documented with recordings, photographs, and motion pictures. The second nest Kuhn discovered was in a dead oak, two miles south of the first nest, but the next day a black squirrel had seemingly displaced the pair. The third nest Kuhn had found was about one mile northwest of the first, but he was unable to relocate it with Doc Allen on May 9, in part because they heard no birds in the vicinity. Hearing an ivory-bill was key to finding it. The fourth nest was near the old Foster Plantation, seven miles south of the first nest. Allen and Kuhn had found this nest on May 10 and saw the ivory-bill pair carrying food to the hole, but four days later, it had been abandoned.

Out of these nesting attempts, no young were apparently produced. Two years later, in an account he published in *The Auk*, a quarterly journal published by the American Ornithologists' Union, Doc Allen could only speculate about what might have happened to the four nests and the one Kuhn had observed in 1933. One thing was becoming clear: if finding an ivory-billed woodpecker was hard, finding young ones was almost impossible, even when active nests were located. Kuhn, an experienced woodsman, could only remember seeing young ones twice in his lifetime. They looked, he said, like the female but not so black and with more white in their plumage. Three of the nests—the first and fourth found in 1935 and the one Oastler had investigated with Kuhn in 1933—contained eggshell fragments. Allen believed that the critical period in a young ivory-bill's life, a time of high mortality, came soon after hatching.

"Whether this is due to predators or to innate weakness in the stock has not, of course, been determined, and there are arguments to be advanced on both sides," Allen wrote. Predators rarely bothered the nests of pileated woodpecker, but since an ivory-bill's nest entrance is larger, could a raccoon or opossum, great horned or barred owl snatch a young ivory-bill? Yet, none of the nest holes examined showed any signs of marauders. A black squirrel had been found in the second nest located in 1935, but whether it had contained young was unknown. While mites had perhaps caused the first 1935 nest to fail, there were no evidence of them in the others. The rediscovery of the ivory-bill had opened a Pandora's box of baffling questions.

Doc Allen's greatest concern had to do with the scattered nature of the species, which inhabited widely dispersed patches of old wooded swampland. Habitat loss had forced the birds into ever smaller family units living in isolated pockets. Could this have led to inbreeding or out-of-balance reproductive cycles? Individual ivory-bills had little choice in selecting mates. Were their young genetically weak, unable to survive for more than a few days?

The plight of the ivory-bills was that of many species facing possible extinction—a dilemma well summarized by David Quammen in his book *The Song of the Dodo*. Citing work by physiology professor Jared Diamond, Quammen writes, "Within any bounded area, a carnivorous species will usually be less numerous than a herbivorous species; a large-bodied carnivore will usually be less numerous than a small-bodied carnivore; and a habitat specialist will usually be less numerous than a generalist. The specialist and the carnivores, in particular the large-bodied carnivores, will consequently face a higher risk of extinction. Big populations don't go extinct. Small populations do. It's not surprising, but it is significant. Otherwise put: Rarity is perilous."

In 1935 ivory-bills were obviously not extinct. But the birds were large-bodied insectivores, and existing data seemed to indicate that they were also specialists and perilously rare. With so many unanswered questions cropping up, Doc Allen concluded that efforts should be made for a more complete study of the species. That research would have to come later. For now, the Cornellians had an itinerary to keep, and they needed to move on. Doc Allen had two months left of his sabbatical; other adventures awaited.

Chapter 8

Westward Ho

From Oklahoma our expedition moved north and west through the barren, windswept prairies of western Kansas into the verdant irrigated stretches of eastern Colorado, and thence to Colorado Springs and Denver.

—Arthur A. Allen

After coastal marsh, swamp, and grassland, it was time to head to the mountains, but first a return trip to the prairie was in order. This time Allen, Kellogg, and Tanner found Oklahoma noticeably different. It was wetter, too wet in most places. When they arrived back in Ardmore it was raining, as it had been when they left fifteen days earlier. The team hoped for a few more quiet days to observe the lesser prairie chickens before moving farther west.

On Saturday, May 18, they found all the steams swollen and water standing in the fields. Rivers that had been dry just two weeks earlier were now running full. The weather cleared for a while in the middle of the day only to reveal considerable flooding. A breached levee upstream had sent a surge of water downstream. The team arrived at Clinton, eighty-five miles west of Oklahoma City on the fabled Route 66, at about 1:00 PM Water was starting to cover the road, and the principal bridge was closed just after they crossed it. Farther west, near Sayre, they were pounded by yet another heavy storm. If a Dust Bowl–weary farmer had prayed for rain, his prayers had been answered and then some. Finally arriving back at the Davidson Ranch at seven o'clock, the trio learned that it had rained seven inches in the past five days—the first real precipitation western Oklahoma had seen in three years. Call it a drought breaker, but it was only a reprieve. Dust Bowl conditions would actually last until the early 1940s, when weather patterns finally changed and normal rainfalls returned.

Sunday, May 19, was perfect, clear and bright from beginning to end. In the morning Kellogg and Tanner recorded a scissor-tailed flycatcher and Cassin's sparrow, two species with very limited ranges, and despite the wind, they later succeeded in getting audio of a western meadowlark's clarion calls. The next morning, Tanner went with Allen and Davidson back to the tooting ground of the prairie chicken, but as Jim noted, "The birds tooted more spasmodically and there was less fighting than earlier. . . . Doc was certain that the chicken's have sexual cycles similar to grouse."

"They live in the shinnery, right on the ground," Tanner observed. "Their song is ordinarily given in the air. They fly diagonally upward, bursting into song almost immediately. The song is completed as they half hover in mid-air, wings fluttering and tail pointing upwards. The song is a thin trill, slightly varied, followed by two lower, clear notes. When it is completed, the bird volplanes [glides] and flies back to the earth, always to the ground."

Wednesday, May 22: Kellogg and Tanner attempted to record a white-necked raven early and were back at the ranch and ready to leave by late morning. "The roads up to Kansas were rough from the rains, but we had no trouble," Tanner wrote in his field notes. "All of the country between Arnett and Garden City had been badly hit by the drought. Many fields were nothing but dry dirt. Several farms had been abandoned. All we saw of Kansas was flat and dry. Once we crossed into Colorado, irrigation made things greener and brought more birds." The road from Garden City, Kansas, follows the Arkansas River upstream toward its source. The eastern third of Colorado is part of the High Plains, the elevated region of America's Great Plains. West of the one-hundredth meridian, the region is generally drier than Kansas and Nebraska, but irrigation, as Tanner noted, had "greened" up that part of the state for farming. Although the land seemed as flat as a billiard table, it actually had a significant tilt. Allen, Kellogg, and Tanner climbed about twenty-two hundred feet in elevation in just over four hundred road miles. At the end of the day, the trio spent the night in Pueblo, east of Royal Gorge. The Colorado Rockies loomed, snowcapped and majestic, to the west.

The next morning they drove north through more rain to Colorado Springs and the Antler's Hotel, a courtly Queen Anne–style structure with twin bell towers. Lofty Pike's Peak—all 14,115 feet of it—dominated the background.

Shortly after their arrival, Allen, Kellogg, and Tanner met with Robert J. Niedrach, curator of birds at the Colorado Museum of Natural History and the future coauthor of *The Birds of Denver and Mountain Parks* (1939). The Cornell group's goal was to locate and record golden eagles and prairie falcons, and Niedrach's help proved invaluable. After an informative lunch with Niedrach, they followed him to his cabin, twenty-three miles south of Denver.

"The cabin or house is perched on the edge of a ravine and commands a view of the Platte Valley and the Rockies. Colorado Springs and Denver are just east of the Rockies, just before the foothills rise from the plain and plateau," wrote Tanner in his journal. "The level country, as one goes westward, gives a foretaste of the mountains by being broken up into ravines, arroyos, draws, canyons. The foothills are in ordered ranks, projecting towards the plains, covered with scant timber. Behind the hogback foothills stand the rugged peaks, obtuse pyramids, snow blanketed." Niedrach's cabin became the expedition's headquarters for the next two weeks. Denver is a prairie city, situated a mile above sea level and only twelve miles from the rugged foothills. It was originally built on barren land, but by the 1930s the large number of shade trees planted along city streets gave it a woodsy appearance. Every tree, shrub, and lawn had been transplanted, however; otherwise it would have been as bare as the High Plains surrounding it. The native trees of the region—cottonwood, box elder, black willow, wild plum, choke cherry, gooseberry—were only found along the more moist stream valleys.

Friday, May 24, dawned clear and cool. Niedrach took Doc Allen and Tanner to a golden eagle's nest near the Colorado Springs Road. It was located seventy feet above the ground about three-quarters of the way up a Douglas fir. As Tanner recorded:

> I climbed to the nest and cleared branches out. There were two young birds, perhaps three-quarters grown, the white down almost all replaced by black feathers. One of the young was pugnacious. He walked or crawled to the edge of the nest and glared at me. Whenever I came too close, he struck with his wings and tried to grab with his talons. His pose of defiance showed him a true eagle. Leaning back against his tail and breasting, he spread his wings, turned his head and glared from one eye. The other bird only sulked on the edge of the nest, lying flat. In the nest there was half of a cottontail and a few magpie feathers.

Tanner had experience with golden eagles, having once nursed one back to health. As a teenager in Cortland, New York, he became known as the town's bird expert. When an impaired golden eagle was found a long way from its normal range, the ailing raptor was taken to the young Tanner. He named the bird "Chris" and fed it rodents until it recovered.

After Tanner climbed down, Niedrach took him and Allen to a second eagle's nest in a tree just below the cliff rim. Niedrach expected the eagles to use that nest the following year. Golden eagles mate for life. Both the male and female build the aeries and may have two or more nest sites they use in alternate years. The nests are bulky, made of sticks, and lined with leaves, grass, moss, and weeds. Each year new material is added; in time the nests become rather substantial affairs. Both sexes incubate, although the female spends more time on the eggs. The female also stays with the young after they hatch. Meanwhile, the male hunts to feed the family until the eaglets are about half grown, at which point the female joins her mate in the search for food. Golden eagles scavenge less than bald eagles. They eat primarily small mammals, but as Tanner discovered, they will also prey on birds like magpies, grouse, and even cranes. The mated pair often hunt together, with the second swooping in to grab prey that might elude the first.

The next morning, Niedrach took the Cornell trio to a third eagle's nest east at Castle Rock. Built on a ledge fifty feet down from the edge of a cliff, this one was also active. Its location seemed ideal for recording, and the Cornellians planned to lower a blind from above to observe the nest from nearby. They spent the rest of the day and all of the next scouting for other birds to photograph and record. High on their list were mountain plovers, which they finally located on nests east of Denver. Mountain plovers are misnamed anomalies. Their preferred habitat is open grassland and prairies, not mountains; they are also shorebirds found a long way from any water in the open dry country of the High Plains. Because the first specimen was collected near Sweetwater, Wyoming, on the central tableland of the Rockies, they received the name mountain plover, although prairie plover would have been a better fit. Limited in range to only a few western states, their populations are declining as natural prairies give way to farmland. The sand-colored plovers are found on featureless plains, skittering about among the yucca, cacti, and drought-resistant grasses. They nest in shallow depressions in loose soil, often near a conspicuous object such as a pile of cow dung.

On Monday morning, May 27, the Cornell team recorded a black-headed grosbeak and Virginia's warbler, both western species found in limited ranges. The grosbeak is one of the few birds that can eat monarch butterflies, which are laden with milkweed toxin. The warbler is grayish and rather nondescript; its common name honors the wife of Dr. William Anderson, who discovered the species in New Mexico in 1858.

Allen, Kellogg, and Tanner found both the grosbeak and the warbler near their borrowed cabin. Afterward, they drove back to one of the plover's nest where, as Tanner recorded, "We planned to set up the blind and let the bird come back before going in, but the bird refused to leave the vicinity of the nest and even settled on the eggs with us but a few feet away. We took several feet [of film] without a blind. Then set up the blind and kept moving it nearer until it was almost on top of the nest." Tanner also noted an approaching storm:

Teenager Jim Tanner with the rescued golden eagle he named Chris. (Photo courtesy of Nancy Tanner.)

It soon began to rain in the southeast, making such a roar as to be heard by us. A little later I entered the blind. The bird returned immediately and sat but three or four feet away. She was so tame; it was difficult to get any pictures but of her incubating. All of a sudden a gust of wind came and blew the blind over, and hail started to pelt down. The plover scared off, but it was obvious that she wanted to return, so we cleaned up quickly. The hail came down harder, some of the stones as big as the plover's eggs. All the birds around were scared of the hail, but there was no natural

> shelter. A meadowlark and two lark buntings flew under the car. Inspired by them, we moved the car forward until it sheltered the sitting plover from the stones.

As Doc Allen observed, the sheltering truck became quite an attraction for not only the plover but for other birds as well:

> Then birds started flying to us from all directions, especially the showy lark buntings, and soon there were some twenty of them sitting beneath the truck. Then came a western meadowlark, pitifully frightened. He longed for the shelter of the truck, but he was a timid bird and each time he approached within ten feet of the car, and could see us inside, his courage deserted him and he ran back. Three or four times he advanced as hailstones hit around him, but just as often he retreated.
>
> At last, summoning all his courage, he made a rush for the car and slipped safely beneath with the other birds. And when he found himself secure at last, he loosed his feelings in one of those clear, beautiful songs that endear this bird to all westerners.

The next morning the team came into Denver early and despite a misty rain, managed to record a house finch singing. At the time, this cherry-faced passerine was a western species, but they were being sold in eastern pet stores. Their cheery song made them a favorite caged bird. In 1940, when this practice became illegal, New York pet shop owners merely released their stock to avoid prosecution. The species spread throughout the east and now are found coast to coast.

After breakfast the Cornellians drove northeast to property owned by the Mile High Gun Club, which maintained seven ponds closed to the public and all clustered within a three-eighths-mile radius. The team soon located several avocet nests, and although it rained off and on, the dry intervals allowed them to record both an American avocet and a yellow-headed blackbird, two more western species not found in the east. American avocets are long-legged waders about eighteen inches tall. These elegant birds feed by strolling through shallow water, sweeping their long, thin, upward-curved bills from side to side beneath the water's surface.

The movie footage the team took shows a graceful avocet delicately wading through shallow water, its steps as measured as a dancer's. Allen and Tanner also filmed a pair exchanging places on a nest containing four speckled eggs hidden in the grass. "Avocet nests," Tanner wrote, "were fairly common, some located on high ground, some in marshes. Those in wet places were built up more with grass and cattail stalks."

The Cornellians also found Wilson's phalarope, American coot, and magpie nests. Tanner described settling into a blind and watching flocks of black terns, coots, shovelers, pintails, and gadwalls come and go. The next day brought mixed weather to the Denver area—rain, wind, and even a dust storm—that prevented recording. The team spent the night in a hotel and had dinner with Niedrach, reporting their progress.

The unusually heavy rains brought flooding to Colorado Springs, but in Denver the rivers managed to stay within their bounds. On Friday, May 31, with Niedrach accompanying them, the group drove sixty-five miles to Fort Collins, through rain and hail into semimountainous terrain, which as Tanner observed, was "cut up by rolling hills, ridges, escarpments, ravines, canyons; littered with large boulders of granite or soft sandstone; partially wooded with yellow pine." A walk of two miles led them to the cliffs above the lower end of Box Elder Canyon. About sixty feet below the top of a red sandstone cliff was, Jim wrote, "an eagle's nest with two black and white young. . . . We started a blind above the nest, dug the sound truck from the mud, and camped nearby over night."

The next morning Allen photographed the eagles. "Never," he recalled, "shall I forget the experience of lying prone for four hours on a flat rock at the edge of Box Elder Canyon . . . watching and waiting for a golden eagle to return to its eyrie. Directly below me, the cliff fell away 750 feet, while the nesting ledge was only 60 feet down. I was covered with one of our grass blinds so that the eagle would not see me and, unknown to me until I tried to shift my position, the boys had piled so many rocks on the edge of the blind to keep me from falling off the cliff that I could not even roll over." Finally, Allen's long wait was rewarded: "At last the majestic bird sailed in with a jack rabbit in his talons and the young eagles screamed with anticipation at his approach. The picture impressed upon my mind was well worth all the fatigue of the journey up the mountain and the long wait on the hard rock at the edge of the canyon."

Sunday dawned with high expectations. The team went to a golden eagle's nest below the rim of a cliff in Willow Creek Canyon. Kellogg lowered the microphone over the edge to record sounds from the nestlings, while Tanner eased himself down the rocky precipice, hoping to get photographs of the adult eagles in flight as they came and went from their aerie. But the birds didn't cooperate. They kept their distance, circling high overhead. The eaglets occasionally pecked at the mike, but since it wasn't food, it didn't interest them. They also exercised their wings but did little else without their parents' encouragement.

Meanwhile, Doc Allen set up a blind at a long-crested jay's nest. These are handsome birds with bad reputations as nest-robbers and cannibals. Known as Steller's jay today, this black and dark blue bird of the western forests nests almost exclusively in evergreens. Leery of the blind and taking a cue from the eagles, the jay didn't return to her nest either. The eagles and the jay lacked the parental tenacity of the mountain plover. Disappointed and with little accomplished, the Cornell trio packed up and returned to Niedrach's cabin.

A new day brought another challenge, something perfectly suited for the young, athletic Tanner. Niedrach led the team to a ranch where Kellogg recorded canyon and rock wrens and tried to get audio of a Lazuli bunting. All three are western species. With Niedrach's help, the Cornellians then rigged up a block and tackle to hoist Tanner up the side of a cliff. Allen shot movie footage of Jim sitting in a sling with Kellogg and Niedrach tugging on a rope. Each tug raised Tanner several feet up the craggy, weathered cliff face until he reached a prairie falcon's nest on a ledge high overhead. The western raptors are similar in size to peregrine falcons but paler in color. They are found in open prairies and grasslands with suitable cliffs, bluffs, or rocky outcroppings for them to nest. Their dusty, sandy coloration allows them to blend into the cliffs. They are not nest builders but prefer simply to lay their eggs on a rocky ledge. Once Jim reached the aerie, he discovered the downy young tucked two feet back into the rocky surface. He carefully moved the feisty threesome closer to the edge to photograph them. "The young were fine and active, fighting and scratching when they had a chance," he later noted.

That evening the team dined at the Cactus Club, a literary and artistic society founded in 1910, and showed its members some of the motion-picture footage they had taken thus far on the trip. It met with overall approval, although some in the audience wished it were in color.

The success of the day before led to a more ambitious venture. It was Tuesday, June 4. This time Doc Allen was hoisted up the cliff face to the narrow ledge, where he shot a hundred feet of movie film showing the young prairie falcons being fed. This parent was not camera shy. The result was some remarkable footage made even more remarkable by where it was recorded.

The trio then returned to the golden eagle's nest on Willow Creek, a more convenient location. The men could actually drive the trucks to the cliff's edge. "We padded the microphone, lest it strike a rock, and let it down about 60 feet on its cable to the nesting ledge," Doc Allen wrote. "Then, concealing the trucks in a grove of pines near by, we spent the night on the bunks within them." In the sound truck the researchers eavesdropped on the avian chatter through a set of headphones. They couldn't see the young birds, but they could hear them.

"The first morning we worked by lying in bed," recorded Tanner. "There was no sound when we first listened in. Other birds could be heard, robins, swifts, swallows, doves, etc." It was early Wednesday morning, the weather ideal. "About 7:00," Tanner continued, "the young birds began to talk and we could see an old bird over the canyon, but it didn't come in. About an hour later, while I was getting breakfast, the old bird circled in carrying a rabbit."

Peering through the truck window, the team could see a parent coming from the east. As Allen described it:

> In majestic circles it sailed over the canyon, looking the ground over to make sure that all was safe. Now the screams of the hungry eaglets became more and more excited as, in narrowing circles, the old bird dropped lower and lower. Finally, in one long graceful sweep, it disappeared below the rim of the canyon and a moment later we heard the crash of twigs as it landed on the nest. There were no cries from the old bird; silently she came and silently she left. Only the calls of the young were recorded.
>
> Contrary to popular belief, these eagles are shy birds and only because of their extreme wariness have they been able to persist in most parts of the Rocky Mountains region. Usually they nest on inaccessible ledges, but occasionally in the tops of tall trees.

Doc Allen's reference to the birds' wariness and persistence is significant. In the 1930s eagles were, like other birds of prey, persecuted creatures. Farmers and ranchers, overprotective of their small livestock, would shoot the raptors on sight.

Later in the day, Allen and Tanner returned to Castle Rock to the golden eagle's nest high in a tree. They hid inside a blind, but the parents did not return. Although they could hear one "yipping" from somewhere up the slope, it seemed reluctant to come any closer. Tanner then climbed the tree to inspect the nest. He later wrote:

> Just as I stuck my head over the nest, one of the young scrambled to the edge and flew, sailing down the mountain side until he hit a tree, then falling to the ground. The other remained in the nest, and I took several photographs.
>
> While I was working there, I suddenly heard Doc yell and then came a loud rush of wings. One of the old birds, apparently not knowing we were there, dove in with food, passing only 20 feet from Doc. Just at the moment Doc yelled, she apparently saw

> me, and I saw her, him, or it. Its wings were stretched wide, a dark golden brown bird, banking vertically and traveling like a bullet. The rabbit it was carrying slipped from its talons and catapulted sideways and then earthward. The eagle shot out over the valley and then soared away. Unforgettable speed and rush are what I mostly remember.

With Tanner back on the ground, he and Allen caught the young eaglet that had leaped from the nest. Returning to the cabin with the captive, they found Niedrach and Alfred M. Bailey waiting for them. Director of the Denver Museum of Natural History from 1936 to 1969, Bailey was a pioneering bird photographer and cinematographer noted for his fieldwork. He would later coauthor the two-volume *Birds of Colorado* with Niedrach.

Early the next morning Kellogg and Tanner drove back to the site of the prairie falcon's nest and successfully recorded the song of a lazuli bunting, perhaps the only bird named for a gemstone: lapis lazuli. Both bird and gem are an intense ultramarine blue. The lazuli is the western counterpart to the indigo bunting. The two birds are closely related, with similar behavior and appearance, except that the lazuli has white underparts and a cinnamon-colored breast. The lazuli's song is a buzzy *see-see-sweet, sweet-zee-see-zeer.* Bailey and Niedrach soon joined Kellogg and Tanner for a climb to the falcon's nest to get more photos.

In late morning Kellogg and Tanner met Allen back at the eagle's nest. Doc brought the nestling they had rescued the day before. The young bird was almost fully grown. Its leap from the nest created a fortunate opportunity. In addition to obtaining close-up photographs and sound recordings, Allen set up the cumbersome Akeley to get motion pictures of the eaglets. Tanner climbed the tree again to retrieve the second nestling. Reuniting the nest mates on a nearby rock, they got excellent photographs of the pair. They determined that one was a male, the other a female.

"The male young is smaller but well developed; the female is larger, heavier, with bigger feet and bill and has more down and less well developed flight feathers," Tanner noted. "We dubbed them Christopher and Christina." As with the golden eagle called Chris that Jim had once nursed back to health, the names were derived from the birds' species name, "chrysaetos" (kris-AY-ee-tos), which comes from the Greek—chrysos meaning golden.

"In the afternoon after both birds were down, the adults never came around to our knowledge," Tanner wrote. "It may be that the young do not leave until they are ready to fly and more or less take care of themselves." Perhaps realizing that they had disrupted the natural order, the Cornellians decided to take the nestlings and care for them until they fledged. That evening they met with Niedrach, Bailey, and Robert Rockwell at the home of noted outdoor photographer Clark Blickensderfer. Rockwell was a founding member of the Colorado Biological Society and frequently wrote about birds for *The Condor*, *The Auk*, and the *Denver Sunday Post*.

Blickensderfer had been experimenting with the new Kodachrome 16mm movie film, which impressed Tanner. "The stuff looks darn good," he wrote. Sold by the Eastman Kodak Company, it became popular in the 1930s for producing slide shows and color movies. Noted for its sharpness and brilliance, the process would be the gold standard in color photography for years, required by publications such as *National Geographic*. Unfortunately, it came along too late for the Cornell expedition. Kodak introduced Kodachrome first in 16mm movie film in early 1935; 8mm movie film and slide film in 35mm and 828 formats followed a year later. No doubt the Cornell men wished they had possessed it when they were photographing the ivory-bills in the Singer Tract.

The trio's visit with Blickensderfer wrapped up their stay in Colorado. Despite a few rainy days, it had been a big success. All of their target birds—golden eagle, prairie falcon, mountain plover, avocet, and several other western species—had been found and recorded. But it was time to move on to other challenges. Doc Allen wanted to find at least one more vanishing bird on his list, but before doing that, he had a few classes to teach.

Chapter 9

Swansong

The song season was nearly over . . . northward and then westward through arid Wyoming the expedition wound over the mountains to Logan, Utah.

—Arthur A. Allen

Back at Cornell, students were beginning their summer break. Nearly eleven hundred got their degrees at commencement exercises held outdoors at the eleven-year-old football stadium known simply as The Crescent. But for the traveling Cornellians, there was still work to do. Allen, Kellogg, and Tanner had been on the road for almost four months. They left the Denver area just after two o'clock in the afternoon on Friday, June 7, enjoying beautiful weather for their day's drive. The trio spent the night in a cabin in Laramie, Wyoming. They also traveled with a pair of guests: the two eaglets. Fearing the parents had abandoned them, they felt obligated to care for the two young birds until they fledged. Again, Tanner's golden eagle expertise came in handy.

On Saturday, June 8, the men left Laramie at 4:20 AM. They fed the young eagles "road-killed rabbits" found along the way. Their route, U.S. Highway 30, took them through the Great Divide Basin, a 3,860-square-mile drainage basin that averages over six thousand feet in elevation. The little precipitation that falls there stays there, not draining to either the Atlantic or Pacific oceans. Water almost always drains somewhere, but here it either soaks into the ground or evaporates. The arid basin is home to some grasses, an occasional shrub, and a few small trees in some of the ravines. Tanner did not note seeing any birds.

Jim did record a change in scenery, though: "Soon after entering Utah, we met marshy lands, and then climbed. Bear Lake was an intense copper sulfate blue, surrounded by reddish, ravined mountains, which were sprinkled with spruces. We climbed a long ways from the lake, and then came down through Logan Canyon, which showed some picturesque and grand scenery on a promising trout stream."

Logan Canyon empties into the beautiful Cache Valley. The Wasatch Mountains are to the east, the Great Salt Lake and desert to the west. Doc Allen was scheduled to give a two-week course in ornithology at Utah State Agricultural College in Logan. After arriving in the college town in late afternoon, the Cornell trio met Professor J. S. Stanford of USAC's Department of Zoology and spent the night in a dormitory. For the next two weeks, Logan was their base of operations. The campus was scenic, home to several welcomed species of western birds: lazuli bunting, Cassin's purple finch, lark sparrow, and black-headed grosbeak.

The first morning on campus, Tanner slept in for a change. Being back in a college dorm might have led to his relaxed state. Or perhaps, after 116 days on the road, he was tired. Allen, Kellogg, and Professor Stanford left early and recorded a willet, a large shorebird in the sandpiper family. It was a welcome sight, since the population of the species had declined dramatically in the late 1800s and early 1900s because of overhunting and habitat loss. In the afternoon the professor took Allen and Tanner to Brigham City and on to the Bear River Migratory Bird Refuge near the Great Salt Lake. The location had garnered an unfortunate notoriety in 1928 when an outbreak of avian botulism occurred, killing hundreds of thousands of birds, principally waterfowl. The public was horrified, prompting Congress to pass legislation to make the Bear River Delta a National Wildlife Refuge and initiating a conservation effort to alter the conditions that support the paralytic disease.

Avian botulism occurs when a bird ingests a toxin produced by the bacterium *Clostridium botulinum*, which is widespread in soil but generally dormant. The microbe requires warm temperatures, a protein source, and an anaerobic (no-oxygen) environment to become active and produce the deadly toxin. Decomposing vegetation combined with warm temperatures can provide an ideal nursery for the botulism bacteria to activate. Thus, in 1931 fifty miles of dikes and water-control structures were completed at the Utah site to help mitigate the conditions that caused the 1928 outbreak. "The refuge is about 20 miles long and a mile wide, containing shallow ponds and marshy land along the river," noted Tanner. "The water had once been brackish, but by damming off the salt lake, the marshes are made fresh."

The Cornell team would be kept busy during their stay in Logan. Tanner made a long list of the species that had been observed at the refuge. These were possible birds to record, but as always, positioning the sound truck would be the challenge. Because Doc Allen was tied up during the mornings lecturing, Tanner had time to explore. After helping Kellogg with recordings early in the day, he would then look for nests in the refuge. Finding them made recording and filming the birds the next morning easier.

On Tuesday, June 18, Doc Allen and Tanner drove back up into Logan Canyon to search for water ouzels, now known as American dippers. They did find a nest with two young, but inspecting it would be hard. The bird's nursery was located on a big rock in the middle of a fast-moving mountain stream. Equally at home above and below the water, the dipper is unique—the only truly aquatic songbird. The North American variety is one of only four species in the world, and it is found along swift streams in the western mountains, from Mexico to Alaska.

Dippers have dense feathers with a thick down undercoat, well-developed transparent nictitating membranes to protect their eyes underwater, and a large preen gland for waterproofing their plumage. Because their blood can store more oxygen than that of other passerines, they can remain submerged for extended periods. Their wings and tails are short and stubby, making them good swimmers, even in turbulent water. The fearless little songbird can actually walk on the bottom of a streambed looking for its favorite food: aquatic worms and insect larvae. "Its domed-over nest of moss is fastened to precipitous walls close to fast moving water where the spray keeps it moist," wrote Robert Niedrach.

"Famed for its mockingbird-like song," Doc Allen noted, "the dipper presents a difficult problem for the microphone because, with normal amplification, the noise of the stream drowns out all other sounds."

After exploring the canyon again on Wednesday, Kellogg and Tanner returned the next morning at daybreak, hoping to record the dipper. They had noticed that one of the charcoal gray birds had a favorite rock on which to warble its song before beginning its search for food. "We set the mike on the small rock, propped so as to face the bird," Tanner noted. "The Dipper came and sang in the place, loud enough to drown out the water noise. When it came again, it perched *on* the mike, a good story but not good for recording."

The Cornell team spent the next three days recording and photographing other birds in the area: sage thrasher, lark sparrow, Brewer's sparrow, horned lark, kingbird, and Forster's and Caspian terns. They returned to the canyon twice to observe and take pictures of the dippers. By Sunday evening, with Doc Allen's ornithology course having ended, they were ready to hit the road again. Their stay in the Cache Valley had been productive, resulting in good recordings of 15 species. Tanner noted seeing 109 species of birds in and around Logan during the two weeks of their stay.

On Monday morning, June 24, after an early breakfast at the Bluebird—how could they not eat at a restaurant named such?— the Cornell trio drove north. During the last week of June, the group's itinerary took them to eastern Idaho in search of trumpeter swans. Large, white, and stately, these elegant birds were on the brink of extinction because of egg and feather collecting and overhunting. "It is thought that only about 75 individuals remain alive in all the United States," Allen reported. Clearly, the disappearing bird was among the country's rarest.

"Cache Valley fertility soon disappeared, and sagebrush aridity took its place," wrote Tanner in his journal. "Just after leaving St. Anthony, Idaho, we got a magnificent view of the Tetons; then we drove thru a large fir forest, some of it quite wild. We turned west from the main road and went to Henry's Lake. From the road we saw three or four swans; we asked at the nearest house, found it to be a dude ranch in the making, so we stayed the night." Finding the trumpeter swans when so few existed was not utter serendipity. Allen had done his homework, consulting with bird experts all across the country, always posing the standard query: "Where's the best place to look?" And now his inquiries had paid off.

The Bar L Ranch was on the west side of the lake and operated by a man named Ed Fisher. Tanner described the ranch house as a two-story affair with a rustic exterior and home-like interior. The lake, surrounded by the Centennial Mountains on the Continental Divide, was named in honor of Andrew Henry, an early trapper in the region. It was roughly circular, about three miles across. The Cornell team spotted a few more swans and located the sound truck on the lakeshore before dark.

The trumpeter is one of two swan species native to North America; the other homegrown species is the tundra swan. Both migrate seasonally. The swans commonly seen on eastern lakes and ponds in this country are nonnative mute swans. Although not actually mute, they are mostly quiet and do not migrate. Native to Europe, these graceful waterfowl were brought to America in the late 1800s because they were pleasing to the eye. They served as living lawn decorations for lofty mansions along the Hudson River in upstate New York.

The native trumpeters are the largest species of swan in the world, weighing from twenty to thirty pounds, with a wingspan of up to eight feet. (A Canada goose, by contrast, weighs about ten pounds and a whooping crane about fifteen.) Trumpeters must remain near open water to obtain their preferred diet of aquatic plants. A full-grown, active adult will consume up to twenty pounds of wet herbage every day. Trumpeter swans are noted for their resonating, far-reaching *ko-ho* honks, which remind some of the *oo-ga* horns on vintage automobiles. It was these calls the Cornell group wanted to record for the first time.

Early the next morning, Doc Allen and Fisher went out on the lake, hoping to spook the swans into trumpeting, but the birds merely flew away. Allen counted nineteen of the snow-white birds and got within ten feet of a molting, flightless one but found no nests. The molting swan was an indication that nesting season was coming to an end. The challenge with the trumpeter was getting close enough to record one. As with the ivory-bill and golden eagle, finding an active nest would be helpful. That afternoon Allen and Tanner drove to Red Rock Lake; they found a few more swans but couldn't get close to them.

Wednesday, June 26, dawned fine and quiet. Two honking swans flew around, but their calls were too soft to record. In mid-morning, Allen, Kellogg, and Tanner packed up and drove to Lower Red Rock Lake in Montana. Jim was no stranger to that state: during the previous summer, he had worked as a naturalist at Glacier National Park.

Inquiries led the Cornellians to Ed Stanley, caretaker at the Montana Gun Club, who invited them to the clubhouse. Like the Big Sky Country itself, the house was large and dusty, having not been used in two or more years. But its position was ideal. From its roof the Cornellians spotted seven swans, including a pair that appeared to be nesting within a half-mile of the building. Borrowing a duck-boat, Allen and Tanner rowed to the site and found the nest.

"It was a pile of vegetation two feet above the water, surrounded by tussocks of grass," Tanner wrote. "A channel led from the nest to the open water. Buried in the top of the nest were two eggs, gray and lightly speckled, each nearly five inches long. Fragments of eggshells were in the nest, and we could see the once inhabitants of these eggs swimming along behind their parents. Nevertheless, we set up the blind on a convenient muskrat house." As Allen noted, "We were now quite hopeful of being able to secure a recording of the voice of the trumpeter swan, although we could not get the sound truck within a half mile of the nearest pair."

Roughly four miles long and three wide, Lower Red Rock Lake is located in the high-elevation Centennial Valley in southwest Montana. The valley runs east to west, bordering snowy Baldy Mountain to the south and Patchtop to the north. Dotted with innumerable islands, Lower Red Rock Lake is west of Upper Red Rock Lake. Allen and Tanner rowed around the rest of the afternoon, exploring the scenic marshy wetland. "The fields around the lake slope up to the mountains on the south and hills on the north. Thru a gap in the hills can be seen the rugged Madison range," Tanner observed.

The team had no luck recording the swans the next morning. Later Tanner rowed Allen out to the blind near the nest, where he waited for the trumpeters to come ashore. "The swans did not return to the nest, so Doc wanted me to herd them," Tanner recalled. Every twenty to thirty minutes, the parents took the young to dry land to brood them. While Allen hid in the blind, Tanner used the rowboat to maneuver the family of swans in his mentor's direction. He managed to move them across the lake, but for some reason they were reluctant to go ashore at the old nest.

Despite the lack of success, young Tanner's expedition résumé had a new listing. In addition to driver, cook, mechanic, wood gatherer, photographer, audio technician, chronicler, scout, nest finder, tree climber, cliff cragsman, and eagle caregiver, he had become a swan wrangler.

That evening around ten o'clock, the swans trumpeted, but it wasn't loud enough to record. The team stayed at the clubhouse for four days, microphone ready, but except for that lone trumpet call late in the evening, the swans were quiet.

On Friday, June 28, with their last morning at hand, the team concocted one final scheme: kidnapping, or in this case, cygnet-napping. Constructing a screen cage, the Cornellians placed it in shallow water with a string fastened to the top as a quick release. Concealing the sound truck behind a building, they ran the cable with the sound reflector to the lakeshore near the cage. They also set up a blind with the cameras, including the big Akeley inside. It was now or never.

As soon as the light was good enough, Allen and Tanner slowly rowed separate duck-boats to the opposite end of the lake. The emphasis was on stealth: they didn't want to alarm the swans. Working in tandem, the professor and his protégé surreptitiously avoided the swans until both positioned themselves upstream from the mated pair with their two young cygnets. The swans were wary. As Allen and Tanner began to move downstream toward the blind, the swans moved as well. The swan herding took two hours, but in time the wranglers outmaneuvered the pair, separating them from their young, which they quickly captured, transporting the pair to the wire screen cage. Tanner then distracted the adults as Allen climbed into the blind. Kellogg was already in position, having waited the last two hours in the sound truck.

Tanner's journal recorded the action: "I rowed back upstream, and soon one of the old birds started back to the young. It became tired of swimming and flew part of the way, landing a short distance from the young. Comparatively unafraid, it gradually came nearer. The other bird, probably flightless [beginning its molt], was much more cautious and took a long time to come to the young. The two of them swam around, calling and trumpeting shortly. When enough pictures had been obtained, Doc pulled the string and released the young." The reunited family was vocal. After four days of stalking swans, never getting close enough for decent results, the team finally triumphed—and all in a matter of minutes. Allen got photos and two hundred feet of motion picture film, while Kellogg made audio recordings of the young's lisping calls and the adults' hoarse trumpets.

Finding an active nest of a trumpeter swans in a remote valley was a major accomplishment, but their celebration was short lived. The group soon went back to work, although they must have been relieved. To come so far and be so close, not recording the swans would have been disheartening. Allen and Kellogg spent the rest of the day rowing around the lake, searching for more birds and finding another swan's nest. Meanwhile Tanner staked out and photographed a hatching coot's nest.

At one of the swan sites Kellogg and Allen took photographs of each other by the nest, with the lake and a snow-topped mountain in the background. Gone were the Ivy League coats and ties they wore when they had left Ithaca in February; now they each looked as roughhewn as any backwoods explorers. They also looked happy, understandably so.

The next morning, the team put one of the duck-boats into the truck, hoping to explore the upper end of the lake, but they couldn't find an easy place to put it into the water. They located and photographed a mountain bluebird that was using an abandoned cliff swallow's mud nest to raise its own family. Later they heard that a noted naturalist, E. J. Sawyer, was in the area, and Kellogg went to find him. Thrilled at a chance to visit with the Cornell ornithologists, Sawyer spent the night with the group.

Edmund Joseph Sawyer was a character—a rugged backwoodsman born in 1880 who lived like John Burroughs, throwing his creative energy into his art. Sawyer served as park naturalist at Yellowstone National Park and later field ornithologist for New York State. He was widely known for his detailed paintings of birds in their natural habitats. About a dozen of his works appeared on the covers of Audubon publications. A Sawyer painting of an American robin singing on a bough of apple blossoms was the first color plate in the society's series of educational leaflets.

On the last day of June, it snowed in the morning, making the high mountain peaks that surrounded them even more dramatic. The group broke camp and drove west towards Monida, a place that gets its name by its proximity to the Montana-Idaho border. There they turned south to visit Sawyer's home site. The naturalist's son was homesteading about a half-mile from the road with his wife, another Cornellian, and baby son. Sawyer himself had two cabins up in the hills: an eight-foot-by-ten-foot winter cabin with an attached woodshed surrounded by spruce and aspen and a summer place on a hillside over a small draw. Both were remote. For more than two years, the wildlife artist had lived there, making hundreds of drawings and paintings of birds. The Cornell team spent the night with him, looking through his portfolio and talking about birds. Sawyer's cabin was the farthest point west the expedition ventured. Tanner's list of birds seen while they were in Montana totaled forty-eight species, including thirty-four trumpeter swans found on four lakes and another four reported from Elk Lake.

Monday, July 1, was a big day. It was time for Allen, Kellogg, and Tanner to return home. Saying farewell to Sawyer, they drove into Idaho and headed toward Yellowstone, crossing into Wyoming as they entered the park from the north. After a stop at Mammoth Hot Springs, they spent the night in Roosevelt Lodge. Established in 1872, three years after the transcontinental railroad was completed, Yellowstone was the world's first national park. Although noted for its wildlife, it was set aside to protect the region's geothermal curiosities: fumaroles, mudpots, hot springs, and geysers. Commercial development would have ruined these wonders. Beside these active geological caldrons, Yellowstone's 2.2 million acres contain some of the most stunning landscape in the country, and the Cornell team allotted two days to explore it. That was hardly enough, but they made good use of their time.

Early the next morning, Kellogg recorded a western tanager, Audubon's warbler, and Lincoln sparrow, while Doc Allen filmed a Townsend's solitaire and Williamson's sapsucker. He was disappointed that they were unable to get audio of the solitaire's beautiful, prolonged song, but so late in the season, it was quiet. In the afternoon they drove south, visiting Tower Fall, Mt. Washburn, and Inspiration Point. Although the road over Mt. Washburn was not yet open to the public, the Cornellians got permission to use it. The road had been dug out from the snows of the past winter, and the remaining drifts towered over both sides of the trucks. Photographs taken of the group on Mt. Washburn show three fatigued travelers a long way from home. A sign in the background notes that they were 10,317 feet above sea level—the highest point of their long expedition. Afterward, they spent the night in Canyon Junction.

The next morning they drove north about six miles to a spruce forest and recorded a Clark's nutcracker, named in honor of Captain William Clark of the Lewis and Clark expedition. After breakfast in Canyon Junction, the trio saw Old Faithful and other points of interest before once again turning toward home. Driving east on Highway 20 through Cody, they spent the night in Worland, Wyoming.

On Thursday, the Fourth of July, the group started long before daylight, driving east through Wyoming, but within twenty miles of Casper, an axle on the sound truck broke. While waiting for repairs, the trio located and photographed a McCown's longspur, a prairie species of very limited range found in the northern Great Plains. By 3:30 PM they were back on the road, which was fortunate, considering it was a national holiday. They spent the night in Chadron, Nebraska. The next morning, the pull of home must have been strong, for the threesome elected to drive through the night and into the next day. Fixing a bed in the sound truck, they fell into a rotation whereby each man could drive for four hours and sleep in the back of the truck for two. Highway 20 took them through Sioux City and Dubuque, Iowa; through Elgin, Illinois;

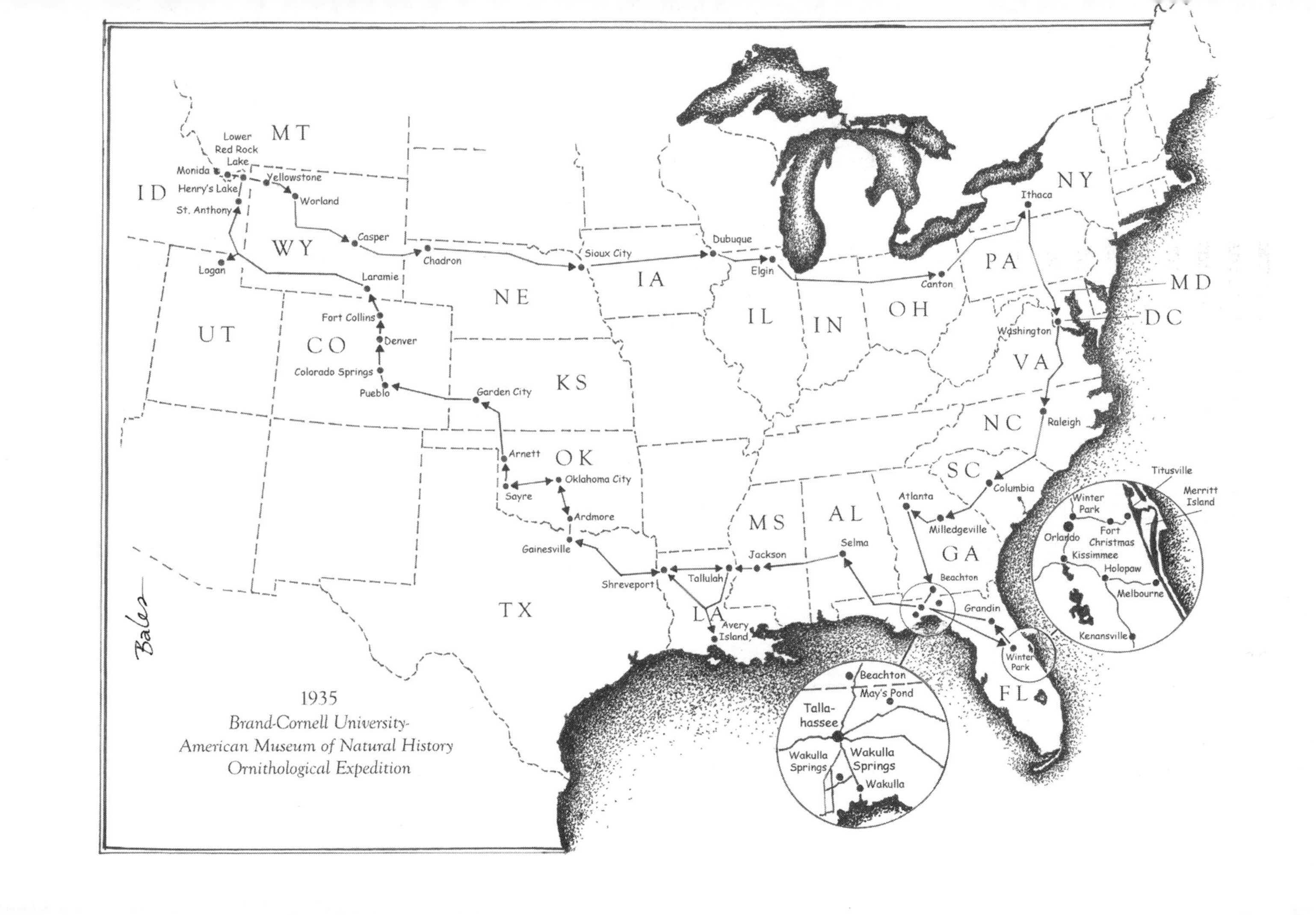

1935
Brand-Cornell University-
American Museum of Natural History
Ornithological Expedition
ID
MT
WY
UT
CO
NE
KS
OK
TX
IA
IL
IN
OH
PA
NY
MD
DC
VA
NC
SC
GA
AL
MS
LA
FL
Lower Red Rock Lake
Monida
Henry's Lake
St. Anthony
Yellowstone
Worland
Casper
Logan
Laramie
Fort Collins
Denver
Colorado Springs
Pueblo
Chadron
Sioux City
Dubuque
Elgin
Canton
Ithaca
Washington
Raleigh
Columbia
Milledgeville
Atlanta
Garden City
Arnett
Sayre
Oklahoma City
Ardmore
Gainesville
Shreveport
Tallulah
Jackson
Selma
Avery Island
Beachton
Grandin
Winter Park
Titusville
Merritt Island
Orlando
Fort Christmas
Kissimmee
Holopaw
Melbourne
Kenansville
May's Pond
Talla-hassee
Wakulla Springs
Wakulla
Bales

and on through Indiana and into Ohio. It was an extraordinary marathon drive, passing through five states and covering about fourteen hundred miles, a great distance in the days before interstate highways. They finally stopped at a hotel in Canton, Ohio, to get some rest and clean up.

Leaving the Buckeye State early on Sunday, July 7, the group arrived back at Cornell in late afternoon, just in time for one of the heaviest rains ever to hit Ithaca. Ten inches fell in only a few hours, producing one of the biggest floods ever recorded in the region. "The hillside road leading to my home was entirely washed out," wrote Doc Allen, "so that after a successful journey of 15,000 miles, our trucks finally became marooned in my own yard."

The 145-day expedition had been a success. Allen, Kellogg, and Tanner had taken hundreds of photographs, exposed ten miles of motion picture film, and recorded the songs and calls of roughly a hundred species of birds, including some of the rarest in North America, among them the South's noted ghost bird. The group's footage and audio of the ivory-billed woodpecker were by themselves an extraordinary accomplishment—records of image and sound that would be played over and over again, millions of times, in the decades that followed.

Their findings also sparked a desperate need to know more about the species. James T. Tanner's ivory-bill adventures had only just begun.

Chapter 10

On His Own

Much of this work had to be done in the range and haunts of the bird, and therefore extended trips were taken throughout the South to investigate areas from which ivory-bills had been reported, to search for new areas, and to examine the localities where the birds once lived.

—James T. Tanner

If only John James Audubon, that pioneering chronicler and painter of avian life, could have lived to see how far his legacy would extend. Of French ancestry, Audubon was a true American original—equal parts ambition, élan, and genius. During his lifetime (1785–1851), he had little inkling that a renowned society dedicated to protecting birds, other wildlife, and ecosystems would one day bear his name.

The original Audubon Society had humble beginnings. It existed only in the pages of *Field and Stream*, which was not only the foremost hunting and fishing magazine in the United States but also a publication with a conscience. In 1886 its editor, George Bird Grinnell, began writing articles about the need to protect and conserve bird life in this country. The wholesale slaughter had to end. Grinnell's rallying cry was in a sense a call to *put down* arms. In proposing an association "for the protection of wild birds and their eggs, which shall be called the Audubon Society," Grinnel declared, "Its membership is to be free to everyone who is willing to lend a helping hand in forwarding the objects for which it is formed."

His passionate views found an almost instant audience: 39,000 members soon pledged not to molest birds. This support was so significant that Grinnell launched a separate publication, the *Audubon Magazine*. Grinnell's venture was an overnight success, too much so. At six cents a copy, or fifty cents for a year's subscription, the periodical sold well, but with no staff at *Field and Stream* to handle the additional correspondence and administrative details, the magazine had to fold after only one year.

The movement's second coming began in Boston, in the home of society matron Harriet Hemenway. To a very real degree, if the movement was to continue, it had to find just such a champion because it was the women's fashion industry, specifically the milliners, that was pushing many bird populations across the country to the brink. In the late 1800s no well-dressed woman could be seen in public without a feather-adorned hat, the showier the better. It was estimated at the time that roughly five million birds were killed each year in the United States just for their feathers. The nuptial plumes of herons and egrets were especially prized, with the snowy egret that E. A. McIlhenny helped save being one of the most persecuted species.

On February 10, 1896, at an organizational meeting in her home, Hemenway hosted two principal groups of people: conscionable ladies of fashion and men interested in ornithology and field sports. The group's bylaws identified its main goal: "to discourage the buying and wearing, for ornamental purposes, of feathers of any wild bird except ducks and game birds, and to otherwise further the protection of native birds." Thus the Massachusetts Audubon Society was formed.

This time the movement blossomed. The Pennsylvania Audubon Society was founded later that same year, followed by likeminded groups in New York, New Hampshire, Illinois, Maine, and Wisconsin. In many cases, the clubs coalesced around a prominent woman who, like Hemenway, called for an all-out boycott of feathered hats.

As odd as it sounds, not everyone agreed with the Audubon objectives. At the time, the august and scholarly American Ornithologists' Union (AOU), founded in 1883, was already quite aware of the dangers facing many bird populations. The AOU comprised many influential ornithologists who defended the collection of birds. In 1902 Charles B. Cory, the group's president-elect, refused to attend a meeting of the District of Columbia Audubon Society, stating, "I do not protect birds. I kill them." Old ways die hard.

Grassroots America also entered the picture. With the growing support of everyday people and at least one very prominent American—sportsman and naturalist President Theodore Roosevelt—the Audubon objectives began to find a broad audience. The movement grew through a widespread letter-writing campaign driven by citizens. Many church associations, which distributed the message by word of mouth and in local newsletters, also helped the cause. Ultimately, the fervor led to the passage of laws that protected birds and ended the plume trade. An early example was the 1910 New York State Audubon Plumage Law, banning the sale of feathers of all native birds within the Empire State.

In 1898 local clubs in Ohio, Indiana, Tennessee, and other states west of the Mississippi joined the growing ranks of independent Audubon societies, and by 1901 thirty-six clubs were scattered from coast to coast. Some were strong and active; others were not. This imbalance illuminated the need for a unifying organization, working together with local groups on projects around the country and presenting a strong national voice. On January 5, 1905, in New York City, the National Association of Audubon Societies (NAS) was incorporated for the protection of wild birds and animals. Soon a constitution was adopted, bylaws written, officers elected, and a board of directors formed that included representatives from various state societies. The local clubs around the country remained independent chapters, with their own officers and dues-paying members. The new national headquarters was located at 141 Broadway in lower Manhattan. Although the NAS constitution brimmed with legal phrases, the group's first president, William Dutcher, simplified its purpose in the pages of *Bird-Lore,* its newly named magazine. His manifesto was straightforward, if a bit elitist: "The object of this organization is to be a barrier between wild birds and animals and a very large unthinking class, and a smaller but more harmful class of selfish people. The unthinking, or, in plain English, the ignorant class, we hope to reach through educational channels, while the selfish people we shall control through the enforcement of wise laws, reservations and bird refuges, and the warden system."

The term "wildlife sanctuary" entered the national lexicon, and NAS began to look for parcels of land needing protection. One of the oldest is the Theodore Roosevelt Sanctuary and Audubon Center in New York, established in 1923.

For two decades, NAS thrived, but by the 1930s the early momentum was waning. Amid the Great Depression, membership dropped from about 8,400 in 1929 to just 3,400 four years later. And like the rest of he country, NAS had its share of financial woes.

To rejuvenate the organization, the board of directors named board chairman John Hopkinson Baker as the new NAS executive director in 1934. Baker was an ardent birder, a member of the Wilson, Cooper, and Nuttall ornithological clubs; but he was also a businessman, having engaged in industrial and banking pursuits since graduating from Harvard in 1915. While acquiring properties for wildlife sanctuaries was vital, Baker believed, much could also be done through education, especially with children and schoolteachers. He saw too that publishing field guides and other books about birds and animals could generate new revenue. John B. May's *The Hawks of North America* (1935) became NAS's first hardcover book. Soon, in association with New York publisher Alfred A. Knopf, Audubon Field Guides became important parts of every naturalist's library.

Why some species were on the decline while others were not became a key question for Baker. Very little was known about the life histories of most of the disappearing species. He conceived the idea of the Audubon Research

Fellowship Plan to gather information about rare birds before it was too late. At the annual NAS meeting in October 1936, Baker presented his thoughts behind the plan: "As yet biological science has not undertaken many studies on the ecology of threatened animals for the express purpose of working out conservation techniques. Conservation of rare species should mean not only preservation from extinction through protection and establishing of refuges, but also active measures to increase their numbers and distribution."

Baker knew that for his plan to work, he needed partners: "The Audubon Association therefore proposes, with the cooperation of interested organizations and individuals, the establishment of a series of Audubon Fellowships. The plan involves the cooperation of selected universities where the research work would be carried out in detail by well-qualified, mature students, working for a degree, under the supervision of professors especially qualified to direct the project."

Baker proposed that each research project should last three years and that NAS would provide fifteen hundred dollars annually to cover the students, plus their travel expenses, and that the universities involved should contribute one thousand to fifteen hundred dollars in services and equipment. With money from well-to-do Audubon members, Baker initially engaged two universities to carry out thorough studies of two key endangered species: the majestic California condor and the reclusive ivory-billed woodpecker. For the former, Baker partnered with the University of California at Berkeley, and for the latter, he turned to Arthur Allen and the Cornell Lab of Ornithology. After all, the biggest coup of Doc Allen's recent, highly successful expedition to record bird sounds was the rediscovery of the ivory-bill in the Louisiana swamps.

After returning from the expedition with Allen and Kellogg in July 1935, Jim Tanner turned his attention to his graduate-level coursework at Cornell in September. (He had completed his bachelor of science degree in zoology and ornithology in February 1935.) In grad school, Tanner majored in ornithology with a minor in physics. True to his work ethic, he completed his master's degree in June 1936. In his thesis, titled "Sound Recording for a Natural History Museum," he was able to call upon all the experience he had acquired recording birdsong on the road. He also addressed the division between the old shoot-and-stuff museum men and the new breed of field researchers who studied wildlife firsthand.

Quoting from *Romeo and Juliet,* Tanner's thesis began, "The old style museum well fits Shakespeare's description of an apothecary's shop, 'a tortoise hung, An alligator stuffed, and other skins of ill-shaped fishes.' Such museums displayed curious objects in a haphazard fashion, and were little concerned with research or the public." Jim noted that modern museums were becoming storehouses of knowledge, bringing together not only specimens, but also field researchers, scientists, and explorers, ultimately creating libraries of scientific publications with the ultimate goal of education. The rest of his thesis explored the importance of the new science of sound recordings made in the field for use as educational tools.

By the fall of 1936, when Baker contacted the Cornell Lab about his new research fellowship and the need to gather more information on the ivory-bill, Doc Allen, not too surprisingly, knew just the right student to tackle the study: twenty-two-year-old Jim Tanner, who was away from Cornell at the moment serving as an Audubon warden during the hawk migration at Cape May, New Jersey.

And so it was that by the closing days of December 1936, doctoral candidate Tanner found himself looking forward to three years on the road. These days were jubilant and busy, filled with meetings and preparations for his upcoming quest for the ivory-billed woodpecker. He spent the time collecting advice and pulling together his modest supplies. The day before he left, a telegram from Doc Allen arrived with last-minute instructions and details about his funding. A letter of introduction, also written by Allen, was straightforward: "To whom it may concern: You will find Mr. Tanner extremely reliable and trustworthy, and if you prefer that your information should get no further than him, I know that he can keep a secret when it concerns the welfare of the ivory-bill."

Doc Allen and Tanner also worked out the goals of the mission:

1. Learn all that could be discovered about the historic range of the ivory bill.
2. Discover where they still could be found.
3. Study the ecology of the species: what were its favorite foods, how did it raise its young, where did it nest and roost, what kinds of trees did it prefer. In short, learn everything possible about its life history.
4. Create a detailed plan on how to save the vanishing species, something that conservationists could use to protect the ivory-bills that remained.

Allen knew that Tanner could more than handle the job. Jim was resourceful. Three years was a long time, and for much of it, he would be alone, cut off from family, friends, and colleagues. He had to solve his own problems, fend for himself, literally bake his own bread, and live as a vagabond, often in backwoods locales with no permanent address.

Tanner's long, rambling peregrination across the South started as the old year was waning. While others were celebrating the New Year, he was pulling together the last bits of information he needed to begin his research. He drove from New York to Philadelphia to Washington, D.C., with meetings in every city. His field notes began simply enough: "In search of Kents." It had not been quite two years since the start of the Cornell expedition that had changed his life. But that trip had been a state-of-the-art affair: everything was new and shiny; the team had the latest technology at their disposal. Tanner's one-man expedition would be more of a seat-of-the-pants enterprise. There were no movie cameras, no parabolic mirror, no erector-set platform on the roof of his vehicle. Jim was on a tight budget. This time he was traveling in a 1931 Model A Ford, a car he would get to know intimately.

In its day, the Model A propelled the Ford Motor Company back into the automotive forefront. Introduced in 1927, it enabled the company to recapture the sales leadership it had lost to Chevrolet a few years before. Ever since Charles Lindbergh had flown solo to Paris that same year, America had become technology-conscious. Ford's eagerly awaited new Model A thrilled the entire country.

Unlike its predecessor, the cranky Model T, which was only available in black, the new Ford Model A came in several colors, such as Arabian sand, Niagara blue, and dawn grey. It had nine basic body styles, including the snappy roadster with optional rumble seat, the *très chic* convertible Cabriolet, and the dignified Fordor sedan with landau roof. Sporting such features as a shatter-proof-glass windshield, double hydraulic shock absorbers, a Lincoln three-speed transmission, and four-cylinder engine, the smooth-riding Model A got twenty-five to thirty miles per gallon. (In 1937 gasoline cost twenty cents a gallon.) At a time when the legal speed limit on the country's best roads was fifty miles per hour, the Model A could easily go sixty-five. From 1927 through 1931, Ford sold almost five million of the vehicles.

The roadster—the lowest-priced model—had sold for $480 brand new, but the one Tanner purchased for $175 was used. Lacking a rumble seat, it had plenty of room for Jim to pack his gear. With curved front fenders and rounded rump, it was sporty yet austere, actually having fewer moving parts than the Model T. Perhaps most important, the roadster was tough—almost like a small truck. It could go practically anywhere, as Jim would prove over and over again during the next one-thousand-plus days. For much of the time, the car would also be Tanner's home on wheels. Jim learned early that its bench seat was removable, and on many nights, it would serve as his cushioned bed under the stars. The Model A was also easy to repair. Ford provided an instruction book detailing basic maintenance, something that would come in handy for the mechanically minded Tanner. It was a perfect vehicle for a young man with modest funding on an exploration of out-of-the-way locations.

The weather in early 1937 was spring-like; a coat was unnecessary. On January 10, with his Model A loaded with camping gear, tools, maps, and personal effects, Tanner left Washington, D.C., and headed south on US Highway 1, driving through Virginia and into North Carolina before the day was over. After 380 miles, he arrived in Cheraw, South Carolina, at about 9:00 PM. Rain was falling as he checked into a cheap hotel. In his room that first night, "a steady pressing-on-your-consciousness drip-drip" fell outside the window. The soppy conditions were perhaps a bit of foreshadowing. Wetlands need rain and over the next three years, Tanner would be visiting every major, untouched, wet, and swampy location across the ivory-bill's range, the extent of which Jim needed to establish. If they still existed in the Singer Tract in Louisiana, shouldn't they still be somewhere else? But where? And how many?

In Charleston on January 13, he located Alexander Sprunt Jr., a naturalist, writer, and native son. Sprunt was a tall, lanky man with thinning dark hair and a high forehead. A leading ornithologist in South Carolina's lowcountry region, he wrote a nature column called "Woods and Waters" that appeared in the *Charleston News and Courier* six days a week without a break for sixteen years. He was also a regular contributor to *Bird-Lore* magazine, the NAS's official publication, and served as curator of ornithology for the Charleston Museum.

In 1934 NAS director John Baker hired Sprunt as the association's southern representative. His job was to travel throughout the South, supervising all of the society's southern sanctuaries and game wardens. Sprunt told Tanner that the best places to look for ivory-bills were the Big Cypress and Gulf Hammock in Florida, the Savannah and Santee regions in South Carolina, and along the Altamaha River bottoms in Georgia.

Noting Sprunt's words, Tanner drove south to the Savannah River, arriving at Groton Plantation, a 23,000-acre hunting preserve, on January 14. The tract spanned parts of Allendale and Hampton counties north of the river. Most interested in the part of the floodplain affectionately known as "The Swamp," Jim spent two days exploring the wetland with a guide named Stephen. "The water was high, red-brown and muddy, making it easy to travel by boat. The current was fairly rapid, swirling along between the tree trunks," Tanner wrote. "Stephen knows the swamp like a book; he seemed to know most of the life in it but never has seen an ivory-bill." They found no definite signs of the birds.

On January 18 Tanner drove to the Savannah River Refuge to investigate an ivory-bill sighting reported the year before by a U.S. Fish and Wildlife Service officer. The refuge superintendent took him to the location—a cypress-gum hammock in the middle of a marsh. Hammocks, also known as "heads," are essentially raised islands of vegetation; their origins are something of a mystery. One theory is that they start as floating masses of peat that become anchored and sprout trees. The dominant plant determines its name. If it's cypress, it's called a cypress hammock; if it's sweet bay, it's known as a bay tree hammock, or bayhead. Mixes of trees are simply called hardwood hammocks.

Tanner noted that the ivory-bill sighting in the Savannah refuge had never been confirmed and that the habitat seemed unsuitable. "The place is mostly saw grass, intersected by two branches of the Savannah River and countless channels and canals," he observed. He toured the refuge by motorboat with a local warden, Mannie Carter, who told him that he had seen ivory-bills there regularly but not recently. Carter was the only local Tanner interviewed who claimed to have seen the birds. When discussing his quarry with anyone, Jim had to determine if the person knew the difference between an ivory-bill and the far more common pileated woodpecker. He carried sketches of both to serve as memory cues.

With his explorations in the Savannah area turning up nothing substantive, on January 20 Jim moved on to Baxley, Georgia, crossing the Altamaha River enroute. One local he encountered, J. J. Brown, spoke of the swamplands along the Oconee and Ocmulgee rivers, which converge to form the Altamaha, but the man believed those swamps had seen too many hunters and other visitors to still have ivory-bills. The best swampy habitat that remained was along the Altamaha, south towards Ludowici, where the wetland widened to two miles. J.J.'s son claimed to have seen an ivory-bill there ten or twelve years earlier.

After buying a boat from another local woodsman, Jim made his first solo excursion into a southern swamp. His four-dollar purchase was flat-bottomed, narrow, and about fifteen feet long. For the next five days, he floated down the river, searching the section J. J. Brown had described. Using a paddle carved from a board, Tanner worked to stay in the middle of the river. Generally he just floated in the current, listening for birdsong and looking for groves of old trees: cypresses, gum, oak, and live oak. At times he left the main channel to explore the sloughs and swamplands that formed the floodplain, particularly if the habitat looked even remotely ivory-bill-friendly. He spent pleasant evenings camping out. Describing one stay on a small, sandy island, he wrote that "with the help of a bright moon, I made a hammock from the materials I had brought with me, an old tennis net and some rope. That done, I paused for a little reflection in the moonlight, listened to a dog and a motor somewhere to the south, and then turned in for a sleep."

On Sunday, January 24, a few miles upstream from Doctortown, Jim paddled through the swamp and side channels away from the main river. He observed,

> One stream went off to the left, then a second thru an opening bordered by scrubby, Crataegus-like bushes. I turned in there and then paddled into a good stand of timber of mostly cypress, oak, and live oak. A good many woodpeckers were there. The trees were of fair size; there was little recent timbering. I came out of that place and started generally east along a stream channel lined with fairly large trees, mostly gum and cypress. The bright sun made a pattern of shadow with the brown water, gray boles, and glinting reflections. I heard and saw two pileateds pounding high on a big stub. Right next to the stream stood a big cypress with two oval holes.

Jim carefully sketched the section of swampland in his journal, noting the location of the tree with holes. While finding that flickers and red-headed and red-bellied woodpeckers were fairly common, pileateds were rather scarce. He estimated only one pair every five miles. If there weren't enough old dead trees to support those birds, then there certainly weren't enough for ivory-bills.

Tanner arrived in Doctortown at about noon on January 25. Leaving the boat for whoever might claim it, he hitchhiked back to Baxley, where he had left his car. The next morning he drove to Lake City, Florida, spending the night in a local tourist court. After five nights of sleeping in an old tennis net suspended between two trees, he finally settled into a real bed.

Florida must have been overwhelming to the young Tanner. It was a big state with no highlands; however, swamplands were everywhere from the panhandle down to Dade County near the southern keys. Doc Allen had found a pair of ivory-bills along Taylor Creek west of Merritt Island in 1924, but a month-long investigation by the Cornell expedition in 1935 had found no evidence that the species remained in the state. But was there a stone left unturned? Only time would tell as Tanner began methodically to visit all parts of the state. "The Florida region is far from being uniform, even in the nature of its swampland," Jim wrote. In the northern part of the state, historic records placed the ivory-bill along the panhandle's Apalachicola River, a typical river-bottomland environ, and along the Suwannee, Wacissa, and other neighboring rivers. But these latter areas, having different tree associations, weren't typical bottomland swamps. However, as naturalist John V. Dennis writes, "Swamp is a word that resists precise definition." It can be a tree-studded wetland or simply a tract of spongy land saturated with water. In the Sunshine State, the most common kind of swamp is the "Cypress dome," so called because the tallest trees grow in the center and shorter ones surround them. From a distance it gives the illusion of a rounded hill.

Swamps can also be either river swamps with a surface flow for at least part of the year or still-water swamps. River swamps form in floodplains from the overflow of rivers or streams. The water is usually clearer and less acidic than in still-water swamps. A variety of hardwoods—swamp tupelo, white and pop ash, loblolly bay, red maple (a.k.a. swamp maple), sweetbay magnolia, sweet gum, willow, and certain oaks—are more likely to grow in these floodplain wetlands than in still-water swamps.

Still-water swamps are fed by groundwater or rainwater and have little or no noticeable flow. Most of the time, the soil remains sodden. The discarded leaf litter decomposes more slowly in these saturated places, resulting in a thick layer of peat. Oxygen levels are low and fewer species can survive. Murkier and darker than river swamps, they are often called "black water" swamps, although the term is somewhat misleading. The actual color of the water, when placed in a jar and held up to the light, is more like that of iced tea—a golden amber caused by suspended tannins.

Basically, a swamp is a flooded forest, and in Florida, the one common component of the various swamps are cypress trees—so much so that many believed that ivory-bills were only found in cypress swamps. But, as Tanner wrote, "the dominance of cypress in the bird's habitat is a condition not found outside of the Florida region. Another difference is that ivory-bills in Florida frequently fed in the pine woods bordering the swamps, something that has never been recorded in the region of the Mississippi Delta and only rarely elsewhere."

Cypress is the dominant species in most swamps because it is remarkably flood-tolerant, although the trees require occasional dry spells to allow their seeds to germinate in the mucky, saturated soil. In the South, a cypress is one of the first trees to sprout in newly opened land, taking root in mudflats bordering rivers. Early in its life, it cannot tolerate being covered by water or shade for any length of time, but once established with a thick, buttressed base, it can live up to five centuries, reaching a height of 150 feet. Native Americans built canoes from cypress logs that could hold up to thirty people. Other trees around it may come and go, but the cypress remains steadfast. Although it's a cone-bearing tree, a cypress loses its needles in the fall, which leads to the name "bald cypress."

After spending a few days interviewing people around Lake City, and calling again on W. E. Browne at Manywings in Grandin, Tanner headed south.

Explorations of Blackwater Swamp near Eustis turned up no sign of ivory-bills, though Jim did see several pileateds. Then, after meeting with various people in the Winter Park area, he drove on to Taylor Creek, where Doc Allen had seen ivory-bills in 1924, but he learned of no recent sightings. Moving farther south, he camped out in Osceola County near Deer Park, off Highway 192. The county's name comes from the Seminole war chief Osceola, which means "Singer of the Black Drink," a reference to a ceremonial beverage made from the roasted leaves and stems of the yaupon holly, an evergreen shrub found on raised hammocks and other well-drained sandy soils in the area.

Tanner began February by driving southwest from Melbourne Beach to Tindall Hammock, leased by the Brevard Hunting Club. Conversations along the way led him to a wilderness guide who had lived in the Okeechobee region for nine years but had never seen an ivory-bill. By Wednesday, February 3, following a report of a sighting, Jim had worked his way to Royal Palm State Park, twelve miles south of Homestead in Dade County. Established in 1916 by the Federation of Women's Clubs, it protected Paradise Key, a large hardwood hammock containing many royal palms. (In the 1940s, the land was donated to the federal government and became part of Everglades National Park.) Interviews with a local naturalist conducting a bird study, as well as with a game warden, brought no information about ivory-bills, since both men believed there was no suitable habitat in the area. Apparently they were right. After camping out on the edge of Long Pine Key—a key is a reef or low island—Jim decided that pileateds had been mistaken for ivory-bills there, that the hammock was too small, and that the surrounding country lacked suitable timber. That night he drove back to Miami.

The next morning, Tanner journeyed west on the Tamiami Trail. A local naturalist had reported seeing two ivory-bills along the route three years earlier. The Tamiami Trail—its name is believed to be a contraction of Tampa-Miami—was completed in 1928. Linking the Gulf Coast with southern Florida's Atlantic Coast, the two-lane road sliced through miles of wild, watery environs, including the Everglades, where few had ventured—a home to vast cypress swamps, exotic birds, and other wildlife, including bears, wild turkeys, panthers, and alligators. The completion of the Tamiami Trail opened the area to dredging and ultimately changed the ecology of South Florida, effectively altering the Everglades forever. But in Tanner's day, that transformation was only just beginning.

This portion of south Florida is unlike any other place in the country—exotic, almost tropical. East of Ochopee, Jim met a filling-station attendant who said he had seen an ivory-bill several years before on Lostman's Key located in the mouth of Lostman's River on the western coast of the Everglades. This portion of Florida—the Gulf Coast from Marco Island south to Whitewater Bay—is like a jigsaw puzzle fresh from the box. Known as "Ten Thousand Islands," it is made up of a myriad of tiny bits of land—some rocky, some exposed sandbars. A few are called "keys" and are big enough to have names. Most are so small they're called islets. Despite the name, the islands really only number in the hundreds, not thousands, but they make for a confusing maze of bays, channels, and broken mangroves. In the early days the region was notorious as a refuge for outlaws.

Tanner drove on to Fort Myers, locating outdoorsman Stanley Hanson, known locally as the "White Medicine Man" and beloved by the Big Cypress Seminoles. The admiration was mutual. Hanson respected the Seminoles' ability to coexist with nature, and he served as a translator and defender of their native culture, including the preservation of their Miccosukee dialect. With Hanson guiding him, Jim met various people who might have knowledge of local ivory-bills. He learned that the best remaining habitat was in the Big Cypress Swamp, principally a region known as Kissimmee Billy Strand, approximately twenty-five miles southeast of Immokalee. Sometimes described as shallow, forested rivers, strands are low-lying drainage systems in which the limestone bedrock has been eroded away and replaced by peat. In the Big Cypress Swamp, strands are an important feature and many run for miles. The largest cypress trees are generally found in the center of the strand.

Located just north of the Everglades, Big Cypress gets its name not from the size of the trees but from its vastness. In 1974 the U.S. Congress designated its 570,000 acres as a national preserve. Only about a third of the parcel contains cypress; the rest consists of hardwood hammocks, dry and wet prairies, pine woods, and mangrove swamps. West of Big Cypress is Fakahatchee Strand, a jungle-like 100,000-acre parcel. South Florida is younger than the rest of the state, only lifting itself above sea level, albeit just barely, roughly ten thousand years ago. It's also home to a baffling number of plants, both tropical and temperate. In addition to containing more northern trees such as cypress, red maple, dahoon holly, and sugarberry, it boasts rare orchids, epiphytic air plants, peperimias, and bromeliads blown or washed ashore from farther south. Forty-four species of orchid—six on the endangered species list—can be found in the Fakahatchee Strand alone.

Tanner spent a week exploring and camping in the area, conversing with local backwoodsmen in and around Immokalee south to Rock Island and Everglades City. Tips from locals included an alleged sighting of fourteen ivory-bills about twenty years earlier in the Main Strand of Big Cypress and the information that the three best places to look for the ghost birds were East Crossing, Kissimmee Billy Strand, and Thickahatchie Swamp. After a week of preliminary investigation, Tanner decided to press on, noting his need to return when he could spend more time in the area and was better provisioned. Big Cypress appeared to be one of the largest primitive areas that still remained in the southern states—and one with credible reports of recent ivory-bill sightings.

Following a lead, Jim met with George McCulloch, custodian for the Tosohatchee Game Preserve, in Orlando. McCulloch gave him the freshest report he had yet come across, claiming to have seen a pair of ivory-bills "last December." The two birds were working a dead pine and had flown over his head towards the Bonnet Holes on Jim Creek. McCulloch's report seemed plausible, and Jim got permission to enter the preserve and investigate the sighting. He found more favorable habitat on Jim Creek than on the nearby Tosohatchee. The former had larger cypresses—diameters of two feet seemed common—and plenty of dead trees. He saw several pileateds but no sign of ivory-bills.

On Thursday, February 18, Tanner drove to the Ocala National Forest, where he spent four days exploring promising habitat with local resident J. E. Shannon. Located only a short distance east of the city of Ocala, the national forest of the same name covers 607 square miles. Established in 1908, it is the oldest national forest east of the Mississippi River and the southernmost in the continental United States. The label "forest" is somewhat misleading, for the Ocala comprises a variety of habitats. Bounded by the Ocklawaha and St. Johns rivers, it contains central highlands, coastal lowlands, swamps, springs, and more than six hundred natural lakes and ponds. Throughout are slow-moving rivers and expansive wet prairies filled with water lilies and ringed with cypresses. It also contains much of what remains of Florida's scrub habitat and is noted for its sand pine scrub ecosystem and large stands of longleaf pine, the home of black bears, alligators, wild boars, river otters, whitetail deer, pocket gophers, armadillos, and, in the sandy soil, gopher tortoises. Unfortunately, as Tanner concluded, "Ivory-bills were formerly seen there, but there have been no recent reports and the swamp areas have been completely cut over, leaving no suitable habitat."

This is how it would go for the rest of Jim's time in Florida. With one local referring him to another, Tanner traversed the state day after day, chasing leads from Gulf Hammock, west of Ocala, to Indian House Hammock, west of Orlando. At the latter location, early in the morning on March 4, Jim had one of his most tantalizing—if ultimately frustrating—experiences. Two men led him for several miles to the scene of a reported ivory-bill sighting. The group immediately heard a call that sounded "ivory-bill-like." Jim noted that it was also hawk-like.

"We sat down and waited a while, when the sharp call of an ivory-bill came from just north of us, and then was answered by the rapid, weaker call," Tanner wrote. "I started towards the sharp call, it was repeated several times, then I saw the bird fly in ivory-bill fashion directly away from me." Unfortunately, the sighting was fleeting and from a poor angle. In the afternoon, the group circled the swamp, finding one lone limpkin and one stripped pine. That evening they all agreed to keep quiet, perhaps hoping for a better sighting or more evidence the next day. One of Jim's guides, whom he described as "a good observer," had never seen an ivory-bill in the area, and the cypress swamp had been logged just two years before.

Their reticence proved well founded. Describing their return the following day to the same spot, Tanner's next page of notes began, "Disillusion day." He wrote, "I waited not long when I heard the same *kuh-kuh-kuh* . . . I didn't see the bird at first, then a Cooper's hawk passed over, briefly in view, and the call seemed to follow it. I saw it once or twice more and became convinced that the sharp ivory-bill call came from the hawk."

The confusion was understandable. Bird expert David Allen Sibley notes that the harsh, nasal alarm note *kent* of an ivory-bill is reminiscent of the call of a red-breasted nuthatch but much stronger. Allen and Kellogg described it as like the "tooting of the mouthpiece of a clarinet." Like most birds, ivory-bills also have other secondary vocalizations: calls or conversational phrases. When Tanner first heard the call at Indian House Hammock, he noted that it was "hawk like." He described it as a series: *kuh, kuh, kuh.* Pete Dunne, director of the Cape May Bird Observatory, writes that the Cooper's hawk alarm call is a loud strident *kak, kak, kak, kak.* Recordings of ivory-bills and Cooper's hawks sound remarkably similar. Years later, Tanner wrote, "The ivory-bill has a more prolonged, upward slurring, repeated *kient-kient-kient* and a lower and softer, and continued *yent-yent-yent.*"

Kuh. Kak. Kent. Kient. Yent. What does it all mean? Only that bird vocalizations are complicated and that different species are similar and dissimilar at the same time. Jim also noted that the general character of a bird's call, like most sounds, is difficult to describe in words. In the field, there is also the excitement of the moment and the overlying cacophony of other sounds, both from near and far. Tanner learned a lesson that day in Florida: Cooper's hawks can sound like ivory-bills, especially when heard from a distance. He concluded, "I could hardly believe that there was not ivory-bills hidden someplace; but I saw plainly that I was sadly mistaken."

On March 6, 1937, Jim turned twenty-three years old. It had been two years since he celebrated his twenty-first birthday with Doc Allen, Kellogg, and Joe Howell on the Kissimmee Prairie. To mark the occasion, Jim ventured down Highway 50, which paralleled the lower Suwannee River to the gulf, stopping here and there to ask about ivory-bills. He found no one who had ever seen one. After two days, Tanner camped near the river at a place he called Piney Landing. A group of locals assembling for a "fish catching and frying party" invited Jim to join them. Feeling festive and perhaps a bit isolated, he did so. "While the lines were out," he wrote, "they played games: drop-the-handkerchief; pleased-or-displeased; rush, sheep, rush; hide-and-seek." For supper, the partygoers ate fried fish, baked yams, and biscuits. Although it was a belated celebration, it's hard to imagine a merrier impromptu birthday party.

No doubt Jim could have used some cheering up. In one community after another—places with names like Salt Creek, Cedar Keys, and Cross City—he heard reports of ivory-bill sightings that didn't pan out. Or else it was the discouraging news that no one had ever seen the bird, or if they had, it had been years before. He saw the effects of logging on ivory-bill habitat, and just as distressing were reports of how hunting had diminished the woodpecker's numbers. One man had even told him that the birds were being killed for their "bills of solid ivory." What nonsense! It was a chilling reminder that some still saw nature as a commodity to be harvested.

And then there were those who killed the birds just to have them stuffed and placed in trophy cases. "The collecting of ivory-bills undoubtedly greatly reduced or extirpated the birds of certain localities," wrote Tanner. "This almost certainly happened in the lower Suwannee swamp and California swamp, Dixie County, Florida, when A. T. Wayne collected there in 1892 and 1893. Natives there say that ivory-bills were very rare and non-existent in that area after Wayne's activities. It is impossible to say how many birds have been killed through collecting." In 1901 Florida passed a law protecting non-game birds, thus making it illegal to kill an ivory-bill. But that came probably too late to save the state's dwindling population. And in some areas the law was more or less ignored. (In 1963 Paul Hahn published a report titled "Where Is That Vanished Bird?" Hahn had located 413 ivory-bill skins and mounts and four skeletons in museums worldwide.)

On March 11 Tanner ventured briefly back into south Georgia for a visit at Sherwood Plantation with Herb Stoddard, who believed that while the recent decline in ivory-bills was caused by shooting for collectors, he thought the species had a good chance for survival, thanks to the increase in government-owned, protected land, as well as the public's interest in wildlife. Of course, that depended on whether the ivory-bills could endure the next few years until things settled down.

The next day Tanner returned to Florida, where he tracked down biologist George Van Hyning, whose 1936 and 1937 sightings in the Wakulla Resettlement Project (later the Wakulla National Forest) near Tallahassee were the most intriguingly fresh Tanner had encountered so far. Visiting the locations, Jim saw signs of possible ivory-bill activity—including a dead pine with about ten feet of bark knocked off—but no birds. Still, Jim believed that Van Hyning's report was reliable.

By now, Tanner was planning to leave the Sunshine State and drive to Louisiana where the Cornell team had seen ivory-bills just two years before. After more than two months of fruitlessly looking for the ghost bird, perhaps he longed to see a real one. Florida was a big state, and he would be back. But part of his mission was to observe ivory-bills in the wild, collecting data on their behavior. To do that he needed to go where he had the best chance of finding them. He had been on the road for eighty days without seeing an ivory-bill, but that was about to change.

Chapter 11

Back at Singer

It took me some time to realize that the bird in the hole was a young one, it seemed impossible.

—James T. Tanner

As Jim Tanner was winding his way through the southern United States looking for ivory-bills, the international news was becoming increasingly grim. The darkening political clouds on the other side of the world escaped the notice of many, if not most, ordinary Americans. In Europe, Nazi Germany and Fascist Italy were both in belligerent, expansionist mode, while in Asia the same was true of Imperial Japan. All too soon these powers would unite to form an "Axis alliance" that would plunge much of the world into a devastating war.

On the first day of spring, Sunday, March 21, 1937, Jim arrived back in Tallulah, Louisiana, at 4:00 PM. He found J. J. Kuhn almost immediately; he was standing on a street corner, talking to a local game warden named MacDonald. (By now, young Tanner was comfortable enough to call J.J. simply Jack.) Kuhn had not been to the Singer Tract since November but was eager to go back. Tanner arranged to pay Jack a modest fee to help search for ivory-bills and serve as his guide to the region. "His knowledge of the woods, tireless work, and keen observation more than doubled the amount of work that I could have accomplished alone," reported Tanner. "Because of the nature of the work, it had to be done on foot, including the trip and packing of food from the highway to the camp." Later, Jim met with Ed Cochran, the current timber warden for the Singer Company, who offered the use of his cabin on Methiglum Bayou. That night Tanner stayed in the Montgomery Hotel, a few blocks from the courthouse and Scurria's Grocery Store, where he could purchase supplies.

The next morning, Jim went to see Mason Spencer, the local attorney and state representative with whom the Cornell group had met two years earlier. Spencer believed all the ivory-bills had been "shot out," blaming it not on the shooters but on the birds' "lack of intelligence." Curious. It was the birds' fault they were being shot. Jim spent the next twenty-four hours pulling together the provisions they would need in the swamp. The following afternoon, Tanner and Kuhn drove to local resident J. P. Morgan's place near Sharkey Road, loading everything on a horse and mule. Jim rode the latter. The road in was just as wet and muddy as it had been in 1935—a fact the Cornell group had documented at the time on movie film. Kuhn and Tanner reached their base camp on Methiglum at about sundown. A local named Sam Denton joined the two men, and that night it rained, adding to the sloppy conditions.

Sharkey Road intersects both Methiglum and John's bayous east of the Tensas River and Little Bear Lake. Early the next morning, Kuhn, Denton, and Tanner began to search John's Bayou, the same watery place where the Cornell group had started two years before. But Kuhn knew where to look. They followed John's Bayou upstream almost due north until they reached a sharp turn to the east. The trio soon heard an ivory-bill, and Denton saw one flying away from them. Although that was their only encounter the entire day, Tanner at last was back in the land of *Campephilus principalis*. No ghost birds here. Although the woodpecker had eluded them, Jim was elated to be so close once again. Kuhn told Tanner that twenty-five to forty years before, cowmen had frequently seen and killed ivory-bills in the area, shooting them simply because they were wild. It was reported that one man had killed six in one morning to try out a new rifle. From 1905 to 1920, as Tanner would note in his journal, the Tensas region had been "hunted intensively by large parties, sometimes killing incredible numbers of squirrels, deer, and turkey" just for the sport of it. Kuhn recalled seeing his first ivory-bill in about 1925, and believed that since then, their numbers had actually been increasing.

The next day, despite the group's best efforts, they neither saw nor heard an ivory-bill: the needle in the haystack had moved. On Friday, March 26, Kuhn and Tanner left camp early. At about 5:45 AM they separated, pursuing different paths. Jim noted that it started out as a dreary, most disagreeable day, but the palatability of the morning soon changed. Ninety minutes after leaving camp, with daylight seeping into the forest, Tanner heard ivory-bills near the mouth of Indian Camp Bayou, a small stream that flows north into John's Bayou. "They called and acted nervously when I approached to within 70 yards," Tanner wrote. "Male whammed on stub two inches long, then flew a short distance, whammed and bammed. Female worked on a dead hackberry stub 25 feet high, 18 inches in diameter, mostly skinned and showing many engraver burrows."

After the female found a beetle grub so large that she could hardly close her bill, she flew southeast with the prize. The male silently followed. Jim pursued the pair, finding them in a slash (a section of woods that had been logged earlier) about a quarter-mile away. The birds' interest centered around an oval hole about sixty feet above the ground, on the dead branch of an otherwise healthy sweet gum. Tanner watched the pair all day, noting their activity until late afternoon, when a heavy, cold rain began to fall. Back at camp, he learned that Kuhn had located a pair of ivory-bills as well, near the head of Indian Camp Bayou. "The day had been darn disagreeable and most woodpeckers had been very quiet, so we were doubly fortunate," Tanner recorded.

The next morning, the dreary weather conditions had not improved. In the afternoon, wanderlust got the best of Jim, and he left camp, finding the pair of ivory-bills he had seen the day before. He referred to them as the "John's Bayou pair," noting that they did little feeding; the male seemed to be "huddled up to keep warm."

On Sunday, March 28, it was cold enough for ice to form around the cabin. Kuhn and Tanner ventured outside around noon, each going in a separate direction. Jim found only some peeled, dead hackberry trees, but J.J. reported locating a pair of ivory-bills roughly a quarter-mile north of Sharkey Road. The two birds moved south as Kuhn followed, crossing the rough, muddy road just west of Second Carter's Slough. Tanner spent that night back in Tallulah, gathering provisions to pack into camp the following morning. More rain fell that evening. The swamp was getting swampier.

Tuesday morning, March 30, proved to be a day Tanner would long remember. Returning to the slash near John's Bayou where he had found the ivory-bill pair four days before, he once again located the birds on the sweet gum. But this time he discovered something the 1935 expedition had been unable to locate: a nestling peeking out of the cavity. "It took me some time to realize that the bird in the hole was a young one, it seemed impossible," Jim quickly wrote.

By sheer fluke, in an article that appeared in the April 1937 issue of *The Auk*, literally within days of Jim's sighting of the infant bird, Doc Allen wrote, "At this time it is appropriate to call attention to the fact that in the literature there are relatively few references to young ivory-bills and there is no complete description of an immature bird." In composing the piece, Allen could have had no inkling that its publication would coincide almost exactly with the moment of his young protégé's remarkable discovery—the very discovery that would fill the gap in the scientific record Allen had so scrupulously noted.

Tanner carefully described the details of the find: "The nest is in a dead stub of an otherwise living sweet gum. The tree forks about 45 feet from the ground into a leafy limb and the 18-foot stub. The top of the stub bends sharply to one side, and just below the bend, half under the projecting end, is the nest. The diameter of the stub there is about one foot. The entrance faces east; it's roughly oval, a little irregular."

Jim was ecstatic. If finding a living, breathing ivory-bill was important to the success of his mission, he had just found the Holy Grail: an active nest. He knew the adult birds would remain in the area as long as they had offspring to nurture. "I first realized that the bird in the hole was young when at about 11:15 [AM] the female came and fed it, and also I saw that it was noticeably smaller. The male fed it immediately afterwards. The young bird gave the food call to both parents, a rapidly repeated series of weak nasal calls punctuated by a sharper note."

Tanner immediately began a palmetto blind near the tree and settled in to watch the activity, making careful notes of all he saw. Throughout the day, the male and female returned to the tree with food for the young bird. From time to time Jim noted seeing the nestling stick its head out to look around; at times it would exercise its "woodpeckerness," using its bill to chip away at the lower edge of the hole, creating a noticeable notch. "I would estimate the young about three-quarters grown. Its eye is dark, bill chalky-white, crest apparently short. I can't see enough of the rest to say," he recorded.

Tanner knew that what he was observing was important, so much so that he shouldn't rely on his own handwriting to remember the details. One of the things he carried with him on this trip was an old manual typewriter. For the next several weeks, he typed his notes on the same loose-leaf ruled pages he used in his three-ringed-notebook journal. In effect, he became his own secretary, transcribing his own handwritten field notes.

On the last day of March 1937, Tanner was in the palmetto blind early: 6:30 AM. The adults were away gleaning; the youngster was alone at the nest. Jim was fortunate. This time the nestling was out of the hole, moving about the dead limb. "The young bird handles himself with assurance, climbing about the stub, often peering in the hole, pecking at the wood," he noted. At 7:00 AM the adults discovered Tanner. They "flew to a nearby tree, scolded for about ten minutes; calling *kent, kent, kent-kent,* one and two syllable yaps. Both birds had raised crests, double-whacked several times on the tree. They flew to the nest tree, looked over it and the young, later to come back and scold some more." In time, the pair settled down and went about their normal routine.

Not only was the nestling moving about the nest tree, but it was also flying short distances. At one point, the female flew in and fed it, also peering into the nest hole. A minute later the male came to the stub and fed the young a grub. When both parents flew away, the fledging followed. "The young left the nest that second morning and stayed in the vicinity all day," Jim reported. "It flew well from the start. It was fed regularly by the adults. It never returned to the nest."

For the next three days, Tanner watched the adult ivory-bills care for their fledgling. The family of three remained in the vicinity of the original nest tree, moving from dead branch to dead branch, knocking away bark, the adults looking for food to feed their youngster, which was always nearby, exploring its new world, testing its limits. Jim took note of the kinds of trees—most often sweet gums and striped oaks—and the diameters of the trees or branches the ivory-bills worked. Most of the trees were at least three feet in diameter; the branches could be as little as two inches. Sometimes the entire tree was dead, while at other times the tree was living with only dead limbs for the birds to debark.

On Saturday, April 3, Jim took time to record a detailed description of the fledgling ivory-bill. Knowing the significance of what he had observed, he wrote,

> The young resembles the female, except that the white on the side of the neck seems broader, the plumage is a bit more ragged, less glossy. The crest is well developed, erectile, blunt, has none of the curve of the female, is black. The tail is short and rounded. The eye of the young is a dark red-brown. Every primary, and secondary beyond the largely white secondaries (if there are any), is tipped with white except possibly the two or three outer ones. The white is three-quarters inch long on the inner feathers, about one-quarter inch on the outer ones, tapering gradually to that. The bill is a chalky-white. Feet seem to be a bit paler than adults'.
>
> He handles himself well, climbing about with confidence, often pecking weakly at the limbs, sometimes with vigor. He sometimes makes quite long flights, 100 yards or more, sailing more than flying. His calls, except for the food calls, are like those of the adults but a bit weaker and softer.
>
> When fed by one of the parents, the two birds turn their bills at right angles to each other but in line, interlocked scissor fashion, and young takes the food from the adult.

On Sunday, April 4, Tanner stayed in bed rather late. It had rained heavily the night before; the morning was warm and muggy with a lot of water on the road and in the surrounding woods. Jim was alone. Kuhn had been away, working at his parents' home for three days. "During the last few days, spring has really come to the woods. The leaves have come out appreciably making the forest take on a green tint," wrote Tanner. "Turkeys have begun to gobble in the mornings and afternoons."

Jim noted the overlap of seasonal species as winter gave way to spring. Birds such as the hermit thrush and white-throated sparrow, which spend the cold months in the South, were still in the swamp while the migrating songsters—wood thrush, prothonotary and cerulean warblers—were beginning to arrive from points farther south. "It is odd to hear a Hermit Thrush and an ivory-bill at almost the same moment," he remarked. The thrush's breeding grounds are much farther north: New England, the Great Lakes, and Canada.

After spending several days observing the John's Bayou pair interact with their young, Tanner turned his attention to an even larger task: looking for other ivory-bills, trying to get a sense of how many were in the Singer Tract's eighty thousand acres. This was no small feat. First you had to find an ivory-bill—never easy in the first place—and then follow it as best you could on foot, using whatever high ground was available, hoping to get a sense of the bird's territory. Did it remain between point A and point B? How many ivory-bills could eighty thousand acres (125 square miles) support? No one knew, but Tanner had to find out how many ivory-bills were there; this would give him an idea of the range requirements of the species.

This was really a question of ecology, which, in the 1930s, was a fledgling science, an offshoot of biology. German biologist Ernst Haeckel coined the term "ecology," or *oekologoe,* in 1866, defining it as "the relationship of the organism to its environment." By the 1960s the field entered the mainstream, becoming a hot topic of research. It was also a discipline that would dominate Tanner's thought processes in his later years. But the only ecology that captured his attention in 1937 was the relationship of the ghost bird to its watery home.

Speaking of water, it rained heavily on Sunday night, April 4, adding to the difficulty of the search, but other than a bleak, cloudy Thursday, there was good weather throughout the week. Most of the time, Tanner searched the swamp east of John's Bayou but found nothing. Feeding sign was scarce. Jim returned every so often to observe the original family of three and noted that they remained in their territory, just east of the nest tree. Kuhn returned to camp the second week in April and reported seeing a pair of ivory-bills farther north of Sharkey Road east of the river. He had spotted a female carrying a grub, suggesting that she was feeding a nestling. South of the Methiglum base camp and west of the old Foster Plantation, they found abundant feeding sign but no birds. On Sunday, April 11, Kuhn came across a pair in a region known as Dry Bayou (near John's Bayou) and followed them for three hours. "They dawdled along and acted as though they had no nest," Tanner noted. Nesting birds, by contrast, exhibit a sense of purpose as well as a central location for their activities.

On Tuesday, April 13, after a trip to town to replenish the camp's larder, Tanner returned to observe the original family of three, finding them on a "little bayou east of John's Bayou." As time went on, the familiar trio ventured farther and farther from the nest tree. The same day Kuhn located two additional pairs: one to the west, near the end of the "Slash Trail," and one east of the mouth of

Lake Carters. The next morning Kuhn returned to Dry Bayou, east of Little Bear Lake, and found the pair there attending to a young bird—the first confirmed report of a second family of three. (Tanner ultimately recorded this family of ivory-bills under the heading Despair Bayou.)

By now the John's Bayou family seemed to have established a preferred roosting ground, principally spending the night in a dead ash filled with cavities, east of "Indian Camp" and south of the east-west section of John's Bayou. Tanner resolved to be there at first light to observe their morning ritual. Leaving camp early, he was in position at about 4:50 AM, in time to see the adults coax their young bird from its roost hole. Jim watched the three interact all morning. It had been eighteen days since the fledgling's first flight. "The young now looks almost as large as the adults," Jim wrote. "The crest is longer than when it left the nest, still blunt; tail well pointed; eye still dark. The three kept together, female fed it most often. Young pecked quite a bit, still did not see him find food. He frequently gave the food call."

Time was slipping away, perhaps necessitating that Tanner start his days earlier and earlier. On Sunday, April 18, he recorded,

> When I stepped outdoors about 3:45 [AM] the stars were bright in the dark sky. A cardinal whistled once. We left camp just as it was getting light enough to see where to walk. A Chuck-wills-widow was calling and the chorus of cardinal whistles was just getting underway. A Wood Thrush slowly began to sing, and then went into full song as others joined him. Thrashers *churred* from the thicket, and then almost at once, parula warblers began to sing all over the woods, until the leafy tree tops buzzed with them. The chorus of songs was punctuated once by the cry of a pileated and an owl hoot. It was fairly bright when we heard the first turkey gobble, the high, clear gobble of an old gobbler. One or two others in scattered parts of the woods joined him. By sun up the woods were noisy with woodpeckers, chats, cardinals, several warblers, white-throated sparrows.

Tanner searched the area between Methiglum and Indian Camp, but despite the early start and splendid morning, he found nothing, not even signs of ivory-bill feeding.

After a trip into Tallulah on Monday—a long walk down muddy Sharkey Road in the rain—Tanner investigated the area between Methiglum and the river on Tuesday, April 20. He came across wolf tracks on a muddy trail that reminded him of his utter isolation. He also found Swainson's warblers singing their "ringing, swinging" songs. This bird sighting is of note because the small and rather nondescript, plain olive-brown warbler is considered uncommon, one of the most secretive and least observed birds in all of North America. It skulks close to the ground through thickets and canebrakes, and if it weren't for their distinctive songs, it would probably go completely undetected.

It rained heavily the next morning, a mixed blessing. Tanner got to sleep in, but he knew trekking around the swamp would be more difficult. When it cleared in the afternoon, he decided to check on the John's Bayou family, locating them at the "mouth of south Dry Bayou." The adults were working the dead trees in the area, bringing food to the youngster that was always nearby. Late in the day, he watched the female knocking bark vigorously off one side of a tree, while the young bird, perched on the other side, called incessantly for food in what Jim described as "a weak, rapid, very nasal, *eh-eh-eh-eh*." The plaintive plea worked, because it was fed several times.

On Thursday, April 20, Tanner searched the area between Methiglum Bayou west to Greenlea Bend, north of the damage caused by a tornado. (Jim's hand-drawn map shows a diagonal jagged line running northeast to southwest labeled, "Cyclone of 1931.") He found lots of old ivory-bill sign but nothing indicating that the birds had been there recently. He noted that the timber north of Methiglum and east of Despair Bayou was mostly scrubby ash and hackberry with a few big oaks. At this point, he was still trying to get a sense of exactly what was ideal ivory-bill habitat. The next day, his search was cut short by yet more rain.

On Saturday, April 24, Tanner revisited the John's Bayou family. As the days passed, it became more and more obvious that he had been fortunate to locate the nest hole so soon after arriving back in the Singer Tract in late March. Jim found the young ivory-bill soon after sunrise. It was alone for at least half an hour, pounding the wood but apparently not yet feeding itself. In time, the adults moved in from the east, and the three birds flew off together.

It had now been twenty-four days since the young bird fledged. With Jim's curiosity piqued, he and Kuhn returned to the nest hole that afternoon. What was it like inside the cavity? Spiking the tree, Jim climbed to where the dead stub branched off from the main body of the tree. "Tying myself to the tree, I cut the stub off," he wrote. "It turned as it fell, struck the ground top foremost." The dead branch broke below the base of the nest hole as it hit the ground, sticking into the soft soil. Tanner was climbing slowly back down the tree when he heard J.J. call, "D——, there is a fresh egg in here, all busted to ——." (It was a kinder, gentler age. Jim was much too polite to record Kuhn's expletives.)

"How fresh?" Jim yelled, still clinging to the tree.

"Not more than two days old," replied Kuhn.

Tanner's alarm was noticeable, as he recorded in his journal: "I hurried to the ground, and there in a little pool of water was a crushed egg shell, glistening white, and the contents of the egg mixed with the water but looking perfectly fresh. I knelt and put my arm down the hole that had been the bottom of the nest. The cavity was already filling up with water. At the top of the nest cavity, where it had been shaking by the fall, was a quantity of small chips and feeling around the chips, I found two whole eggs unbroken. I pulled them out, and we handled them tenderly but with dismay. They were wet, looked shining white."

Jim was remorseful: "We were thoroughly disorganized; the birds were nesting again while still caring for young; despite my attempts to keep close track of them, they had got away from me." How could this have happened? Worst of all, he had destroyed their second nesting. Tanner concluded his entry, "We walked home very quietly, carefully taking the two eggs."

A heaviness hung over Jim the next morning. He returned early to the scene of the accident: "I went to the old nest clearing and sat down to wait. I had not heard a thing of the birds on my way there. While I was sitting, a female wood duck flew over the clearing, circled over the old nest tree, and lit in a tree nearby. She sat there for some time, circled over the tree again, then disappeared."

Could it be? J.J. had remarked on the enormous size of the eggs. Were they too big to be ivory-bill eggs? Once the two men had gotten back to the cabin and dried them off, the pair of eggs were not the least bit glossy. Jim had seen ivory-bill eggs; they glistened pearly white. That night Tanner returned to the hotel in Tallulah where he kept his things, including his reference books, and looked up the description of wood duck eggs, which matched the two eggs back in the cabin. He was relieved to learn that no ivory-bill egg had been destroyed. The duck eggs were taken to the home of J. P. Morgan, where they later hatched.

At the least, the wood duck egg episode shows Jim Tanner's honesty. Another graduate student might not have recorded the incident in his journal, choosing instead to hide a potential mistake from his benefactors. The roots of this attitude may have lain with Doc Allen, who was prone to laugh at his own mistakes, asserting, "If this doesn't work, let's try something else." That acceptance of fallibility created a looser learning environment. If you're afraid to fail, you never take the first step.

With a sigh of relief, Jim returned to the task at hand: examining the nest hole he had cut down. Taking detailed measurements, he carefully sketched front and side views in his journal. The stub itself had been partially alive: three feet below the base of the nest was a green branch. The section the ivory-bill pair had chosen was 13 inches in diameter; they had chipped out a cavity that virtually hollowed out 25 inches of its length. The entrance hole was rounded:

5.25 inches high, 4.75 inches wide. The interior of the space was roughhewn, oval, and oblong, 10.5 inches at its widest point. All and all, it was a compact space to house an incubating adult ivory-bill and later, its growing chick. It was much like the nest hole the Cornell group had retrieved in 1935; Tanner found, at the bottom of the cavity, "a quart of loose, small chips, like coarse sawdust. Mixed in with this were a few fragments of droppings, fewer fragments of feather sheaths, at least one small egg-shell piece." But this time there didn't appear to be any mites. And this time the nesting had been a success.

After a day back in Tallulah on business, Tanner spent the next forty-eight hours observing the family of three. The ivory-bills were moving throughout the woods, feeding together west of John's Bayou and working their way north to what was known as the old Tank Road. Jim recorded subtle changes in the young bird since it had fledged twenty-seven days earlier. "When I look directly at the young's eye," he observed, "he seems to have the same eye color: dark red-brown. But seen from an angle, the eye seems to be lighter, a yellow. The bill is losing its chalky whiteness, becoming an ivory color, but it is still naturally whiter than that of the adults."

The last day of April, Tanner and Kuhn searched Greenlea Bend all the way to Rainey Lake and then south, following the river back to Alligator Bayou—a long trip. Moving through the Singer Tract was never done in a straight line, especially if one was searching for a bird that lived in the treetops. Within a two- or three-square-mile area, an explorer might actually travel fifteen to twenty miles in a serpentine pattern. One kept to the high ground, working around the water that was always there but at varying depths, depending on the most recent rainfall. Ivory-bills had been reported in the section; yet all Tanner and Kuhn found was fresh feeding sign—no birds. But the fresh sign was enough to indicate that at least one was there. "There is a variety of timber in Greenlea," Jim recorded, "From second growth in the old fields, to big solid oaks and gums that make a very valuable stand there."

On Saturday morning, May 1, it rained again. "Something that we did not need as the woods are much too wet for any good traveling," lamented Tanner. In the middle of the day, the rain stopped, and Jim ventured farther north to "Amonette," crossing near the John Harris Waterhole to Tank Road. (Amonette is the surname of one of the earliest landowners in Madison Parish.) "The only interesting thing that I saw was a giant and beautiful wisteria vine that had completely covered a small tree," Tanner wrote. "The pale lilac flowers hung in bunches like clusters of grapes, gracing the woods with their appearance and the air with their fragrance." With the arrival of May, Jim had been on the road for four months.

Kuhn and Tanner left the cabin at 4:30 AM the next morning, quickly scooting up John's Bayou in the dark. Jim wanted to check on the family, but they proved hard to find. As the young ivory-bill grew stronger, were the birds covering more ground? Tanner would hear them, but as he grew closer, they would disappear. J.J. and Jim separated, but by the end of the day, neither had a concrete sighting to report.

On Tuesday, May 4, Tanner set out early for John's Bayou: "I left the house about four, even though it threatened rain with thunder and a heavy sky." His need to reconnect with the family superseded any caution about getting caught in a downpour. Tanner may have felt a sense of loss: the ivory-bill family he had spent so much time observing was beginning to slip away. "It rained by the time I reached John's Bayou," he wrote, "but I continued on up to the old roosting ground, got under a big leaning ash, and waited."

Like any good woodsman, Tanner was accustomed to wet weather. "The rain fell steadily and quietly," he reported. "Wood thrush, wrens, cardinals, and others sang as usual around the hour of sunrise. Not a single woodpecker of any kind stirred." Conditions did not improve: "I stayed until after six, then hiked back to camp, stripped and slept till eleven. The afternoon faired some, but still threatened rain, so we stayed in camp." Jim spent the afternoon sitting on the porch, photographing a Carolina wren's nest that was over the door.

Determined to reunite with the ivory-bill family, he returned to their familiar roosting ground early the next day. The rain had passed; it was a quiet, starry morning. "It gradually grew light, light enough to see when I reached John's Bayou," Jim wrote. "I settled down on a log in the roosting ground about five."

The early songbirds began to sing. Jim recorded the order: first came the wood thrush, followed by parula warbler, Carolina wren, and then the cardinals. The first ivory-bill, the young bird, called at 5:15 AM and was answered once from the east. The juvenile vocalized for about ten minutes and then flew quite a distance toward the rising sun. A few minutes later, the adults called and pecked, flying east to join the young bird, and then called again. "After that there was silence and no more woodpeckers for the day," Jim wrote.

Tanner spent the rest of the day searching the region of John's Bayou and an area he called the "white line," finding scattered fresh feeding sign but no birds. Kuhn searched the Greenlea Bend area without seeing a thing. (From time to time, in recording his explorations of the Singer Tract, Tanner referred to either the "white line" or the "blue line." Although the exact meaning of the references remains unclear, these were apparently surveyed property boundaries. The white line seems to be the boundary of the Singer Tract, and the blue, the boundary of the old Sharkey Plantation.)

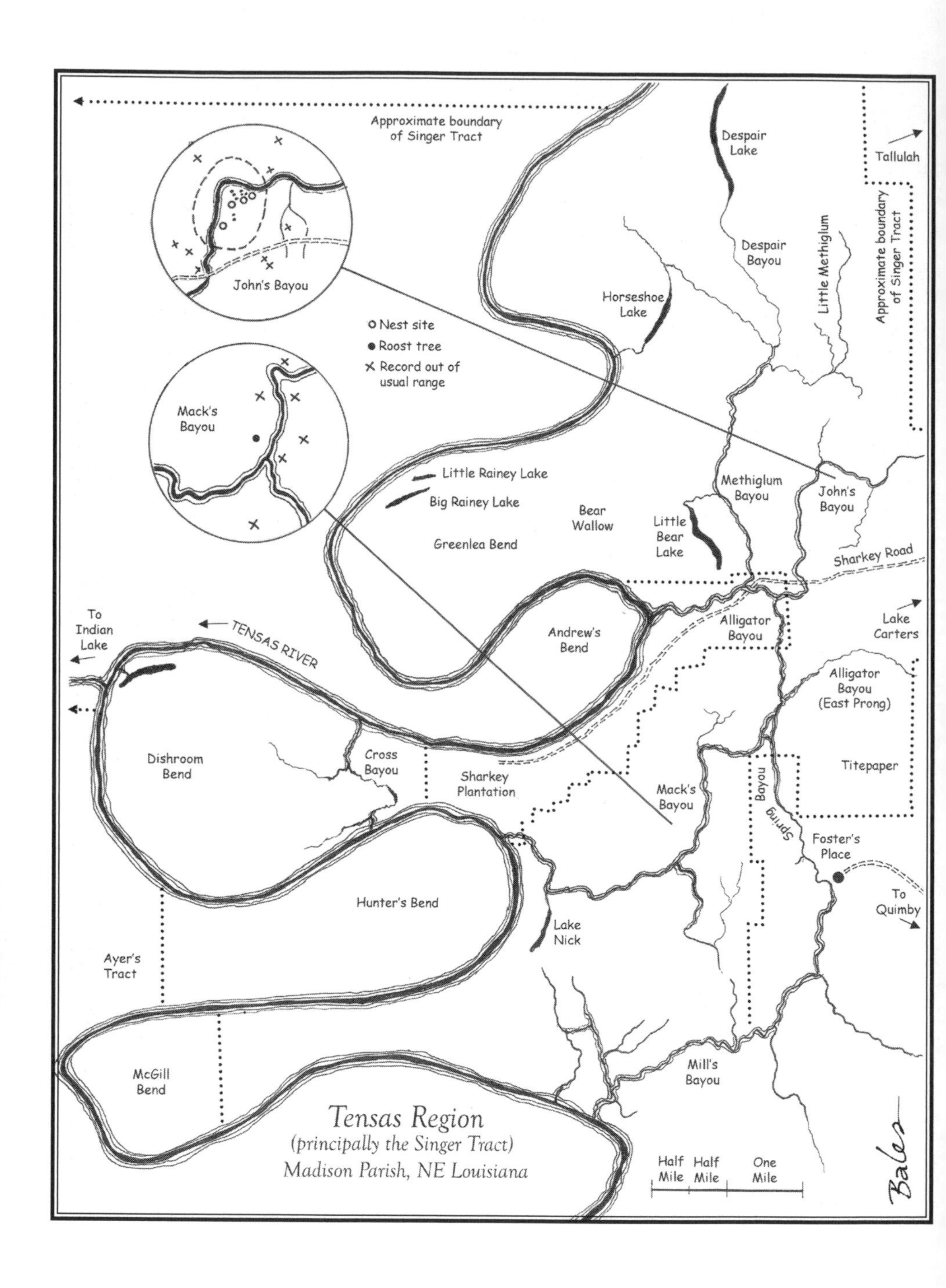
Approximate boundary of Singer Tract
John's Bayou
Nest site
Roost tree
Record out of usual range
Mack's Bayou
Despair Lake
Tallulah
Despair Bayou
Little Methiglum
Approximate boundary of Singer Tract
Horseshoe Lake
Little Rainey Lake
Big Rainey Lake
Bear Wallow
Little Bear Lake
Methiglum Bayou
John's Bayou
Greenlea Bend
Sharkey Road
To Indian Lake
TENSAS RIVER
Andrew's Bend
Alligator Bayou
Lake Carters
Alligator Bayou (East Prong)
Dishroom Bend
Cross Bayou
Sharkey Plantation
Mack's Bayou
Spring Bayou
Titepaper
Foster's Place
To Quimby
Hunter's Bend
Lake Nick
Ayer's Tract
McGill Bend
Mill's Bayou
Tensas Region
(principally the Singer Tract)
Madison Parish, NE Louisiana
Half Mile
Half Mile
One Mile
Bales

Mason Spencer's cabin was west of Little Bear Lake, on the north shore of the Tensas River above Andrew's Bend. On Thursday, May 6, Kuhn and Tanner crossed the river at the cabin to search the area. Ivory-bills had been reported there within the past year, but the only sign Tanner found was near a series of oxbow lakes on the east end of the bend. Jim also noted seeing his first purple gallinule, what birdwatchers call a "life bird"—the first sighting of a species in one's lifetime.

Tanner and Kuhn ended the initial week of May expanding their search south of Methiglum. After packing enough food for an overnight stay, they hiked to Mack's Ranch and pitched camp at Kemp's Bayou. Jim stayed at Kemp's to explore the area for suitable habitat, while J.J. walked farther south to Lake Nick. Both found old feeding sign, a lot of impenetrable vines, and no ivory-bills.

The following day, they hiked to the old Foster Plantation (west of Quimby). Jim searched the area north of the road, while Kuhn explored the south side. Neither found evidence of ivory-bills. J.J. discovered a big bear that had recently killed a "huge" wild boar about four days earlier. The bear had returned to feed once again on the kill. That afternoon it began to rain again, so the pair packed up their gear and walked to Stewart's Camp on the river next to McGill Bend. Buck Guthrie, a local resident, was the only one there, and he had no news of recent ivory-bill sightings. As the rain continued, they were glad to have a roof over their heads that night. The next day Jim and J.J. walked and waded north, returning to their base camp at Methiglum.

The rainfall was becoming a real issue. After replenishing their supplies, Tanner and Kuhn returned to the John's Bayou family. At the birds' roosting ground, the two men separated. Tanner soon heard calls and single "whams." Each time it sounded like a lone bird. Kuhn heard calls as well, and following the sounds, he found a dead stub with fairly fresh feeding sign near the top. A female ivory-bill flew in and disappeared—all but its tail—into a hole carved out of the stub. When Tanner reunited with Kuhn, he took over watching the hole, while J.J. searched to the south. Kuhn soon encountered the family of three, plus a second pair, further supporting the idea that the John's Bayou region was home to five ivory-bills. All vocalized often.

Kuhn encountered the second John's Bayou pair several times between March 28 and May 30 in the John's Bayou region. They appeared to have a large adjoining territory east of the family of three. Apparently they were not attending a nest because every time they were seen, "they did nothing but lazily feed." In Tanner's final report on the Singer Tract activity of 1937, he designated these two ivory-bills as Pair II.

Over the next four days, Tanner divided his time between searching areas in the vicinity of John's Bayou and checking on the original family of three.

They were getting increasingly harder to locate and follow, as they covered more ground every day. The adult ivory-bills seemed to be expanding their territory with the young bird in tow.

On Monday, May 17, with the month half over, Tanner met with Mason Spencer once again. Jim was hungry for any information that would aid his search. The attorney believed that Greenlea Bend and Lake Rainey had historically been home to between ten and fifteen ivory-bills—that is, up to about 1932 or '33. Spencer had long maintained that the birds had been "hunted out" and that Tanner was perhaps lucky to have located those he had found so far. With nesting season winding down, finding ivory-bills had become very difficult, especially with the leaves on the trees.

After spending two days working the area between John's Bayou and the white line and the vicinity of the John Harris Waterhole, Jim and J.J. packed their gear and hiked to Rainey Lake on the northwestern edge of Greenlea Bend. Camping on the upper end of the lake, they spent three days searching for the ghost bird, but what they initially found of note was an enormous alligator swimming up the lake towards them. "He swam with head and body still," recorded Tanner, "only his tail sculling back and forth and making a swish and splash like a boat paddler. It was impossible to accurately judge his size, but Kuhn guessed 15 to 16 feet. " In this part of the Singer Tract, larger alligators were easier to find than ivory-bills: Kuhn and Tanner saw none of the latter, nor did they hear any.

Breaking down, they left the camp on Rainey Lake and crossed the river, walking to Spencer's camp. Late in the day, they heard what could have been a call, but it was dusk and the pair couldn't follow it. Jim noted finding "quite a bit of sign in certain places especially around Turkey and Bearbite brakes." (Brakes were somewhat open places overgrown with bushes, brambles, or river cane.)

Monday, May 24: Tanner walked back to Tallulah for supplies. His weekly overnight trips to town gave him a chance to buy groceries, take a bath, do his laundry, get news from the outside world, and visit the post office. Telephones were becoming affordable in the 1930s, but they weren't widely used. Generally, Jim communicated with his family back home and Doc Allen via penny postcards. He offered succinct messages on how things were going or not going, with perhaps a brief weather report. Conditions had changed since his arrival in late March. As he recorded in his journal, "It is getting to be a hot job now, packing the food back to camp over the rough road and under the burning sun."

Every morning for the next three days, Tanner and Kuhn left the cabin early, having decided that the Titepaper area south of Methiglum was the best place to look. Located east of Mack Bayou, this area of small ridges is cradled by

Alligator and Spring bayous. Disappointingly, they saw or heard no ivory-bills. "There was very little fresh ivory-bill sign in the place, although it looks very suitable," Jim noted. "Pileateds were common, feeding in the high gums where ivory-bills are likely to feed. One of the puzzling things is the disappearance of the Red-heads [red-headed woodpeckers]. Kuhn said that when he first went there this year, Red-heads were so thick and making so much noise that they seemed to be the only bird there. Now I could not find a single Red-head in the place. I have heard but one or two anywhere in the last few days. Red-bellies are calling commonly."

At times, reading Tanner's journal, one gets the sense that he returned to the John's Bayou to reassure himself that ivory-bills indeed remained in the region. At 5:05 AM, on Saturday, May 29, he found the male and juvenile at the ash tree roosting site. Perched high on the dead stub, they preened themselves, occasionally calling *keent, keent.* The female answered, about 250 yards to the east, *yeenh-yeenh,* and flew in to join them. The three then flew north over the bayou. Jim followed, watching them feed together. "The young bird has now a light eye, but not a yellow one," he observed. "The bill is very nearly as much an ivory color as the adults, but still is short. The crest still is blunt. He continually gives the food call when his parents are near."

If Tanner had learned anything during these last few weeks in May, it was that, with the lush green canopy in place, seeing ivory-bills at this time of the year meant being in the right place at the right time—and getting there early. The days were becoming longer. On Saturday, May 30, Jim was in place at the ash tree roosting ground about fifteen minutes after good daylight seeped into the swamp. At 4:50 AM the adult male emerged from his overnight hole, called *keent* one time, and climbed to the top of the stub. He sat there silently, preening and scratching for several minutes. At about five o'clock, the young bird emerged from a roosting hole west of Jim, gave several *keents* in succession, and drummed a double-rap. The adult male flew to the young, and they called together. Then they both flew east, stopping one time to call. As they disappeared into the canopy, Jim did not hear or see the birds for the rest of the day.

Kuhn had better luck. Positioned southwest of Tanner, he had heard the birds early, and by running as fast as he could, he was able to keep the birds within hearing distance. By now, all three ivory-bills were traveling together, making longer and longer flights. When J.J. caught up with the trio, he watched them feed and heard a fourth ivory-bill call from the southeast. Kuhn elected to stay with the threesome, ignoring the fourth. At first, the family had traveled far and fast, not stopping to feed until they were a good distance from the roosting ground; then they settled down to feed in a group of recently dead pin oaks.

It was quite warm when June arrived. After his weekly trip into town, made somewhat easier because the hot sun had dried Sharkey Road, Tanner hiked back to Rainey Lake to search the area where Kuhn had heard an ivory-bill earlier. He camped at Bearbite Brake but heard no ivory-bill. The next day he followed the river upstream to Horseshoe Lake and then into Despair and Methiglum bayous. East of Horseshoe he encountered a slash where he found some sign of ivory-bills.

Back at the cabin, Jim slept until 7:00 AM for the first time in weeks. Perhaps he pondered where next to look for ivory-bills. Even in an area that was still hospitable to the ghost birds, they were proving most difficult to find. Jim was still grappling with the question: how many lived in the Singer Tract?

That afternoon Tanner traveled south to Spring Bayou. Sharkey Road had dried considerably, so he was able to drive part of the way. He did a tree count in the woods around the Titepaper ridges, taking photographs of some tall gums. East of the bayou he encountered a singing Bachman's warbler, a species that has become very much a ghost bird itself. Today it is probably extinct, but perhaps they were never very common. The last reported sightings were in 1961 and then again in 1988, both in South Carolina; the I'on Swamp was its final stronghold. Reverend John Bachman, who gave a study skin to his friend John James Audubon, discovered the reclusive bird in 1832. Its preferred habitats were swampy regions and canebrakes. It was Audubon who lent the bird its original name, "Bachman's swamp warbler."

Tanner heard the bird in the mornings and evenings. "He sings from the tall trees," he noted, "a rapid buzzy song sounding much like a fast chippy's [chipping sparrow]. Then every short interval he will plunge to the undergrowth for a few moments, move round a little there and then fly up to the tree tops again. I have not seen any signs of a female." Returning to John's Bayou, Tanner spent the next couple of days chopping and debarking dead trees so as to study the order of insect infestation: beetle, ant, and termite.

On Tuesday, June 8, Jim arrived at the chosen roosting ground early. He had been watching the interactions of the John's Bayou trio for exactly ten weeks. In natural history annals, this was a first: no biologist had ever had such an intimate experience with a single family of ivory-bills. The first adult stirred, left its hole, and flew to another tree at 4:45 AM. Five minutes later, a call came from a second roost hole, followed by yet another call from somewhere to the east. In short order, the family reunited in a single tree, climbed to the top, and flew off together, north across John's Bayou. Later in the morning, Tanner relocated the family. Both adults were still feeding the juvenile, but the youngster was in turn finding "a few grubs for himself." The adults steadily led the way, calling as

Tanner in front of a sweet gum, May 1937. (Photo courtesy of Nancy Tanner.)

they went, encouraging the young ivory-bill to follow. Three days later, Jim was following the family again as a storm approached. The rain slowed their travel.

"At one time, all three birds were in the top of a dead trunk," Tanner observed, "wind was tossing the tree tops; hurrying the ragged black clouds. The birds surely appeared to be denizens of the dark and dismal swamp." The birds' vitality—their glossy, contrasting plumage—stood in stark contrast to the storm's encompassing gray shroud. A poet might see the gathering storm as a metaphor for the outside threats to the woodpeckers' existence around the Tensas. At that point, it perhaps seemed that these three ivory-bills were the last of their kind, stoically defying the forces arrayed against them.

Over the next couple of weeks, Jim stayed busy. One day would find him doing tree counts and taking photographs around the nesting site; on another he would explore other parts of the Singer Tract for ivory-bill sign. He made inquiries about sightings in an area called the Ayer Tract, a parcel west of the Singer; meanwhile, visits to other areas proved fruitless. He was no doubt most troubled by new threats to the ivory-bills' habitat. The Singer firm had recently sold logging rights on their property to Chicago Mill and Lumber, and during a visit to their timber camp, he learned that cutting had begun in the area. He had seen it before in other parts of the South, and now it was happening here. The clock was ticking.

By Saturday, June 19, he was back at John's Bayou but didn't spot the ivory-bill family of three. The profusion of leaves had made it ever more difficult to find dead branches high in the canopy. Kuhn, however, had seen the three birds, still together, west of the bayou a few days earlier.

Tanner realized that to learn more about ivory-bills, he needed to know how a tree dies and decays. Meeting with Bill Pierce, a neighboring property owner, he got permission to "girdle" a few big trees: hackberry, gum, and pecan. "Girdling" means removing a ring of bark from around a tree, a process that ultimately kills it.

On June 22 Tanner camped at Indian Lake, which lay across the river, west of Greenlea Bend. The following day, he worked his way south into the Ayer Tract. It had already been cut over: the big oaks and gums were felled. Tanner believed the trees had been down for about a year, and he noted the split, loosened condition of the bark. Venturing north to Africa Lake, Jim found no ivory-bill sign but managed to get his car mired "almost out of sight." He spent the night with a local sharecropper named Levi Jefferson, who lived four miles away. Jefferson had been there for nineteen years and had never seen an ivory-bill west of the river. The next morning, with the help of Jefferson's horse, they were able to pull the car out of the mud but with great difficulty. The differential and ring gear were damaged, which meant a slow drive back to Tallulah.

The damaged car was only a minor setback, as Tanner was used to such. The larger issue was one of time. With the arrival of summer and the increasing difficulty in finding ivory-bills, where should he look next?

Chapter 12

A Need to Move On

Hunting for localities where ivory-bills were, and in these localities trying to find the birds, was like searching for an animated needle in a haystack.

—James T. Tanner

With the lateness of the season—it was the last week in June—Tanner was feeling the need to move elsewhere. The past several days in the Tensas region had been more or less fruitless; even the John's Bayou family of three had become increasingly hard to find. While he waited for his car to be repaired, Jim queried Harry Anderson of Chicago Mill and Lumber about the swamplands of the Atchafalaya Basin in south central Louisiana and the names of people who might aid in his search for ivory-bills.

Back at camp at Methiglum, Tanner arose early to visit the John's Bayou trio one more time before his trip south. He was in position at their favored roosting ground when he heard the first bird call at 5:00 AM—a soft *cape, cape, cape* coming from the direction of the female's favorite sleeping hole. A second bird flew silently overhead to join the first. Thirty minutes and a few more calls later, the birds flew southwest and disappeared. Though brief, the encounter felt good, energizing Tanner. Afterward, he traveled to Foster to work on deadening the trees he had received permission to kill for his impromptu study. The afternoon heat forced him to quit around two o'clock. A fire had already killed a few trees near this section of the white line, and he noted some possible ivory-bill sign.

Tanner drove south to Ferriday on Tuesday, June 29, stopping along the way to inquire about possible ivory-bill sightings. He visited Fisher Lumber Company in Ferriday and Three Rivers Lumber Company in Jonesville, learning where timber had been cut. At a Texaco Station, an avid hunter and fisherman named A. M. Beard recommended that Jim look at Cocodrie Lake and on the east side of the Black River. Over the next couple of days, with more local guidance and advice, Jim made his way into both areas, but saw no ivory-bills and very little promising sign. East of the Black River, the big trees had already been removed, and a timberman reported that he had never seen an ivory-bill there. Rain finally forced Jim out of the woods, and he drove to Alexandria, where he spent the night.

Tanner had now been alone and traveling throughout the southeast for six months; if he was road-weary, he didn't record it in his field notes. He began July by driving north from Alexandria to Catahoula Lake and then to Saline Lake. Lumbermen at Simmesport knew of few old-growth woods in the Red River area and nothing of ivory-bills. Jim found willow and cottonwood along the river's banks; the woods in the bottomland were second-growth, mixed slash with large trees removed and overcup oak flats, all of it poor ivory-bill habitat.

After a night in Baton Rouge, Tanner drove across the Atchafalaya Swamp to Opelousas. At over half a million acres, the low-lying basin—a combination of lakes, bayous, wetlands, and river delta that surround the Atchafalaya River south to where it converges with the Gulf of Mexico—is the largest swamp in the country. Historically, because of repeated flooding, it was sparsely populated with few roads leading into the region. Today the waters have been "tamed," with protective levees built along its entire length, corralling the shallow basin, which is roughly 20 miles wide and 150 miles long.

In 1937 Tanner's visit to the Atchafalaya was brief; he was in a reconnaissance mode planning next year's itinerary. Tanner had scheduled a return to Avery Island, arriving there and meeting with E. A. McIlhenny on July 3. Little had changed since the Cornell Expedition's 1935 visit to McIlhenny's Bird City, especially with McIlhenny, who was always eager to talk about birds. He told Jim that ivory-bills had once lived in the swamps extending from Avery Island east to Morgan City, an area about four miles wide and forty-five miles in length. Within that region, McIlhenny believed, the ivory-bills had historically moved around quite a bit. He had seen one ivory-bill in 1937, none the year before that, and two in 1935; however, the last nesting he had observed was around 1927. With most of the cypress cut from the swamp, McIlhenny surmised that proper habitat for the species was now gone. (J. J. Kuhn said he had never seen an ivory-bill *in* a cypress but, rather, in the trees associated with them.)

Tanner spent the Fourth of July on the road, exploring the wetlands east of Avery Island: Weeks Bay at Bayou Sale. Mostly it was coastal marsh; the big trees inland appeared to have been cut out about twenty years before. It was a Sunday, and, as was often his habit on the Sabbath, he did a little sightseeing. He drove out to Cypremont Point, where a ridge of live oaks, fringed with marsh, led out to the bay. Jim spent that night in a tourist camp in Franklin, south of Grand Lake.

After breakfast the next morning, Tanner visited the May Brothers Lumber Company, where he learned that all of the Atchafalaya Basin had been cut over, with nearly all of the cypress and much of the gum, the two most common trees, removed; however, some good stands of timber remained. The company still owned a big tract of virgin tupelo north of Shadyside and Calumet. The swamps along Bayou Sale Road were pretty well cut over. The lumbermen considered the large woodpeckers beneficial; the local trappers, however, had shot them for bait. Tanner met an old swamp man, "Capt' Ben," who was still active in the Patterson area and remembered seeing ivory-bills from many years before.

The next morning Tanner drove to Morgan City. Stopping at the Norman-Breaux Lumber Company, he met with Kennedy Breaux, a "big hearty French man who was very free with his time and information." He told Tanner that there was very little virgin swamp in the southern end of the Atchafalaya Basin, as most of the region had been cut over. Thus, it was hard to find any woodpeckers in the swamp between Lake Verret and Elm Hall Junction north to Old River.

In New Orleans, at Tulane University, Jim located the widow of Dr. George Beyer, who had reported seeing ivory-bills in July 1899 in a swamp between the Tensas River and the Bayou Maçon in Franklin Parish, southwest of the Singer Tract. Mrs. Beyer knew of no field notes left behind by her late husband. It was a long shot, but Tanner had to try. Beyer had done more than just see ivory-bills in Louisiana in 1899; he had also shot several, as he noted in an article for *The Auk* in 1900: "Our hunt was quite successful, as I obtained seven specimens in fairly good plumage. The old pair which I found with one of their young in the nest, I mounted with all their belongings." Until Mason Spencer shot one in 1932, those had been the last seen in the state. It was more old-school thinking: an ornithologist who would rather kill the state's last ivory-bills and turn them into museum specimens than actually watch them live—exactly the paradigm Doc Allen and his protégé Tanner sought to change.

The next morning, from three taxidermists at a Royal Street museum in the French Quarter, Jim learned about a possible ivory-bill sighting two or three years before in a remote swamp on the Pearl River, a little fragmented place that could only be reached by boat.

That afternoon Jim drove north to Tangipanoa Parish, where a game warden, Dan Lavigne, offered to take Tanner into the Ponchatoula cypress swamp the next day. The trip through Manchac and out to Lake Pontchartrain proved uneventful. Later Jim met with a man at the Louisiana Cypress Lumber Company, learning that the last parcel of virgin timber north of the lake, between the railroad and Tangipahoa River, was being cut. (Today, this section is part of the 16,394-acre Joyce Wildlife Management Area, a wetland within the Lake Pontchartrain Basin that consists primarily of cypress-tupelo swamp.) Jim also interviewed several locals who lived along the edge of the swamp; all knew of pileateds but none had ever seen an ivory-bill.

Those observations were borne out early the next morning, when Jim visited the swamp with the game warden he had met the day before. "Black gum outnumbers cypress ten to one, but the cypress are much bigger. All of the cypress, much of it hollow, and the larger gums are cut, leaving a scanty forest of slender small gums," he observed. Dead trees were scarce, and Jim saw only a few red-bellied woodpeckers and one pileated. "I feel quite certain that there is no ivory-bill there," he concluded. "The pineland nearby is comparatively young and quite healthy."

Afterward, as Tanner drove through Baton Rouge to Plaquemine and then, the next morning, to Grosse Tete, he queried various locals along the way, but none had knowledge of ivory-bills. Finally, he drove back to Tallulah in the rain. His twelve-day trip to southern Louisiana had produced nothing definite other than the reported sightings by McIlhenny. In his notebook, however, he listed people and places he needed to visit in that part of the state at a later date.

Saturday, July 10: Tanner went back to the camp at Methiglum. It must have felt like something of a homecoming, as J. J. Kuhn and J. P. Morgan were there. Kuhn reported finding a lone male ivory-bill several times in the Andrews Bend area, but he was unable to follow it for long, saying that the bird was skittish and called only when disturbed. Each encounter sent the bird flying away in the direction of Turkey Brake on Greenlea. Still, it confirmed that at least one lived in that area. Earlier they had found only fresh feeding sign.

Morgan reported finding five ivory-bills feeding together on Lake Carters near the white line on June 27, supporting Tanner's belief that that many remained in the John's Bayou area. Early the next morning, July 12, Jim went to the adopted roosting area of the family of three. At 5:20 AM he heard their calls east of the location, but by the time he reached the site, they were gone. He hunted the area that day but found nothing. Two days later, back at the same location, the birds first called at 5:15 AM, and Jim soon located all three, together in the same tree. "They called a little bit, then flew east, swung north across John's Bayou to a nearby dead big gum," he noted. "They fed there for some time, then traveled west with frequent stops for feeding until I lost them at 7:15, quite a ways east of Indian Camp and the Tank Road. During their traveling they had called only occasionally, when about to leave and when disturbed." This would be the last time he saw the family during this visit. "The young is now showing red in his crest, eye is yellow, bill ivory," he added. "The crest is nearly like the adults, but is a bit ragged and blunt. The white tips to the outer primaries are nearly worn away. He fed himself regularly, but still gave the food call when near a parent."

Tanner spent the next three days revisiting various locations in the Singer Tract, including Rainey and Little Bear lakes, having one last look but finding no ivory-bills. But this mattered little: his first solo trip to Madison Parish and the Singer Tract had been overwhelmingly productive. He had observed ivory-bills for fifteen consecutive weeks; no one in the history of bird study could make such a claim. On Saturday, July 17, Jim packed up his Model A, left Tallulah early in the morning, lunched in Selma, Alabama, and arrived in Macon, Georgia, around dark—an uneventful trip of 497 miles. He spent the night in the Milner Hotel, noting that hundreds, even thousands, of purple martins flew over Macon at dusk. The next day he drove to McClellanville, South Carolina, and stayed at White Gables, the home of a Mrs. Graham.

Around 1930 George Melamphy, a biologist working on a wild turkey project in the Santee River Swamp, had reported seeing an ivory-bill. When the National Association of Audubon Societies sent Alexander Sprunt and Lester Walsh, John Baker's personal assistant and secretary, to investigate in early 1935, the pair found one ivory-bill and possibly heard two more. They then leased a portion of the swamp, hiring a local, Hollie Shokes, as a game warden to guard the site. Shokes subsequently saw the ghost birds several times on Wadmacon Island in the Santee River. "The Santee swamps," according to the famed bird expert Roger Tory Peterson, "were more extensive in those days; hundreds of square miles of cypress. Sweet gum, and pine embraced the muddy yellow river, swamps known to few men other than a handful of hog herders and trappers."

Tanner met Shokes early on Monday, July 19. In a cypress dugout fitted with an outboard motor, the pair traveled upriver to Steward's Neck in the Wadmacon section of Santee Bottoms. It rained heavily, and the men saw no woodpecker of any kind. They spent the next four days exploring up and down the lower Santee. Tanner wrote,

> Simply described, the Santee there is a river swamp cutting thru sandy pineland. Next to the rivers and creeks are ridges bearing sweet gum, water and willow oak, maple, some overcup, birch, elm, and occasional pine. Big cypress stand in or on the banks of the creeks. Back of the ridges are flat swamps of tupelo and pole cypress. This turns almost abruptly into the hills with pines and blackjack oak.
>
> The northern end of Wadmacon Island is uncut, and has many fairly large sweet gum and oaks, some very large pine, and many old cypress. The best hill pine is east of Shokes place. Steward's Neck is a high ridge, some of it old field, lying between two swamps and bearing pine and scrubby oak. This kind of country extends for miles from the river.

During his five days on the lower Santee, Tanner recorded seeing fifty-two species of birds—including several red-bellied and red-cockaded woodpeckers, plus an encouraging twelve pileateds—but he found no real sign of ivory-bills. His entry for Saturday, July 24, ends succinctly: "An uneventful day for the last of the season's ivory-bill hunting."

Since leaving New York on the last day of 1936, Jim had been on the road alone in his cramped Model A Ford for 205 days. It was time to go home.

Chapter 13

On the Road Again

Winter was the best time to search for ivory-bills. The birds were active and called frequently, their calls carrying far through the leafless forest, and the same bareness made it easier to see and follow them. We searched every day, trying to follow and count the birds before spring made it harder and also made it necessary to concentrate on nesting studies.

—James T. Tanner

It was early December 1937. Jim Tanner repacked his Model A Ford and picked up where he left off: the Santee Bottoms. The recent sightings reported by Alexander Sprunt and others were tantalizing. With the leaves off the trees, hunting would be easier. The Palmetto State was much colder than when he left it in July. Temperatures dropped below freezing every night, but it was sunny during the day.

"Most of the swamp was about ankle-deep," Tanner wrote. "The deepest creek I waded was half-way up my thighs. None of the deeper creeks were long. Here and there were low and small ridges, carrying sweet gum, a little laurel oak, etc. Bird life was scarce." The Steward's Neck and Wadmacon sections of the Santee were fairly large stretches of virgin tupelo and mixed swamp. Ivory-bills had been reliably sighted in the region regularly for several years, up to the winter of 1936–37. But one year later, Tanner spent ten days there and found none. Where had they gone?

On Saturday, December 11, Jim broke camp and drove to Georgetown, South Carolina, and then on to Atlanta. It was clear and cold, but having grown up in western New York, the temperatures didn't bother him. The next day he drove to Birmingham and on to Tallulah via Highways 11 and 80, checking once again into the Montgomery Hotel. Finding J. J. Kuhn at home the next day, Tanner learned that he had been "making a not-so-good living by fishing." Kuhn was eager to help Jim look for ivory-bills, having encountered a group of three early one morning in September in East Carroll Parish (due north of

Alexander Sprunt Jr. and Jim Tanner in the Santee, late 1937. (Photo courtesy of the family of Alexander Sprunt IV.)

Madison Parish). However, he had been unable to follow them for very long. Tanner soon reconnected with Mason Spencer, Ed Cochran, and J. P. Morgan, but learned nothing new.

Then it was back to Methiglum Bayou and the cabin he had left in July. Sharkey Road was almost passable, but a car bogged down in the mud a short way in convinced Jim not to risk driving to the camp. Carrying his provisions, Tanner got there on foot. "Camp was in fair shape, clean and with some wood," he reported. "Outside was a clear, moonlit night, quiet as a desert, but for occasional bat chirps and owl hoots."

On Tuesday, December 14, with the chill of late fall in the air, Tanner left camp before sunrise; a waxing moon lit the way. "I started out in the half light of early morning, reaching the ash roost hole in John's Bayou about 6:30," he wrote. "At near 6:45 the male called short notes from the top of the stub. He then flew to a nearby tree. Several minutes later the female called from the east and then came flying rapidly to the same tree, calling loudly *kient, kient* as she flew." It was the first ivory-bill pair he had seen in several months. "The two called from that tree," he continued. "Then they flew north with but one short stop. That was the last I saw of them on that day. I walked around the east White Line to Sharkey Road, then up to the Tank Road and back to camp."

Kuhn joined Tanner the next morning, and over the next five days they searched for ivory-bills but found none. One "bad" morning he hiked out to Tallulah and decided to drive his car back in, knocking the muffler off in the process.

On Sunday morning, December 19, Kuhn located three ivory-bills—one male and two females—foraging together east of Methiglum. J.J. pursued them as they moved quickly towards Despair Lake west of Tallulah, eventually losing them in late morning. They had traveled about three and a half miles. Kuhn observed, "The three kept together and called a lot. The male and one female stayed together, close, all the time. The other female stayed to one side."

Tanner and Kuhn spent the days leading up to Christmas searching some of the same places they had searched the spring before. It was overcast off and on, with an occasional shower or light drizzle. Jim carefully noted the number of pileated woodpeckers he encountered each day, the time he spent during his search, and the amount of ground he thought he had covered. Judging distances was always difficult because one could not really walk in a straight line. Since it was late December, nightfall came early, sometimes too early.

"I misjudged time and distance in coming back and dusk caught me following the old road in the brake at the end of Rainey," Jim wrote on December 21. "Coming out of that road, I somehow made a mistake and turned the wrong way on the road that leads along the lake. I realized that something was wrong, but could not understand how it became wrong. I called once, but heard no reply. Finally the road became so dim that I could not follow it." Looking at his compass, Jim found that he was not lost, just misplaced and soon realized he needed to retrace his steps. The Tensas had grown quite dark, and Tanner was beginning to think he was going to have to spend the night in the woods.

"Just then a single wolf, way down in the bend, opened up with a lonely, mournful howl," he wrote. "'Nice company,' I thought. After several minutes of walking, I saw the cypress that rimmed Rainey Lake, and then heard the ducks talking. I called, and Kuhn answered from not far ahead. That sounded good to me." J.J. had also misjudged the time, and darkness had caught him as well. Together they walked out and found the car. Neither had found an ivory-bill, yet, both knew they were probably there.

Christmas Eve: Tanner left the cabin early, walking to the roosting trees at John's Bayou. It was warm and damp. Spring peepers called along the way. Occasionally, there was a break in the clouds; and while the waning gibbous moon broke through, sunrise was hidden behind the clouds. At about 7:15 the male ivory-bill came out of his hole and hopped to the top of the stub. The magnificent bird was silent, and without calling, he soon flew to the east. Jim followed. A quarter-mile away, he found the pair together picking and preening. The female pounded the tree twice in quick secession. Ivory-bills use their strong bill to pound on limbs or dead stubs with hard blows. Sometimes it is a single rap and sometimes a hard double rap—*BAM-bam*—with the second blow sounding like an immediate echo of the first. The double rap was the ivory-bill diagnostic behavior that Tanner listened for; no other woodpecker does it. Jim had grown used to hearing the loud *BAM-bam*. Shortly, the mated pair flew east. Tanner followed but soon lost them. The juvenile they had raised earlier in the year had apparently moved elsewhere. The early-morning sighting, albeit brief, was the one holiday present Tanner was most grateful for receiving.

Jim stayed in the woods until past noon but didn't see or hear the pair again that day or, as it would turn out, that year. While in the woods, he conducted a Christmas Bird Count, totaling 638 birds and 34 species, including the ivory-bills. That afternoon he packed up and returned to town, spending a quiet Christmas in Tallulah. The heavy rains that fell the last week of December left all the secondary roads impassible, preventing any further work in the swamp. Tanner drove back to Atlanta, and after arranging to store his car, he took a train to New York to welcome in the New Year. Tanner would return to Louisiana only a month and a half later, but first there was a report to write for the National Association of Audubon Societies. Though reserved, Tanner's summation did carry the upbeat news that the vanishing ivory-bills had been found.

"The major problem in the study of the ivory-bill is to discover the cause for the diminishing numbers and threatened extinction of the species," Tanner's official 1937 report began. After a year on the road, he had pinpointed only a few places where the ghost bird *might* still live: the Big Cypress, Gulf Hammock, and lower Apalachicola River swamps in Florida and possibly parts of the Santee region of South Carolina. It was decided, however, that he should focus his energy and attentions on the Singer Tract in Louisiana. This site, he continued, "was chosen as the place to study the birds during the breeding season, because more was already known about the ivory-bills there than anywhere else, and with that knowledge, it was thought that the birds could be more easily found and that new facts could be better interpreted."

During 1937 Tanner and J. J. Kuhn had only been able to make a thorough search of the eastern portion of the Singer Tract. Through direct observations and other evidence, they concluded that six pairs of ivory-bills still lived in the section. (Later, Tanner modified this to two pairs and one juvenile in John's

Bayou, one pair and one juvenile in Despair Bayou, one pair in the Titepaper/ Mack's Bayou section, one pair in Hunter's Bend, and a single male in Greenlea Bend for a total of thirteen birds.) Jim designated the two birds in John's Bayou with which he had spent so much time "Pair One"—and that was perhaps the same pair discovered and photographed in 1935 by Doc Allen and the Cornell expedition.

Tanner submitted his report against a grim backdrop of international and national news. In Europe tensions were steadily building. The previous September, at the Nazi rally in Nuremburg (an annual event since 1933), some 600,000 German troops had paraded before Adolf Hitler in a bellicose show of force for all the world to see. At home, meanwhile, the U.S. government released its first national unemployment census on January 1. It revealed that 7.8 million Americans were jobless, and the total was expected to climb to over 10 million since the survey's actual completion was in late November 1937. Twenty percent of the country's workforce had no gainful employment.

Still, it could have been worse. Up to 2 million workers were engaged in Franklin Delano Roosevelt's Civil Conservation Corps (CCC) and Works Progress Administration (WPA), both part of the president's New Deal initiatives to combat unemployment during the Great Depression. Created by Roosevelt in 1933, the CCC soon became one of his most popular programs, engaging young men—and roughly 8,500 women—from underemployed families to build dams, bridges, and roads in all forty-eight states and several territories. Similarly, the WPA, created in 1935, built many public buildings and roads, as well as operating large media, drama, arts, and literacy projects. It also fed children and distributed clothing and arranged housing. It was all paid for by the government.

For his part, Jim Tanner probably counted himself lucky to be employed, albeit meagerly. And what an odd job it was: living like a gypsy, out of his car, often sleeping under the stars. But at least he had a purpose—a mission, in fact.

Chapter 14

A Second Nesting Season at Singer

The vistas between the widely spaced forest giants were quite open, and the tangles of catbrier and poison ivy that barred our way were easily circumvented. We were in the higher, drier part of the swamp, the "second bottoms." The trees whose massive crowns towered 150 or more feet above our heads were sweet gum, Nuttall's oak, and ash. In the lower parts of the swamp grew the pale green cypresses, their knobby "knees" emerging from the dark, coffee-colored water. Never, said Kuhn, had he seen an ivory-bill on a cypress.

—Roger Tory Peterson

In early February 1938, Tanner was anxious to get back to Louisiana. He arrived in Atlanta and retrieved his car from storage on February 12, driving the next day to Livingston, Alabama, southwest of Birmingham and just east of Mississippi. There had been rumors of ivory-bills in the swamps of Tombigbee Bottoms in Sumter County. These accounts amounted to little more than hearsay, but still Tanner needed to check out their credibility. As he had learned the year before, local lumber companies were good sources of information. They had knowledge of the current state of the woods and knew the old-timers and their stories. At the Allison Lumber Company in Bellamy, south of Livingston, Jim learned of previous efforts to find ivory-bills in the area—attempts that had located nothing. Ultimately, Jim found neither good territory nor anyone there who had seen the birds.

On February 15 Tanner drove on to Tallulah. Once again, Ed Cochran gave him use of his cabin at Methiglum. The weather had been warm, almost summer-like. Most of the roads were fairly dry, but Jim knew there were more cool days ahead. He left his car with a local farmer and arranged for the use of a horse to carry his gear into camp from a Dr. Speaker, the local veterinarian, who lived near Quimby.

Returning to the cabin he knew so well must have been satisfying. Although sparse, its confines would be home for the next few months. Its roof would keep him dry during the wet days that were sure to come, and its stove would keep him warm. Winter in Louisiana can consist of days of steady rain that flood the bayous and sloughs; or it can be bright and clear, cool in the morning but warm in the afternoon.

Anxious to reconnect with "Pair One," Tanner was at their favorite roost hole in the group of ashes in John's Bayou at 6:30 AM on February 17. Nothing happened. Had the birds moved on? Disappointed, Tanner began to search the area and an hour and a half later, he found the ivory-bills in the general vicinity of the previous year's nest. He noted,

> They left and I waited. About 9 [AM] they came back and for 40 minutes hung around. The male was carrying a big grub for a long time. Once the two birds got close together, the male pointed his bill upward, and gave a call much like the notes they made at nest-changing.
>
> Twice, when the male was carrying food, he flew to a partly dead maple which had much scaling on it. An hour or more later, 10:45, the female flew to that tree, climbed to a fresh hole, looked in a few times, entered, came out, went half way in again, came out, looked around, flew off.

It was mid-February, but spring was already coming to the swamp. Tender green plants were peeking through the soil. Red haw shrubs were beginning to show new leaves, and the American elms and red maples, known in parts of the South as swamp maples, were in full fruit (called samara). Jim's luck of being in the right place at the right time held true. On his first day back in the Singer Tract, he had found an active nest. But could this be possible so early in the year? For the rest of the day, he observed the interaction of the pair, noting their behavior. He soon realized that they *were* feeding young. The male and female came and went from the new cavity all day. Tanner estimated that the 1938 nest was roughly 150 yards to the west and 300 yards south of the 1937 nest.

Over the next several days, unless it was raining, Tanner watched the nest from a blind he built about 70 yards away. The spring-like conditions gave way to cold, gray skies, but the nest activities continued. Jim sat quietly, recording the comings and goings of the mated pair, noticing a pattern:

> The usual procedure is for the bird with food to fly to a tree in the vicinity of the nest, often a tall slender ash about 30 yards from

Site of the 1938 ivory-bill nest in the top of a dying red maple, fifty-five feet above the ground. (Photo courtesy of Nancy Tanner.)

> the nest hole, a tree which has been scaled quite a bit. It may call from there. Then it flies to the nest tree, climbs up to the left of the entrance, may call and look around from there. Then it slides around and pauses just below the hole, looking sharply from side to side. It goes up to the hole, peers in, and then half enters the hole so that only the rear part of the body is visible. It emerges and re-enters three or four times. Often it jerks as though pumping or tearing food. Usually it stops on the nearby tree before going on. Most of their feeding seems to be done west and southwest of the nest.

Although Tanner was squirreled away inside a blind, the birds seemed aware that he was nearby. As Jim recorded, "The amount of calling varies. If they are aware of me, they call quite a bit, nervous yaps."

Tanner had not seen the young ivory-bill tucked away inside the tree, but he knew it was there. The nestling was not mute, as Jim observed on February 23 after watching the brooding activity for a full week: "Call of the young: a rapidly repeated 'chirp-chirp . . .' mostly moderately pitched, occasionally rising in pitch and intensity. It is much like the call of a nestling sparrow hawk [today known as American kestrel]."

The following day, Tanner decided he needed to investigate the nest. In late morning, he was halfway up the tree, driving metal spikes to climb as he went, when both parents returned from foraging. Caught in the act, he froze, watching the parent birds watch him. At first, they flew from tree to tree, calling. Then the male flew into the nest tree and "looked me over," wrote Tanner. When the male bird flew to another tree to get a different perspective, Jim scrambled down the tree. Afterward, the ivory-bills settled down and continued to feed the young as normal.

Believing that the parents were wary of him but not overly upset, Tanner climbed the tree a second time after the adults flew away to forage: "When they left I spiked the rest of the tree, and reached the nest. It was shallow, from tip of fingers to elbow. It contained one young, half grown, tail feathers were one and a half inches long. Cavity felt very warm. I could feel no eggs or anything else. The young was silent until I put my hand in the hole, then a scraping buzz." (Birdsong expert Donald Kroodsma has noted that the nestlings of flickers, also members of the woodpecker family, "buzz like bees" to scare away predators.)

The female ivory-bill flew back into the area as Tanner was climbing down the tree. She made a few sharp calls, but after Jim was safely on the ground, the wary mother returned to her normal routine. His close inspection of the nest yielded the following description:

> The nest is in a red maple, 55 feet up. The tree is about 27 inches in diameter breast high. The trunk slants upward, bearing several small branches, and is straight except for one sharp bend where a dead stub projects. There is one large living branch within eight feet of the hole, but the several small branches near and above the nest are recently dead.
>
> The entrance faces west. The hole is oddly shaped, roughly triangular-oval, with the upper apex rounded-out into nearly a Roman arch. It is slightly higher than wide. Because of two branches below the hole, the birds approach the nest from the north side of the tree. The bark on that side of the tree near the hole has been worn so smooth that the birds sometimes have trouble grasping there.

From the size of the nestling and the length of its tail feathers, Tanner surmised that the young bird had hatched around February 10. (Tanner admitted that this was a rough estimate based on the time it takes for a pileated woodpecker chick to develop. No one actually knows the exact time it took for an ivory-bill to grow from hatchling to maturity.) If Tanner was correct, this meant that the egg had been laid in late January, a very early date. Historically, only one other ivory-bill nest had been recorded earlier: January 20, 1880, at the mouth of the Withlacoochee River in Florida, a location much farther south than Madison Parish, Louisiana.

The John's Bayou nest site was somewhat typical of the region. Near the swamp maple nest tree were some large sweet gums, Nuttall's oaks, American elms, and several medium-sized green ashes. The undergrowth was a tangle of *Smilax* and other vines. The ground around the tree was primarily covered with shallow pools. Young green leaves were beginning to appear throughout the forest. Tanner was keenly aware that what he was observing was special. He also feared that if he spent too much time in the area, the adults might desert the nest. Although he stayed hidden in a blind or at other inconspicuous locations, he felt the parent birds were aware of his presence. Jim's loyalties were divided. He also needed to search the surrounding bayous for other nesting pairs. Consequently, he would come and go, giving the birds their privacy.

Yet, ultimately Tanner decided that it was important to observe at least one entire day, from daylight to dark, and record everything that happened. That day was Tuesday, March 1. Leaving the cabin before 5:00 AM, he arrived at the nest tree a little before 6:00. It was a bright and sunny day, quite warm. The cold and frost of the week before had given way to spring-like conditions. The first birds to greet the new day were the cardinals, followed soon thereafter by Carolina chickadees. At 6:25 AM, with Jim in place in the blind, the male ivory-bill's head appeared at the hole entrance. The only call came from the juvenile inside the nest. Soon the female flew into view, and her mate left the cavity. "They talked a few seconds in the soft notes heard at nest exchanges (yuck, yuck, yuck . . . with a 'toot' quality)," Tanner wrote. The pair then flew west together. For the rest of the day, Jim recorded their feeding visits to the nestling. Most of the time they carried large beetle grubs. As was their normal routine, they were more active in the morning and later in the afternoon. Midday was quiet. In all, the male made thirteen trips with food, the female seventeen. Their day ended almost twelve hours after it had begun, at 6:03 PM, when the female entered her roost hole in a dead ash one hundred yards away and the male climbed into the nest with the juvenile. The male always spent the night with the young and occasionally brooded during the daylight hours as well.

Over the next four days, Tanner divided his time between watching the nest and searching for ivory-bills in other parts of the Singer Tract. The weather was warm, and the first lizards and fireflies of the season had appeared. Early in the afternoon on Saturday, March 5, Jim came across a lone male ivory-bill near a freshly dug hole, fifty-five feet up a dead ash. It was north of Mack's Bayou, roughly five miles south of the John's Bayou nest site. The bird soon flew, but Jim was able to follow it for over an hour before he lost it.

Sunday, March 6, was Jim Tanner's twenty-fourth birthday, and even though he was a long way from home and family to celebrate, it proved to be a most memorable day. In Tanner's own words, the day "started with an augury of good fortune." Early that morning, as he stepped off the porch of the borrowed cabin, a large bird took flight from a nearby tree at the mouth of Methiglum. Recalling the injured bird "Chris" he had cared for in high school, Tanner recognized it at once: an immature golden eagle. Mobbed by a group of crows, the raptor circled the area several times as it slowly gained altitude. Golden eagles were very rare in Louisiana. Was it an omen of good things to come?

It was a clear and cool morning when he reached the nest. Tanner had asked Kuhn to meet him there because he felt he might need help: he wanted to mark the nestling for future research. No one had ever put a lightweight-metal, numbered leg band on an ivory-billed woodpecker before, but the information that could be garnered from thus tagging the bird outweighed the risks. If the bird were retrieved many years later, ornithologists could gain further insight on how long an ivory-bill lives and how far an individual travels. Both facts were unknown by science. (Both are still unknown.)

Marking birds had been done since the ancient Greeks began tying messages to the legs of pigeons, and medieval falconers sometimes placed metal rings of ownership on their birds. In 1899 a Danish schoolteacher live-trapped some starlings and attached numbered aluminum bands to their legs, and the method has been used ever since to track birds.

Tanner had already made one important preparation for banding the nestling, having spiked the tree for his climb to the nest ten days earlier. He also knew that the young bird would be leaving the nest soon and the opportunity of easily placing a numbered band on its leg would be lost. The risk was in getting caught by the parent birds and what their reaction would be. Would they desert the nest? As the nestling matured, the intervals between the feeding visits had been growing longer and longer. Close to fledging, young birds were fed as little as twice an hour; also, toward midday, the parents made fewer feeding trips. A thirty-minute, even a twenty-minute, window should give Jim more than enough time to band the young bird.

When Tanner and Kuhn arrived at the nest at a quarter past ten, the parents were nowhere to be seen, but the female soon arrived with food, followed in short order by the male. After both fed the nestling, they flew away—a long flight. Tanner did not hesitate; he knew the task at hand and that speed was of the essence. He quickly climbed the tree. "Just as I put my hand up, the young bird jumped out, but I caught him, and then banded him," Tanner later wrote. "He struggled and squalled some, but I had little trouble handling him. When I finished, I returned the bird to the safety of the nest hole." (Jim's banding kit is today on display at Ijams Nature Center in Knoxville, Tennessee.)

Here Jim once again revealed his honesty, admitting in his journal that he could not be exactly sure of the band number. He took two bands with him that day: numbers 36-527264 and 38-401012. One he secured to the bird's left leg and the other he lost; he wasn't certain which was which. He was nervous, but his banding adventure wasn't over. His journal entry continued:

> I then started to cut off the branch which obscured the nest hole. Just as I got it loose and threw it down, the young bird jumped from the nest and fluttered to the ground. He landed in a tangle of vines, where he clung, calling and squalling.
>
> Down the tree I went, as fast as I could. I surely thought that I had messed things up right now! I picked the young bird up, still squalling loud enough to be heard to Sharkey Road, or I thought so. Kuhn took it in his hands, and I unlimbered my camera and started taking pictures. I had taken six before I realized that I had not focused the camera. Jittery and nervous as all get-out.
>
> Shaking like a leaf and wondering how far away the adult woodpeckers were, I loaded another film pack into the camera and made a few more photographs, then realized that the diaphragm

> setting was wrong. This time I conquered my buck fever, checked everything on the camera two or three times, and got some good pictures.

Tanner's camera did not use roll film but film packs. Each negative measured 2.25 by 3.25 inches. According to photography historian Don Dudenbostel, in those days the preloaded packs were available with either twelve or sixteen sheets of film. Between each click of the shutter, Jim had to pull a paper tab that would rotate the exposed sheet and its paper backing to the back of the pack, leaving a fresh sheet of unexposed film in position. This action would have taken a few seconds. Afterward, Jim would have had to look through the viewfinder once again to compose his next image.

Tanner's field notes continued,

> Kuhn first held the young bird in his hands. Then it perched on his wrist, lengthways as on a limb. It had ceased its calling by then, but it was scared, and it viewed me with great distrust. It climbed up Jack's arm, bit by bit until it reached his shoulder. Jack kept slowly turning to keep it in a good position for pictures. It sat for some time on his shoulder, and there gave a few sharp taps on Kuhn's cap. Kuhn raised his hand once, and the bird hit it hard enough to break the skin.
>
> On upwards the youngster climbed, until he sat perched on the top of Kuhn's cap. He sat like the bird of last year. His big feet partly on either side of the limb or arm in this case, resting back on his legs. He held his head up and back, and most of the time he kept his crest on end, making his head look large. He held his wings normally, occasionally extending them to keep his balance, or when one of us reached towards him, as if to appear more imposing.
>
> His coloration was the same as the bird of last year: eye a dark brown, wing feathers tipped with white, tail short and squared. His bill was chalky white, and the upper mandible had a short hook on it. There was no striking coloration to the inside of his mouth. Jack thought that the black feathers were bluer than an adults, and that the feet were a lighter color.
>
> When we had used up all the film, I wrapped the young bird in two handkerchiefs, put him inside my shirt, and climbed again to the nest. He struggled some, but quit before I reached the top.

Recently banded ivorybill nestling perched atop J. J. Kuhn, Sunday, March 6, 1938. (Photo courtesy of Nancy Tanner.)

> Once there I slipped him out of the handkerchiefs and into the nest hole. I was probably as glad as he that he was back there.

Back on terra firma, Tanner and Kuhn moved a good distance away from the nest tree. There they waited. Luck had been with their enterprise: the adult ivory-bills had stayed away for a considerable length of time and remained so for another twenty-five minutes until the female swooped in to feed her young one. She appeared to hesitate, perhaps because of the missing branch that once was so prominent below the nest hole.

After the female fed the newly banded bird, she moved away to preen in a nearby gum, giving several "resounding double-raps" to state her position. Soon the male flew in with a mouthful of food; after feeding the young one, the family's patriarch climbed inside the hole and stayed. Wishing to give the woodpeckers their peace, Tanner and Kuhn left. Later, Jim received a report from a neighbor named Baker of a second active ivory-bill nest west of Little Bayou.

It had been more than a good day. In addition to banding a young ivory-billed woodpecker (the only one ever banded), Jim had gotten some unexpected—and remarkable—photos. Agitated, the young bird had bounded about on the arm, shoulder, neck, and head of the cap-wearing J. J. Kuhn. Since then, some of the impromptu pictures Jim took that day have appeared in numerous magazines, including *Audubon, National Geographic,* and *Bird Watcher's Digest.* Also, two of the photos appeared in Tanner's *The Ivory-billed Woodpecker,* two in Jerome Jackson's *In Search of the Ivory-billed Woodpecker,* and three in Phillip Hoose's *The Race to Save the Lord God Bird.* A total of six photos have been published and republished in various forms.

For me, a postscript to this story came on Friday, July 3, 2009. Books such as this are assembled from thousands of shards and pieces, like an explosion in reverse. I had gotten a phone call from Nancy Tanner two days earlier. She had found an envelope of old ivory-bill prints and negatives of which she was previously unaware. Jim had donated almost all of the original material to Cornell or the Tensas River National Wildlife Refuge—those latter items are now archived at LSU—in the late 1980s. Nancy and I agreed to one of our customary lunches, which she prepared for me. With a Wimbledon semifinal match on TV in the background, we discussed a wide range of topics. (If there's anything Nancy loves more than discussing a wide range of topics, it's tennis.) Afterward, we cleared the dining-room table, and I began to sort through the material. I soon came across the first precious slice of history, one of the original negatives of J. J. Kuhn and the young ivory-bill, but it was an image I had never seen. Soon I found another and then another. My heart began to pound. The exact whereabouts of all of the original negatives had been a mystery; only two are archived at LSU. "Goodness, Nancy, do you know what these are?" I said.

By the time I worked my way through the stack of material, we learned that Jim had actually taken at least fourteen photos that day. Yes, fourteen! I asked Nancy, "Does anyone in the world know this?" And at that moment, we both realized that perhaps we were the only two people who did.

Thus, on his twenty-fourth birthday, March 6, 1938, after calming his jitters and "buck fever," Jim had been able to snap more than a dozen black-and-white photos, which amounted to some of the most memorable shots in the annals of natural history: a series of images that show the frenzied nestling close up, outside the safety of its nest hole. Until that morning, few people had ever even glimpsed an ivory-bill nestling, much less held one. In a matter of minutes, the excited young male *Campephilus principalis* had climbed all over woodsman Kuhn like a hyperactive cat on a scratching post.

After a quick trip to Tallulah on business the morning after banding the young ivory-bill, Tanner was anxious to return to John's Bayou in the afternoon, arriving just after three o'clock. At the site, Jim found the female ivory-bill perched near the nest, preening. When she flew away, Tanner climbed to a higher blind he had rigged in a nearby gum with a better view of the cavity's entrance. With the troublesome branch now removed, his line of sight was unobstructed. When the male arrived to feed the nestling, Jim accomplished another first, taking a Dufaycolor photo of the bird just as it reached the nest hole—the first full-color photograph ever taken of an ivory-billed woodpecker. Dufaycolor was an early British and French additive color photographic film. In 1938 it was only available in a few different-sized formats for motion picture and still photography. For a young grad student on a tight budget, it would have been an expensive luxury.

For the next several days, Tanner tried to get additional photos from a high blind but the lighting conditions were poor: overcast with frequent rain. The parents continued to feed the young, newly banded bird that was beginning to show itself more, even venturing outside the nest cavity. Jim and J.J also periodically searched the Little Bayou area for the ivory-bills reported by the man named Baker but had no luck. On Friday, March 11, Kuhn and Tanner broadened their search, traveling due south to Titepaper. "I had been sitting still for several minutes in some thick palmettos and vines, when I heard something coming towards me," wrote Tanner. "I watched in that direction, and in a moment saw what looked to be a small black horse coming straight to me. Then it came a little more above the palmettos and turned its head, and I saw a coal black wolf."

The 81,000-acre Singer Tract was a bastion, a lost world—in many ways an island surrounded by men with saws. One of the largest pieces of old timber left in the South, it still contained nearly all of its original fauna: deer, turkeys, panthers, and ivory-bills, which were gone from most of the surrounding country. As Jim noted, only the Carolina parakeet was missing. By the 1930s wolves had been driven from many of the forty-eight states. Yet here they still roamed.

Tanner remained still, breathlessly watching the black wolf. "It had been walking on a log," he continued. "It leaped down from that and disappeared behind a tangle, going to the windward of me. I partially straightened up to get a better look, and saw him well as he crossed an open place. He was only about thirty steps away. . . . He was a handsome, powerful but a swift appearing animal, self-confident and yet, alert. He was all black, deep-chested, small-bellied." Like their more familiar cousin, the family dog, gray wolves vary in color from pure white in the Arctic to mixes of white, gray, cinnamon, brown, and, farther south, black. Some individuals are uniformly black.

Returning to the business at hand, Tanner found no fresh ivory-bill sign around Titepaper. The disappointment sent him scurrying back to John's Bayou, where he knew he could watch a live ghost bird family. Along the way, he encountered the first rattlesnake of the year.

The next morning, Saturday, March 12, was clear and cool. Tanner and Kuhn ventured south again, this time to Mack's Bayou. Crossing Sharkey Road, they saw the golden eagle again. The year before, Tanner had ultimately decided that one pair of ivory-bills probably lived in the Titepaper/Mack's Bayou region. The habitat was right, and it was roughly four to five miles away from the John's Bayou pair. By 8:40 AM they reached a promising hole discovered by Kuhn a week earlier and soon heard a male ivory-bill rap and call to the west. When it flew, Kuhn pursued the bird while Tanner searched the area for other sign. He recorded finding "another new, big and oval hole in a dead ash stub about 150 yards west of the first," and added, "The woods around there contain many old holes and lots of feeding sign." Was there an active nest? Tanner and Kuhn weren't sure; they neither heard nor saw a female and left the area late in the day "puzzled as to just what was going on."

Tanner spent the next day observing the John's Bayou birds. The adult ivory-bills spent considerable time near the nest, the male working to create a new hole in a live oak about one hundred yards away. The female also worked on a hole high in a striped oak. The pair interacted, with Jim noting how the "male lit below the female, climbed up past her, gave the *toodle-toodle-toodle* call. They touched bills twice." At times their nestling could be seen with its head completely out of the nest hole, watching the scene that unfolded around him.

Tanner stayed, observing the bird's activity until early afternoon. The following day, Jim bought a horse named "Charlie" from the veterinarian, Dr. Speaker. Acquiring Charlie enabled Tanner and Kuhn to cover more ground, with one man on horseback and the other on foot; also, the horse allowed them to carry camping gear for longer trips. For the next four days, the two men divided their time between John's and Mack's bayous. During the afternoon of March 17, Jim took two more color photographs at the established nest. (The location of the original negatives is unknown.)

Whether what was happening in Mack's Bayou signaled an active nest was still unclear. The area was east of Hunter Bend and the old Sharkey Plantation. Kuhn left the cabin soon after 3:00 AM the next day to find the male they had seen six days before. Kuhn was there when the bird climbed from its roost hole, called, and flew away. J.J followed it. Tanner arrived around noon with Charlie and their camping gear. Late in the afternoon, Jim found the lone ivory-bill, half a mile south of the bayou. "I followed him as best I could for half a mile or more," he wrote, "Until he took a long flight and I never did catch up with him."

Back at their new campsite, Tanner and Kuhn settled in for the night until distant thunder woke them shortly after 11:00 PM. Not prepared for heavy rain, they broke camp and returned to their Methiglum cabin. They had to locate the trail, which was "hard to find and follow even in the day," with a flashlight. "Kuhn finally found it, and then we set the horse on it." wrote Tanner. They had

Tanner's horse, Charlie, and his 1931 Model A Ford. (Photo courtesy of Nancy Tanner.)

been lost in the woods at night before but never in a thunderstorm. Kuhn led the way slowly for a while but then decided that the horse could make better time, perhaps arriving back at the cabin before the bedding got wet. Tanner mounted Charlie and proceeded north into the gathering tempest.

"That horse," Tanner continued, "followed that trail exactly as he had come down it. . . . He went around stumps, holes, vine tangles without a bit of hesitation. It got darker then and I could see nothing but the treetops. Finally I dropped the reins on the saddle horn and held my hands before me like a plow to ward off vines and branches. I could see nothing of the trail, and it was the oddest feeling to feel Charlie turn and twist beneath me."

Without Jim touching the reins, Charlie found his way north to the cabin. "The rain hit as we turned to cross Sharkey," Tanner wrote, "coming in cold driving drops that soaked thru clothes immediately." Thunder and lightning cracked and flashed around them. The heavy downpour slowed after about ten minutes, and shortly thereafter Tanner was back at the cabin. Unpacking the gear, Tanner fed the horse and was starting a fire when Kuhn arrived, "just as wet as I was, but the bedding was dry, the roof tight, and as soon as we were warmed up, we turned in at about 2:30 and slept till near noon." Outside, the rain continued to fall. Trying to sleep on the ground in Mack's Bayou through the deluge would have been pure misery.

In late afternoon the weather cleared and was noticeably cooler. Tanner went to the John's Bayou nest, noting that everything looked greener—the light yellow-green of spring. At the nest site he was surprised to see the nestling had fledged while they were away. He worked the area with his parents; the shiny band Jim had placed around his leg thirteen days earlier was clearly visible. The parents were attentive. "The three stayed in the vicinity of the nest," Jim noted. "The adults fed near the young, and fed it regularly. The youngster occasionally took fairly long flights and when he did so, the adults would fly to him immediately."

On Sunday, March 20, Tanner returned to the nest. The hike was sloppy, the heavy rain the day before having flooded the woods. Low-lying bayous were swollen, and places that had been dry were now ankle-to-calf deep in water. But that was a typical spring in the swamp. Jim found the family of three in the vicinity of the nest. The young bird was noticeably thinner than his parents. Since the nest hole was no longer being used, Jim removed the high blind in the nearby gum. He then climbed the spike ladder up the nest tree once again to inspect and measure the cavity. It was shallower than the nest hole of the year before, and its entrance just a bit smaller as well. Jim gathered the debris from the bottom—feathers, droppings, and bits of shell—for later study.

It rained off and on over the next four days. During the drier spells, Tanner alternated between visits to observe the new ivory-bill family and trips on horseback to nearby sections. But outside John's Bayou, no ivory-bills were found. As conditions got wetter, Charlie proved to be a valuable asset, keeping Jim out of the mud. Tanner made one quick trip into Tallulah for mosquito repellent and a headlamp. He knew he was going to need one or both, depending on the weather to come.

On Friday, March 25, Tanner and Kuhn packed up their gear, loaded Charlie, and left Methiglum early. Crossing the Tensas River, the pair went to Hunter's Bend and the camp of a local named Drew Denton. It was an area not owned by the Singer Company. Tanner had heard several recent reports of ivory-bill sightings, certainly credible enough to be investigated. Denton's camp—shack, pen, and small pasture—was a good one. He kept cattle there from time to time and reported that he used to see ivory-bills near what he called Blue Lake, which was now mostly cut over. Denton's brother told of seeing two or three ivory-bills regularly in the winter around Big Board Brake, while another local claimed to have seen four near the same area recently.

"In the afternoon, we walked over to Blue Lake," wrote Tanner. "The cut-over country is the darndest place to get thru, tree-tops in every direction, cat-roads [meandering trails] winding around, every depression full of water, and where a cat-road crossed water was a boggy trough."

Walking through this section was a slow, laborious trek. If an ivory-bill flew over, it would be nearly impossible to follow. "We saw some good looking sign at the edge of Blue Lake," Jim continued. "Here there was a pecan top that had been scaled very freshly of the flaky bark. The bird had even worked on the limbs resting on the ground. The bark was full of grubs. Right next to this was a slender gum stub which had been really worked over."

The freshly peeled bark was encouraging. The next day the pair ventured out to Big Board Brake, separated, and spent the day searching, trying to get a sense of any recent activity. The section was much like the area around Rainey Lake on Greenlea Bend: brakes and deep slashes alternating with gum and oak ridges. Tanner found lots of older evidence of ivory-bill activity but very little of recent vintage. Kuhn's report was more encouraging, as he had found some sign of fairly recent activity northwest of an old logging camp. A boy who was also staying at Denton's camp thought he had heard an ivory-bill farther south below the camp on Dishroom Bend, west of the old Sharkey Plantation.

Living in the backwoods for a sustained period of time brought its own unique set of problems. Generally, Tanner had to make a trip into Tallulah once a week for supplies. Now that Charlie was part of the group, the horse's needs also had to be met. Jim rode into town on Sunday, March 27, and returned to Methiglum the following day. This time he had to transport a five-bushel sack of oats. It was cumbersome, so Jim divided it into two sacks, tying one to each saddlebag. The load dragged the ground on both sides and slowed the trip. Eventually, holes were torn in the sacks—first one, then the other—spilling oats along the way. Makeshift repairs fixed the leaks, but a long trip had become even more arduous.

Arriving back at base camp late in the day and frustrated by the lost time, he hurried to John's Bayou and found the fledgling at the old ash tree roost hole—"noisy and active," with the adults close by. Seeing the woodpecker family again relieved Jim's frustration. As he summed up, "Back to camp and found everything O.K. Oats in my clothes, scattered here and everywhere but 'nearly' five bushels in the barn."

The following day, Jim needed to rejoin Kuhn at Denton's camp on Hunter's Bend, which meant fording the Tensas River once again with Charlie and supplies. Luckily, Tanner reached the river just as a herd of cattle was being moved through the water, so he could watch their passage and determine the safest place to cross. He found some ivory-bill sign in Dishroom Bend due west of the old Sharkey Plantation, but it was scattered about. There was no concentration to suggest a sustained presence. "Drew Denton reported hearing two that day in that bend, nearly one-half mile above Dishroom Brake," Jim noted. "In the evening I worked back of camp for a while and found a good lot of fresh sign at the edge of the cutting, in some tall timber left standing there."

On Wednesday, March 30, the weather turned foul. It was windy, and rain fell periodically through Thursday. On Friday it rained much of the day. "We managed to get some looking done," Tanner wrote, "but felt that the weather hindered too much to say that we had done real hunting. There is abundant fresh sign at either end of Big Board Brake. It is spotty and hard to understand."

Was it a pair of ivory-bills or just one? If two, were they nesting in the area, feeding young, or just passing through? "The timber too is spotty," Jim observed. "Here and there are big gum ridges, alternating with brakes or low slashes, and on the same ridges are places where there is but a scattering of trees. We are both sure that birds are there, and if good weather comes when we can hunt, that we will find them."

The weather broke a bit on Saturday, but it was cool and windy. Tanner decided to return to base camp for supplies, in part because Jack had other work to do elsewhere. The pair planned to return to Denton's Camp on Monday, hoping that good weather would arrive as well. On Sunday the temperature remained in the low forties, a cold day in the swamp.

At John's Bayou, Jim found the family of three feeding near the ash roost holes. The young bird seemed slightly more mature. As Tanner noted, "There had been no change in color except perhaps that the dark marks on the ridges of the bill have disappeared some. Its tail is more pointed than before. It gives the food call, a low 'che-che-che.' Both adults fed it, often calling to it with a low call similar to the 'kient-kient' call." The adult female spent time scaling an overcup oak, a dead limb on a live sweet gum, and some dead limbs on an American elm. Meanwhile, the adult male worked on a slender dead stub on a sweet gum.

As planned, Tanner and Kuhn returned to Hunter's Bend on Monday, April 4. This time they loaded Jim's car with gear and drove to the Tensas settlement, leaving the car parked at the home of a family named Firth, who lived in the last house on the dirt road. From there they packed the stuff into camp. The hope for improved weather didn't materialize. The following day, the pair renewed their search of Big Board Brake, finding nothing. That night it started to rain again—heavily—and continued with only an occasional break for the next three days. "Most of the time there was little to do but sit in the house. The yard outside was a sea of mud, there was water standing everywhere in the woods; brakes and bayous were full. The river rose about four feet," Tanner noted, also taking time to list reports of recent ivory-bill sightings—five good accounts from reliable people in different locations in the area.

Considering the conditions, the camp was a hubbub of activity, full of people who had come to round up all the cows in the area to be tested for Bang's disease, also known as brucellosis or undulant fever. The disease is a highly contagious (though treatable and rarely fatal) bacterial infection that affects both animals and humans. The testing activity that Tanner encountered was part of a larger federal/state effort begun in 1934 to eradicate the disease. By the spring of 1938, the testing of cattle for the infection had reached Hunter's Bend, and the sloppy weather did not stop the process. Despite the rain, mud, and standing water, the assembled cowhands managed to pull together all the cattle.

Friday, April 8, dawned cold and cloudy with the dark threat of more rain to come. Kuhn had hiked out to retrieve Charlie, thinking his services would come in handy when the rains stopped. "The cattle testing bunch reached camp about noon, started right to work, and finished around three o'clock, testing about 100 cows," Tanner recorded. "I helped by writing down the tag numbers and description of each one tested. Kuhn kept busy with cooking fish and biscuits for the bunch, which ate as soon as we were thru."

Afterward, Tanner decided to take advantage of the assembled manpower. Sure that his car was mired up in Tensas, he wanted to move it out to a more stable, gravel road. He did so with the help of Kuhn and others. The mud-slicked road had ruts and ridges a foot and a half deep. Reaching the bridge and eventually crossing the river took the help of a tractor belonging to sharecropper Blois Laughton, plus ten men and several horses. Jim's car was muddy but in fine running order, another testament to the ruggedness of the Model A.

With so many local men together in the swamp, inquiries about ivory-bills began to surface. From Louisiana to South Carolina, Jim had met dozens of swampers in the past year. They were good folks, resourceful and helpful if your car was stuck in the mud, but for them money was hard to come by. Mostly they earned a living by gleaning whatever they could from the watery woods. They farmed, hunted, fished, and even poached if they had to. Naturally, their curiosity about the big woodpeckers centered on monetary value.

"Just how much is one of those birds worth?" inquired one man named Joner.

"How much is dey worth? They worth three or four hundred dollars, ain't they?" replied another man, Top Bolden.

One local had heard they were valued at six hundred to a thousand dollars; and if that were true, he told Tanner, "he was going to find one, follow it until it went into a roost hole, climb the tree and catch it."

Blois Laughton claimed to have heard ten or twelve men say that "since all the publicity about the birds had come up a few years ago, they had shot and killed one just to see what they looked like." If this were true, ten or twelve dead birds made for a sizable loss. Obviously, this wasn't something Tanner wanted to hear. His estimate of the ivory-bill population in the Singer Tract just the year before was only thirteen birds; the killing of only one or two to satisfy someone's curiosity was alarming to think about. Laughton himself confessed that he had intended to kill an ivory-bill but had never seen one, although he said he had changed his mind about this when he learned of Tanner and Kuhn's research. When queried about an ivory-bill's worth, Jim replied that the birds had no real value and suggested that a big fine could be levied for harming one. But did the threat of a fine outweigh curiosity?

With the excitement of the cattle testing over, Tanner and Kuhn returned to Drew Denton's camp on Hunter's Bend and had the place to themselves. Even Denton was away, so Jim and Jack took care of his hogs and dogs while they were there. The weather had finally improved: it was fair but windy, but with all the rain, mosquitoes had become an issue "and would have been impossible if there had not been some wind." They spent the entire week methodically searching the area. They explored Hunter's Bend on Monday and Tuesday and spent the rest of the week combing Dishroom Bend.

"We had two good days to hunt in Hunter's Bend," Tanner wrote. "We saw or heard not a bit of the birds, and the fresh sign we had seen earlier had gotten old and we could find no new sign around Big Board Brake, no fresh scaling of bark was troublesome. Where were the birds feeding? Or had they been shot?" As Jim saw it, two possibilities were likely: "one is that the ivory-bills making the sign have come from some such place as Hamilton Bayou; the other is that at this time of the year pileateds do quite a bit of feeding by scaling." Troubled and frustrated, he continued:

> Last year we had almost a similar experience in the vicinity of Mack's Bayou. We found no sign, no holes, or anything of much account in Dishroom Bend. Two to four birds were seen in there around Long Slough and Eagle Brake last winter by Bud Smith. We covered nearly the entire bend without finding anything.
>
> Dishroom has some of the finest trees that I have seen in the Singer. There are ridges thick with big tall gum, other places with much oak, many cypress brakes. It gives the impression of being relatively healthy timber, few dead trees and dead tops. Game was not abundant, but hogs were.

Even after a week of fair weather, water levels were still high, making travel difficult. Rain began to fall again on Saturday, April 16, and it looked like foul weather might be settling in for several days. Tanner and Kuhn decided to work their way out of Hunter's Bend and go back to their cabin on Methiglum. Kuhn packed Charlie and rode on to camp, but Jim had to retrieve his car before driving into Tallulah for provisions. He also got permission to stay at the big house on old Sharkey Plantation for a week. It was located farther west than Methiglum and would afford them easier access to some of the sections they needed to search.

Tanner made it back to the ivory-bill family at John's Bayou the following Tuesday. He had been away for several days, watching it rain on Hunter's Bend. The gloom persisted. Jim reached the site of the roost holes at 5:10 in the predawn hour. It was a gray, misty morning. He heard no ivory-bills, but all the woodpeckers were quiet that day. Meanwhile, Kuhn hiked south, looking for the lone male they had nicknamed Mack's Bayou Pete. Jack heard it call but lost the bird as it flew east. Late that evening, Tanner and Kuhn relocated to the old Sharkey Plantation. For much of the next day, they slowly searched the section north of Mack's Bayou from Hamilton Bayou to Brook Trail. The area was low-lying and very wet at the time, much of it covered with scattered rock elm or overcup oak. They found nothing to indicate the presence of ivory-bills.

Thursday, April 21: Mack's Bayou lay southeast of Sharkey Plantation, flowing west into the Tensas at Hunter's Bend. Jim left the old Sharkey house before four in the morning. Using a headlamp to light the way, he arrived at what he believed was Mack's Bayou Pete's roost hole at around 5:20. Was he at the right location? Thirty minutes later Tanner rapped a dead root with a stick. The male ivory-bill peeked out of his roost hole, looked around and then disappeared back inside. Yes, Pete was at home. "Five minutes later he looked out again, then came out and climbed to the top of the tree," Tanner recorded. "He called 'kient-kient' once, and then made a few short flights in the vicinity. He yapped at me, pounded a few singles and doubles, preened. Finally he flew off almost due west, high above the trees, and that is the last I saw that day, even though I hunted that western place most of the morning." The single and double raps, resounding drum beats of the swamp, were music to Jim's ears. *BAM-bam.*

"They frequently double rap when they are disturbed, either by the presence of persons or when one of the pair is absent," Jim wrote. "Twice I saw the female of a pair mount to a tall dead limb when the male had been absent some time, and call and double-rap for a few minutes until the male returned. The single male in the Mack's Bayou area of the Singer Tract made many single raps, even when it apparently was not disturbed." Surprisingly loud, the sound of the raps carried a long distance. Both the male and female rapped when they needed to and would move to a hard dead limb, often pecking or tapping as they looked for just the right place. "Occasionally I was able to make ivory-bills answer by imitating their pounding with a club on a hard dead stump or similar place, making either single or double raps as loudly as I could," Tanner continued. "They sometimes answered with calls, sometimes by pounding. Once I heard some birds rap and pound in response to the chopping of wood."

High water remained in the area. Even though Tanner had found Pete the day before, working the remainder of Mack's Bayou east of the old Sharkey house was difficult. Jim and J.J. could scarcely find a place to cross the flooded bayou, but they did find a way to cross the river north into Andrew's Bend, where they spent a few hours. But there they found no sign of ivory-bills.

Due east of old Sharkey Plantation is Alligator Bayou. It has two prongs, both flowing west into Mack's Bayou. Below the eastern-most prong is the region known as Titepaper. On Saturday, April 23, Tanner and Kuhn planned to search both sides of Alligator, if it was accessible. They split up. Jim worked the area just north of the bayou, finding nothing. Jack, however, had better luck, locating a family of three ivory-bills just south of Sharkey Road, a half-mile west of Lake Carters. "They did quite a bit of feeding low to the ground in hackberry stubs; did some scaling too," Kuhn reported. "The young bird was not fed for some time in the morning, and then the female found a good place on an oak tree, knocked and pried up the bark, picked out the larvae, and in about fifteen minutes fed the young bird 38 times. A few minutes later he was fed some by the male."

Searching Mack's Bayou for ivory-bills had been problematic from the west, so the duo traveled to Foster (the site of an old plantation), settling in with locals Belvin Brown and Sam Denton at a cabin Jim called "Pearce's Place." It proved to be ideal for accessing both Mack's Bayou and Titepaper region from the south. They spent two days combing through the environs south of Mack's all the way to Mills Bayou, finding "ragged timber standing in an ocean of vines and bushes." There were many dead oaks and gums standing but surprisingly few signs of woodpecker activity and rare indication of what could be the work of an ivory-bill. Most of the live trees were rock elm, overcup oak, and pecan. (Today, Mills Bayou forms the southeastern boundary of the Tensas River National Wildlife Refuge.)

On Thursday, April 28, Tanner left Foster early, hiking to a place near Lake Nick where he had seen some "fair" holes, but found nothing. The longer he looked at the finely chiseled cavities high above the ground, the smaller they became and the less likely they appeared to be of ivory-bill origin. By 6:30 AM Tanner was about a mile south of Mack's ranch when he heard Mack's Bayou Pete call and peck. Jim followed the sound, trying to establish the limits of the lone bird's territory. "I found him and followed him for about three or four short flights. He yipped and pecked, double-rapped a little, pecked in a hole in a pecan stub but apparently ate nothing," Tanner recorded. "He finally disappeared north. That was all that I saw that day." Meanwhile, Jack had worked the area north of Mack's Bayou, closer to Sharkey Plantation, without finding anything.

Tanner's journal entry for Friday, April 29, is succinct, even parsimonious, perhaps out of frustration: "We worked out Titepaper thoroughly, but found just nothing. That is except hordes of mosquitoes and hundreds of ticks." Although both were routine annoyances in the swamp, this marks one of the few times that Jim mentioned either in his field notes.

Their last planned day in Foster began early. Kuhn found Mack's Bayou Pete just after eight o'clock feeding on a deep-banked bayou. The bird flew north. Tanner circled around Hamilton Bayou and Mack's ranch and encountered Pete around 2:00 PM about a quarter-mile east of Largent's Bayou. The independent sightings made the extent of the Pete's territory a bit more clear.

In the days that followed, Tanner and Kuhn's excursions around the area of Lake Despair, which lay some three miles north of the John's Bayou nest site, were more disappointing. Although Kuhn had encountered three ivory-bills traveling together in the direction of Lake Despair just five months earlier, the region revealed little ivory-bill sign. Afterward, Jim stayed in Tallulah for a couple of days, perhaps to gather his thoughts. What next?

Monday, May 9: Tanner retrieved Charlie from Top Bolden's place, where the horse had been boarded, riding him back to the Methiglum camp. That afternoon he looked for pileateds, checking in on two nests he had located. One nest had already fledged. "The young call much like an adult, only perceptibly more subdued," Jim noted. "Most of the time they were quiet and hard to find."

The monitoring of the pileated nests was part of the larger search Jim was conducting. Although ivory-bills were the main focus, Tanner (with Kuhn's help) was also attentive to both pileated and red-bellied woodpeckers. Jim hoped to get some sense of the populations of these other species and how they coexisted with the ivory-bills. By counting pileated and red-bellied woodpeckers on various excursions and factoring those numbers against the estimated distance of his route, he would calculate their density. Although the individual results varied considerably, the averages of several such counts were quite uniform, and Jim really just wanted some general sense of the birds' numbers.

Jim had already figured out that ivory-bills could only be found in areas that supported other woodpecker species. That pileateds, for instance, were far more common than ivory-bills was a given, but why? Ultimately, Jim determined that the pileateds' requirements were more lax: they were not quite the specialists their larger cousins were. They worked trees that had been dead much longer than the ones ivory-bills preferred. Ivory-bills were stronger, able to pry away tighter-fitting bark. Thus, Tanner believed that ivory-bills looked for trees that had been dead for two years or less. Once a tree had been dead longer than that, the pileateds took over. And since older dead trees were more abundant than newer ones, the pileateds had a more reliable food source. In the end, Jim's rough estimates for the Singer Tract were six pairs of pileateds per square mile and twenty-one pairs of red-bellied woodpeckers.

On Tuesday, May 10, Tanner rode Charlie to the John's Bayou nesting territory, arriving at about 5:00 AM. After about half an hour, he heard the ivory-bills calling from the northwest. He followed the sound but never found them. The rest of the day he worked the area, looking for pileateds. In the late afternoon he went to the old ash roosting holes and waited. At about 6:40 PM, one of the ivory-bills called from the east of the old ash; then he heard a similar call from the west. Next, Jim located the young bird he had banded in early March on a second ash. "He still looked like a young bird, a bit ragged, crest blunt, tall not fully formed. Eye was yellow. The band was quite plainly visible," Jim noted. Afterward, the parent birds joined their young one. "The birds yapped quite a bit, but by 6:30 were quiet. It seemed like old times to have three birds yapping around the old roosting hole."

The next day Tanner awoke early to a clear and cool morning. He elected to visit the John's Bayou family one more time before breaking camp to concentrate elsewhere. He arrived at the ash roost trees around 5:15. Twenty minutes later, soon after the sun touched the tops of the trees and every other kind of woodpecker had already stirred, the young ivory-bill came out of the second ash tree; and as Jim noted, "almost the same moment, the male came from near the old ash. A few minutes later they started calling. After a few minutes the female came in from the east. The three got together and went off towards the west, traveling rather fast. I never heard them again after they crossed John's Bayou."

Back at the cabin in the afternoon, Tanner cleaned up a bit, gathering gear and packing it onto Charlie. The work there was finished, at least for the time being. For the next four days, Jim stayed in Tallulah and searched the northeastern sections of the Singer Tract: Horseshoe Lake and Despair Bayou, both accessible from town. He found nothing new related to ivory-bills—a disappointing outcome, given that in the previous year, the area had been home to a mated pair raising a female juvenile. What had happened to those birds? Had they been shot by curious locals itching to get a close look at an ivory-bill?

On Monday, May 16, Tanner drove back to Drew's cabin on Hunter's Bend; Kuhn was to follow on horseback. For each of the next six days, they made separate forays in different directions. It rained intermittently. Sometimes Jim rode Charlie; sometimes J.J. did. But the results were the same: neither found the needle in the haystack. Tanner spent a lot of time in this section because he had received several credible reports of ivory-bill sightings, the most recent having occurred the previous December. Finally, on Sunday, May 22, Kuhn found a lone male at about seven o'clock in the morning in the middle of Big Board Brake on Hunter's Bend across the river from Mack's Bayou.

Summarizing Kuhn's account, Tanner reported, "It first traveled northwest along the brake, and then doubled backed and was last seen near 10:00 AM between the brake and the river and shortly north of the log camp that is on the river. The bird called little, only before flights. It had a voice like Mack's Bayou Pete's, whammed a lot, and altogether acted much like him—almost undoubtedly was him."

For the next three days, the two men ventured farther west, searching the sections south of Africa Lake and into Dishroom and Andrew's bends, all northwest of Drew Denton's cabin. In Andrew's, Jim found a little fresh sign near a spot where a local man said that he had heard an ivory-bill calling four weeks earlier. But the sign was so scant that it appeared a bird might only have passed through the area. By Wednesday Tanner and Kuhn were getting tired of walking all day. Taking it easy, they went to the Tensas settlement, where they encountered John Grey, a minister from Raleigh, North Carolina, who had traveled to Louisiana hoping to see an ivory-bill. Jim could relate to the visitor's situation: he hadn't seen an ivory-bill in a while either. He invited Grey to the cabin on Methiglum.

Thursday, May 26: "We got up at three, ate breakfast, and before four were ready to leave the house. Just as Kuhn blew out the lamp, I stepped out the back door and saw that the yard was lit up by a red glow." Running into the yard, Jim discovered that the roof was on fire near the chimney. He yelled, sounding the alarm: "Kuhn ran to the front and climbed to the porch roof. Grey grabbed the water pail and ran to fill it, and I relit the lamp and set it beside the water barrel." Tanner then scrambled up to the ridge of the roof, and the bucket brigade was started: Grey to Kuhn to Tanner. As Jim poured on the water, he pulled away shingles, discovering more fire. The hole in the roof grew. Bucket after bucket made its way to the roof until the fire was finally and safely put out.

Now that their blood was pumping, it was back to the mission at hand. Tanner and Grey trekked to the ash trees on John's Bayou, arriving at almost five o'clock, but before they reached the favored roosting ground, they heard yapping from the direction of the ash where the young bird had been spending the night. Were they too late to see the birds before they flew from their overnight roosts? Walking slowly to the roosting ground, they waited until a quarter of six without hearing another ivory-bill sound. Tanner and his guest then scouted the area for the rest of the morning but found nothing. Grey left without seeing an ivory-bill. That afternoon Jim took his Model A, which he was now calling "Bosco," to a Tallulah garage for maintenance. Since the car was often covered with dark Louisiana mud, the nickname may have come from Bosco Chocolate Syrup, a popular brand first produced in 1928.

The arrival of John Grey had refocused Tanner's attention on the John's Bayou ivory-bill family. He hadn't expected to see them again so soon, but curiosity overcame him. So, late in the day on Saturday, May 28, he rode Charlie to the preferred roosting ground again. He wanted to be there to watch the bird's return after a day of foraging.

"The three birds lit shortly north of the ash holes, called about 6:40, a few minutes after sundown," Tanner noted. "Then they came to the ash roost ground. They called and fed some, made several short flights in the vicinity. Finally the female apparently went to the south, male somewhere just west of the old ash hole, young in the second ash hole. Young's eye is getting light, crest black and a bit ragged, band visible."

On the way back to the fire-scorched cabin, Jim noted that Charlie was developing a limp. By Monday the condition had become a real concern. Jim left the camp early that morning to walk to the roosting ground, reaching it at 4:45. Twenty-five minutes later, the first bird called and was answered immediately. All three ivory-bills had slept in separate trees, but soon they were together, calling a fair amount before the family flew away to the east and then north across the bayou. The youngster begged for food and was fed by both parents, but it also chipped away bark like the adult birds.

Back at the cabin, Charlie's lameness had worsened, forcing Tanner and Kuhn to fetch Dr. Speaker, the veterinarian, who determined that the horse had a bad case of mud itch, a combination bacterial-fungal infection exacerbated by the damp and muddy conditions. Though the problem could be treated, Charlie would need to stay off the affected foot for a while. This forced Tanner to change his plans. For two days, he and Kuhn treated the horse and walked to Greenlea Bend to search for ivory-bills. Between Grassy Lake and Mason Spencer's cabin, Tanner and Kuhn found "good fresh sign," a positive indication of at least one bird, maybe two, still in the vicinity. Several reliable accounts by people he trusted also indicated the presence of at least one ivory-bill, a male, on Greenlea.

On Friday, June 4, after Jim and J.J. repaired the fire-damaged portion of Cochran's cabin, they turned their attention to the horse. Charlie had improved, at least enough to be moved out of Methiglum for long-term care. This was no small feat, requiring them to borrow a horse trailer and fashion a crude road at the site. They had to reinforce a ford of Spring Bayou with poles to create a corduroy surface and a "good solid crossing." Retrieving his car, Tanner drove to Foster and borrowed a horse trailer from Belvin Brown. Perhaps surprisingly, the next morning's trip out with the horse was mostly uneventful, as they only got stuck in the mud once. Charlie was delivered to Dr. Speaker for convalescence.

With the horse in good hands, Tanner and Kuhn hiked into their old campsite at Rainey Lake on Greenlea, working the country the following day north and east of Turkey Brake. "There is a fair amount of sign," Jim noted, "and that seems to be the center of the sign in that country." An oil derrick was being built on the northeast section of Greenlea, not far from Mason Spencer's cabin. Jim visited the construction site but learned of no ivory-bill sightings by the work crew. Jim's stay on Rainey Lake would probably not have been complete without a nighttime trip out on the water just as he had done the year before. "That evening there was a fair moon, so I fixed a headlight and then paddled the boat down Rainey Lake," he recorded in his field notes. "I saw and got close to one gator about seven foot long. There were plenty of noises, some frogs bellowed, some whistled, some brayed, some chirped and trilled, and fish slashed, owls hooted."

In his year-end report for 1938 to the National Association of Audubon Societies, Tanner used the phrase "one or two birds" when describing findings on Greenlea Bend. He couldn't be sure, but by the time he settled down three years later to write his book, he used the more conservative estimate of one.

After several days of reconnaissance on Greenlea, Jim and J.J. broke camp, returning to Tallulah. Tanner's time in the Singer Tract had almost come to an end for the spring of 1938; he needed to move on and search other locales. On Tuesday, June 8, he drove north on Highway 65 to Sondheimer in East Carroll Parish east of Tensas Bayou, ultimately driving as far north as Lake Providence. At Alsatia he turned west toward the inland watershed, walking alongside a drainage ditch to the Tensas, where he discovered that the country was all cut over. What remained were small ash, middling pecan, and overcup oak. Working his way back south, Jim camped at Bear Lake east of the Tensas River. The next morning he got up at a quarter past four and hurried to St. Mary's Lake, where Kuhn had heard and seen an ivory-bill the previous summer. Jim found nothing, not even any good sign of trees being worked. The area "is all cutover, looking skinned," he wrote. Back at Bear Lake, he parked his car and hiked into a remote location to find a local swamper named Jack Thompson, who was fifty years old and living with a young wife and a three-year-old son. Thompson had seen no ivory-bills but was hungry for conversation. Jim stayed and listened to the man's life story while his wife prepared lunch: greens, fried onion tops, beans, fresh onions, lettuce, radishes, cornbread, and wild honey. (Tanner rarely noted what he ate from day to day, but when he did, he seemed to relish the details of the menu and hospitality he was shown.)

After his meal, it began to look like rain, so Jim hustled out to find his car, not wanting to get it stuck in the mud yet again. He had just reached the road and the cabin of an old-timer named Fred Williams, when a heavy rain began to fall. Williams invited Tanner into his home until the shower passed, and Jim learned that the man had not seen an ivory-bill in the area in ten years. His story and the amount of cut-over acreage confirmed what Jim was already sensing: if the upper reaches of the Tensas bottomland had once been home to the storied woodpeckers, they were now all gone. That evening Tanner drove quietly back to Tallulah in the rain. Even though men like Thompson and Williams were not trained ornithologists, Jim respected and valued their judgment. If they had not seen an ivory-bill in years, then that was that.

By Thursday, June 10, the rain had softened the secondary roads, making them untrustworthy for car travel. Tanner elected to keep to the hard surfaces and drove northwest to explore the Boeuf River, which is located farther west than the Tensas. The Singer Company owned timberland in northern Richland Parish and south West Carroll Parish, where the Boeuf is located. The river gets its name from the French word meaning "bullock," or "young bull." Its slow-moving water originates in Arkansas and snakes southeast into Louisiana, where it joins the Ouachita River in Catahoula Parish west of Sicily Island. In some ways it is a mirror image of the Tensas, which follows a parallel course roughly twenty miles to the west. Tanner spoke to several people, including the Singer company's caretaker for their Boeuf holdings. The Richland Parish land had not yet been cut, but no one in the area had any report of ivory-bills. Tanner found mostly oaks, along with some elm and ash, but located little sign of woodpeckers of any kind. At Oak Grove, Jim visited the E. L. Bruce Lumber Company but again heard no reports of ivory-bills. That evening it rained quite hard, forcing Tanner indoors. He spent the night at the Rex Hotel in Eudora, Arkansas.

The following day was also fruitless. Visiting a local sawmill, Jim was told that there was only one uncut section of Boeuf River bottomland southward from Eudora. Called the McLean Tract, it had recently been sold. Driving south again to Oak Grove, Tanner connected with a local game warden, Jesse Ward, who had seen ivory-bills in the area up to 1912. The next morning he and Jim visited one of those places, only to see that the timber had all been cut over. In the six- or seven-mile hike, Jim heard only one pileated woodpecker and saw no ivory-bill sign.

The upper reaches of the Tensas River bottom had proven a disappointment. Historically, ivory-bills had lived there, but most of the timber was long since gone. The sections that had not been cut offered poor habitat for the woodpecker. If Fred Williams was correct, Jim had arrived in the area at least ten years too late.

On Sunday, June 13, Jim returned to Greenlea Bend, camping at Rainey Lake once again and trying to clear up yet another mystery. Were there one or two ivory-bills living there? The next day he worked the woods between Turkey Brake and Grassy Lake without finding anything new, just old sign.

Tanner's trip to Eudora, Arkansas, five days earlier had turned up one small lead: an uncut area known as the McLean Tract. Driving north once again, he located the parcel west of the Boeuf River about five and a half miles south of Chicot, Arkansas. Noting that it was much like the Richland holdings of the Singer Company, mostly oak with few woodpeckers, he found nothing to suggest that ivory-bills were there. Follow-up conversations with several men in the area turned up no reports. Tanner ultimately concluded that the Boeuf River bottoms shared by Louisiana and Arkansas had no ivory-bills. He found no recent reports.

Tanner's ramblings away from his home base of Tallulah were getting longer and longer. While in Arkansas, he drove farther north to the new White River Waterfowl Refuge located just west of the Mississippi River. It was very remote country with few towns or roads. Established just three years earlier, the protected wetland contained hundreds of bayous, lakes, and sloughs. The region floods annually. Strong currents eat away at the hardpan clay soil, changing the river bends and creating new oxbow lakes. Its profile is swampy and ever changing. The river meanders by the Grand Prairie of Arkansas before it empties into the Mississippi just south of the refuge at Big Island. Its seasonal ebbs and flows nourish the wetlands and replenish the oxbows. Today, the 113,000-acre area is listed as a national wildlife refuge. (In April 2005, the Cornell Lab of Ornithology announced that ivory-bills had been discovered along the Bayou de View in the Cache River National Wildlife Refuge and were believed possibly to be living in the White River swamps as well. The Cache, White, and Bayou de View flow roughly parallel until they all converge in Monroe County.)

On Friday, June 17, Tanner met with the White River refuge's new acting manager and his staff, which included a biologist. Most of the men were new to the area, but the junior manager, Pete Cash, was a native of Desha County. The son of a game warden, Pete knew the whole country very well. No one at the meeting had any reports or records of ivory-bills ever being in the region. If they were within the refuge, the most likely places were the old forests on Big Island and Upper Big Island.

That afternoon Tanner and three of the refuge's staff went downriver by boat to Upper Big Island. It was mid-June, but the water level was still high from the spring floods. The group was only able to walk the island's ridgeline. Tanner found no sign of ivory-bills, but the habitat looked just right: lots of gums and its associated forest type. They did locate one dead pecan that had been completely scaled of its bark. Tanner decided, largely on Pete Cash's recommendation, to come back later in the season when the water level was lower to do a more thorough search. He then left Arkansas for Mississippi, searching areas east of Vicksburg for a couple of days. But again he found neither signs nor recent reports of ivory-bills.

Meanwhile, back in Louisiana at the Singer Tract, J. J. Kuhn had experienced better luck. While out frog hunting on June 15, he encountered an adult ivory-bill pair and two young traveling together near Lake Carters in the Mack's Bayou–Titepaper section. Although the adults seemed wary of him, the juveniles were not, and Kuhn reported that they appeared to be younger than the John's Bayou juvenile that Jim had banded. Where the birds had actually nested was a mystery, although Tanner suspected it was somewhere along Alligator Bayou.

Back from Mississippi, Jim was able to actually drive into the camp on Methiglum on June 23. At 3:30 the next morning, he left the cabin to walk to the ash tree roost holes. An hour later, he was in place. It was overcast, still cloudy from the rain that fell the night before. Shortly after 5:00 AM, the ivory-bill family began their day. "All three of them sat in the dead top of the tree within a foot or two of each other, calling, pecking, and pounding," Tanner recorded. "Light was too poor to see well, but I could see no red in the young bird's crest. The crest was still a bit ragged and blunt, wing tips showed white, the band on the left leg showed clearly." Although Jim at this time often referred to the banded youngster as a male, the definitive sign of the bird's gender—a red crest—had yet to show itself.

Saturday, June 25: Tanner elected to stay at the cabin one more day, hoping to find the family of four that Kuhn had seen ten days earlier. Walking south, he crossed Sharkey Road and followed a cane ridge through Alligator Bayou into the north end of Titepaper. While he found no birds, there was plenty of fresh sign: "Coming back to camp, I cut across Alligator flat and hit the ridge just about where the bayou elbows back to the north. Going along the ridge I came into a considerable area of gum and slash timber that I had never known was there. There was quite a bit of ivory-bill sign there, old and new, and a few good looking holes."

The next morning was Sunday. Jim slept late, not leaving the camp until three o'clock in the afternoon, promptly getting his car stuck in the mud once again. It took three hours to free it. (When Jim made his final report to the National Association of Audubon Societies in the fall of 1939, he admitted with a smile that he took his car into many places he shouldn't have.)

Tanner had done just about all he could do in the Tensas for that season. He had exhausted virtually every lead. On Tuesday, June 28, he drove south to Dr. Speaker's place to explore a section where Kuhn had seen some ivory-bills several years before. But by 1938 the woods were well cut over, and Jim found nothing of interest. That evening he spent the night at Mack's Bayou, hoping to find the ivory-bill nicknamed Pete one more time. Again, no luck. Now Jim knew it was time to load the Model A. There were plenty of other places in the Mississippi River region that needed to be explored.

Chapter 15

On the Road Again, Again

It has a habit of reappearing just when nearly everyone has given up on it. Unlike the Carolina parakeet, the ivorybill is not a gregarious species that readily shows itself before all humanity. Persecution by man caused it to retire ever deeper into the great swamps of the South. From the time of its discovery early in the eighteenth century, it has been an elusive, retiring bird, becoming if anything warier and harder to find over the years. I know from long experience how difficult it is to see or hear one.

—John V. Dennis

Driving south, Jim Tanner left Tallulah early on Thursday, June 30. He had spent almost four months in the Singer Tract, ultimately determining that the resident population of ivory-billed woodpeckers had probably grown smaller since 1937. The birds noted on Hunter's Bend and Bayou Despair the year before were not accounted for in 1938. Had the population really dropped from an estimated thirteen to only nine or ten birds? That was all he and Kuhn had found through either direct or indirect evidence. Young birds were being produced. But if ivory-bills were disappearing from the Tensas swamps, why was that so? Had curiosity seekers killed them, or had they flown to parts unknown?

For now, those questions would have to wait, as Tanner had decided to spend the next few months searching for the vanishing species in other locations. The backwoodsmen he trusted the most could instantly describe the differences between ivory-bills and pileated woodpeckers. Although seasoned swampers may have used any one of several regional names for the bird—pearly-bill, log-cock, log-god, king woodchuck, Indian hen, white-backed woodpecker—they, like Mason Spencer in 1932, knew an ivory-bill when they saw it. Tanner relied heavily on these anecdotal reports because it was not humanly possible for him to search every square acre of swampland himself in three years.

In south Louisiana, Tanner reconnected with A. M. Beard, who had spoken of seeing ivory-bills, some with "white backs," some with black. The latter were obviously pileateds, but Beard seemed rather confident that he had seen the former recently in Black Bear Bottoms in Concordia and Catahoula parishes in the floodplain of the Mississippi River south of Ferriday. Jim had searched some of the region the year before, but there were places he hadn't visited.

On a rented horse, Jim set out on Saturday, July 2, into Hibb's Bayou soon after sunrise. Already it had the feel of another hot day. He rode for miles, finding some fairly large areas of what he believed to be old timber, but most of it consisted of overcup oak flats, a forest type he considered poor for ivory-bills. Despite Beard's optimism, Jim could find no one who agreed with him nor any proper habitat for the white-backed woodpecker. Disappointed, he drove south to Baton Rouge, where he spent the night in a hotel, indoors for a change.

The Atchafalaya Basin is a vast swampy area that dominates three Louisiana parishes: Iberville, St. Martin, and Assumption. Jim's visit the year before had been brief. On the Fourth of July, he drove to Krotz Springs on the Atchafalaya River. At the Sherburne Lumber Company, a man told him there were no areas of virgin timber in the north end of the basin. The timber that had been there was mainly willow and cottonwood, with some sweet gum in the higher places and cypress and tupelo in the lower. To celebrate the holiday, Jim attended a local baseball game that evening.

The next day, Tanner returned to Baton Rouge to visit George Lowery, who had completed his master's degree at Louisiana State University and was now an instructor of zoology there. Lowery was only a few months older than Tanner, and the two got along well. (In 1971, Lowery would present two recent color snapshots of an ivory-bill at the annual meeting of the American Ornithologists' Union. He had received the controversial photos from a man who wished to remain anonymous. The mystery man had allegedly taken the pictures in Atchafalaya Basin. Despite Lowery's reputation, many believed the photos were a hoax.)

Jim was able to tell Lowery all that he had learned in the past two years. Lowery did the same, and with the help of fellow Cornellian Claude Edgerton, a professor in LSU's Botany Department, Jim was also permitted to use the department's darkroom to develop some of the film he had taken recently. (It's tantalizing to think—though Tanner made no note of it—that the famous photos of the newly banded ivory-bill and J. J. Kuhn were developed at this time.) That evening Jim had dinner with the Lowerys, and the trio saw a popular new movie in town, *The Adventures of Robin Hood* with Errol Flynn.

Wednesday, July 6, was the hottest day in five years; in New Orleans, temperatures would top out at ninety-nine degrees. Tanner drove west, back to Krotz Springs to meet with the local conservation officer, Charlie Frederick, at his house near the levee. Jim felt that he probably knew the upper Atchafalaya Basin as well as anyone. Frederick reported that the last ivory-bill had been seen in the region fifteen to twenty years before and that he used to see them in virgin stands of sweet gum and oak along the Bayou des Ourses (Bayou of the Bears) east of Sherburne and the Atchafalaya River. He had not seen one since all the timber had been cut out.

Tanner learned that the construction of artificial cuts and levees along the Mississippi River to channel and control seasonal floodwaters had affected the Atchafalaya Basin. Its water level had steadily increased. Seasonal flooding often raised the water ten feet, which had killed many of the oaks and sweet gums years ago. Since the late 1800s, the official flood-control policy along the lower Mississippi River and associated waterways like the Atchafalaya had been to build higher and higher levees, but the Great Flood of 1927 proved that water could find a way into traditional floodplains. It could not be contained, and attempting to do so was a folly. The Atchafalaya is a "distributary" of the Mississippi and Red rivers. It takes water from both as it flows into lowlands near Simmesport, Louisiana.

Tanner also found no anecdotal accounts of recent ivory-bill sightings in the region. Were all the old trees gone? Could an area as large as the Atchafalaya Basin have been completely cut over by 1938? It was beginning to appear that the Singer Tract in Madison Parish was the only tract of old trees left in Louisiana and thus the last bastion of ivory-bills in the state.

Just when Tanner was about to give up on the Atchafalaya Basin, he learned that at least one eight-hundred-acre tract of virgin timber remained near Pierre Part, one of the most isolated communities in the region, perhaps even in the entire country. Located in Assumption Parish, Pierre Part totaled roughly three-square miles, one third of it water. The Acadian French founded the out-of-the-way settlement after *Le Grand Dérangement*, or Great Upheaval, of 1755, a time when the new British governor of Acadia (Nova Scotia) expelled most of the French population, which resettled in Louisiana. Inaccessible by land, the community they founded remained isolated until the mid-1900s. Before the depression, its inhabitants were mainly fishermen. Afterward, they had to find work in other fields, including logging, levee building, and the state's growing petroleum industry. By 1938 the people of Pierre Part remained predominantly French. At home, they exclusively spoke Cajun French. They had a term to describe Tanner's meandering, day-to-day sojourn: "ro-day," as in "he went ro-day up and down de bayous." (The actual French word is *rôder*, a verb meaning "to prowl.")

On Thursday, July 7, Jim drove south to meet Norman Breaux, eldest son of Kennedy Breaux, who took Jim into the old woods near Pierre Part. They traveled first by motorboat and pirogue (dugout canoe) and finally waded through water and mud. The trees were mostly tupelo and cypress, a serene and primordial setting. Yet, for the entire time they were there, Jim heard only two pileateds and saw no sign of ivory-bills. Norman Breaux had never seen one in the remote section or anywhere near there.

That Saturday Tanner drove north to St. Francisville, the seat of West Feliciana Parish to meet John Parker, who had been Louisiana's governor from 1920 to 1924. A onetime vice-presidential candidate on the Progressive Party ticket, he won the governorship as a Democrat and became one of the first political leaders to take on the Ku Klux Klan. And like his good friend Theodore Roosevelt, he was also an active conservationist, much concerned with his state's natural resources and the environment. After his gubernatorial term ended, Parker devoted his energies to his experimental farm at Bayou Sara near St. Francisville. Tanner described their conversation as interesting but "fruitless." While curious about Tanner's work, Parker could contribute little except his well wishes.

While in St. Francisville, Jim also investigated the rumor of a recent ivory-bill sighting. He spent the rest of the day interviewing anyone he could find—game wardens, wildlife agents, lumbermen—connected to the local environs. A naturalist named Edward Butler knew the woods in West Feliciana well, but by the man's own confession, his only knowledge of ivory-bills came from published records. In the end, Tanner decided that the rumored ivory-bill was actually based on sightings of pileateds.

The following Tuesday, July 12, Tanner arrived in Lake Charles, a brackish body of water on the Calcasieu River in southwest Louisiana. There he met Mark Thomson of the Stanolind Oil Company. Responsible for leasing trapping rights to Stanolind-owned lands, Thomson took Jim on a boat trip into the marshes. The oil company's twenty-five-foot cabin cruiser was a far cry from the dugout that Jim and Norman Breaux had used five days earlier in Pierre Part. They cruised downriver from Lake Charles through the marshes and woods into the Intracoastal Waterway. Though not ivory-bill country, it had plenty of bird life. After motoring onto Black Lake and Black Bayou, going through a group of oil wells owned by the Shell Oil Company, Thomson and Tanner arrived at a communal rookery.

American egrets and Louisiana herons (today, known as tricolored herons) were the most common birds there, but the rookery also included many roseate spoonbills, which thrilled Jim, because at that time the species was declining. As T. Gilbert Pearson, an NAS founder, wrote in 1917: "The birds are extremely rare, thanks to the energy of the plume-hunters and the bird-shooting tourist. But for the wardens employed by the National Association of Audubon Societies they would probably now be extinct in Florida. A few are sometimes seen in Louisiana. Unless public sentiment in that state should receive a radical and sudden shift toward conservation, the bird will probably not long survive." The birds were prized for their pink-to-carmine feathers, which were used on women's hats and turned into souvenir fans for tourists. By the 1930s, according to estimates, only thirty to forty breeding pairs remained in Florida in addition to the handful in Louisiana. Legal protection finally came for the species in the 1940s.

The next day, Tanner sought to photograph the spoonbills, but he had no boat. Driving as close as possible to the rookery, which he could see across a marsh, Jim parked his car at an abandoned house and proceeded further on foot. "It looked to be only a mile across the marsh to the rookery," he noted, "but it must have been nearer three. I left the car about one o'clock and reached the rockery at four, hot as I could be and pretty well tired out. Most of this walking was wading about calf deep in water and knee to waist deep in rushes." Although Tanner had been in many remote situations during the past months, this perhaps was the most daunting.

"The water was so heated by the sun as to be uncomfortably hot," he continued. "I did not have much luck getting pictures; the birds were mostly too old. I waited until almost sunset for it to cool before I started back. . . . It did rain in some places, and it looked as though I was in for a wetting, but it missed me. The moon came out later and I needed it for I did not reach the car until around 8:30." Luckily for Jim, the moon was one day past full, so he had plenty of light. His trek through the marsh and back took seven and a half hours. Exhausted, he camped out that night on the back porch of the abandoned house. The next day, he drove west to Beaumont, Texas, where he spent the night at the YMCA.

Southeast Texas is made up of rolling hills that give way to lowlands. The region drains into the Gulf of Mexico via three principal rivers: the Trinity, Neches, and Sabine. The wedge between the latter two is known as the Golden Triangle because of the Spindletop oil strike that occurred near Beaumont on January 10, 1901. The find marked the birth of the modern petroleum industry in the United States, tripling the country's oil production overnight and making a lot of people wealthy. The term "Texas oil man" entered the American lexicon. Near the coast, the land is flat and marshy. To the north, piney woods dominate the high ground, while hardwoods prevail in the lower areas.

Northwest of Beaumont was the Big Thicket, a densely forested area bounded by the Trinity and Neches rivers. Its name comes from the jungle-like vegetation: diverse plant species, including orchids, cactus, cypress, and pine, all growing in close proximity to each other. It was there that Tanner spent most of his sixteen days in Texas, eventually venturing north to Caddo Lake. He wrote, "The Big Thicket is of second-growth pine, short-leaf, mixed with sweet gum, white-post oak, hickory, water oak, etc. It is all cut over, and fire is kept out so that undergrowth is thick. From the natives I learned that deer are very scarce, turkey gone, and squirrels not common. Few pileateds, I saw none all day."

Jim found only a handful of historical accounts of ivory-bills in the area, and all were from the 1800s except for one sighting on the Trinity River dated 1904. He did investigate a couple of alleged recent sightings, but they proved to have little substance. The most interesting thing Tanner found was "a group of several, freshly-dead, young pines. Most of them had much bark knocked off in irregular patches. While I was watching, a pileated came in and barked a little." Ultimately, Tanner decided that the supposed ivory-bill sightings were actually of pileateds. Such mistakes were common: from a distance the differences between the two species appeared slight, and sightings were often fleeting glimpses.

After logging thousands of miles in his Model A and getting it stuck in the mud numerous times, Jim finally had serious car trouble on the road. Driving north from Beaumont to Kountze, his radiator opened up and spewed its contents. By the time he realized something was wrong, the engine was smoking from all sides, and the heat had burned out the condenser. Walking three miles to Voth, he bought a new one and installed it on the side of the road. With the makeshift repair and some water, Tanner was able to inch his car back to Beaumont where he got the roadster fixed.

Tanner next headed east for a return trip to the White River Waterfowl Refuge in Arkansas. During his previous visit in June, the water level had been too high to do a complete search. On the first of August, Jim arrived at St. Charles on Highway 1, but five days of searching turned up nothing encouraging. So it was back to Tallulah and the Singer Tract.

To earn a living, J. J. Kuhn had spent most of the summer hunting frogs, but he had seen the John's Bayou family of three near Sharkey Road in July. Charlie, Tanner's horse, was in better shape but still needed another month or so of convalescence. Because of recent rain, the road into Cochran's cabin at Methiglum was too wet and muddy for Jim's car, so he walked. Conditions worsened as it rained most of the afternoon. Despite the weather, Tanner encountered a pair of ivory-bills along Sharkey Road, which raised the question: was the juvenile now living on its own?

It was dull and cloudy early the next morning. A heavy sky hung over Tanner as he walked north to the ash tree roost site on John's Bayou, a trip he had made many times. At the site, he heard one ivory-bill call briefly, and that was it. Since 1935, when Tanner first visited the Singer Tract with Allen and Kellogg, John's Bayou had been the most reliable place to find ivory-bills. But why? To get a sense of the woodpecker's habitat requirements, Tanner decided to begin a dead wood survey. The number of dead trees determined the amount of woodpecker food available. He described the process as follows:

> The method used was to count all trees, all trees bearing dead wood, and all standing dead trees and trunks in a circle of sixty-feet radius, this giving a plot approximately a quarter of an acre in area.
>
> The plots were chosen at random by walking one hundred yards from the center of the last plot counted, the end of the one hundred yards being the center of the next plot. Usually four plots were counted in this manner, thus covering a total of one acre in four plots separated over three hundred yards.

Tanner recorded the species of trees in the count circles and also made a rough guess as to how long the wood had been dead, dividing the trees into three groups: dead less than two years, dead from two to four years, and dead longer than four years. "The age of the dead wood was estimated by such signs as the presence or absence of twigs and small branches, the tightness and hardness of the bark, and the condition of the wood," Jim explained. Over a two-day period, Tanner made ten such counts, covering ten acres in the John's Bayou region. He determined that there were 195.6 trees of all types per acre and, of these, 7.5 trees had been dead for two years or less.

Thursday, August 11: Tanner drove into Greenlea Bend, making arrangements to stay in a shack at the Continental Oil site. For two hot, muggy days, he searched the woods west of the location, covering the entire length of the bend all the way to the river and making several dead-wood surveys as he had done at John's Bayou. "I saw nothing of ivory-bills in the bend except some fairly fresh and good-looking sign," Tanner wrote. "Kuhn had reported hearing at least one bird near Baker's Ditch on the other side of the river, about three weeks ago." A Tendal Lumber Company employee reported seeing an ivory-bill in the same area about two weeks earlier.

Three days later, Tanner drove north to West Carroll Parish to look through the woods near Darnell, a section known as the Bruce Tract. It was freshly cut over, more so than Jim had initially believed, and he returned to Tallulah, knowing that he had done about all he could do in the region during this field season. He had followed every lead, spoken to anyone who would listen.

It rained heavily in Tallulah the following day, the tail end of a hurricane that had lashed the Gulf Coast. The heavy rains filled the surrounding woods with water. After the deluge ended, Tanner drove south to Foster, having a hard time getting over the soft road. As he and Kuhn had discovered, Foster was the easiest access point into Mack's Bayou when conditions were sloppy. He ventured into the woods, marking an area where he wanted to do a dead-wood survey, but found no fresh ivory-bill sign. Ultimately, Tanner did very basic dead-tree surveys in three separate areas of the Singer Tract: John's and Mack's bayous and Greenlea Bend. In his book published three years later, he reported his findings in great detail, and suffice it to say, John's Bayou contained, per acre, the highest number of trees dead less than two years. This perhaps explained why it was the most reliable place to locate ivory-bills.

After visiting Mack's Bayou, Jim sold the recovering Charlie to Belvin Brown. In the afternoon he started down Sharkey Road, where he encountered as much water as there had been in winter. With the summer's heat, it turned out to be a "mean hot walk." Tanner worked his way to the John's Bayou roost site, hoping to get a few photos. A little after five o'clock, he reached the ash trees and sat down to wait. It was warm and muggy with little birdsong: a vireo sang a few notes, and a Carolina wren sang one time. Jim heard pileateds in the area, and at sunset, the barred owls began hooting. But no ivory-bills. Was the season truly over? In time, he began to walk out, hoping to reach Sharkey Road before it was too dark to see. After about a quarter-mile, an ivory-bill called in front of him.

"I followed it as best I could, came to a dead oak trunk, half rotten but still standing," Jim recalled. "The bird was peering out of a large hole on the north of the trunk. Disturbed by me, it came out and climbed to the top. Even tho the light was poor, I could see the band." He had found the juvenile he had tagged on his birthday in early March. "The crest has scarlet in it," he noted, "but it seemed a bit ragged." This confirmed that it was a male.

Afterward, Jim worked his way through the sodden woods in twilight, finding Sharkey Road muddy and familiar. With the help of a flashlight, he walked out of the swamp, deep in thought. Finding the banded ivory-bill was a fitting, even comforting, conclusion to the second nesting season he had studied in the Singer Tract.

Tanner left Tallulah and drove to New Orleans by way of Baton Rouge. It was mid-August, and the Big Easy was hot and crowded with tourists. After finding a room at the Greenlaw Hotel on Charles Street, Jim visited the local Southern Forest Experiment Station, where he met with Dr. Robert Winters, a noted forester and photographer. A wing of the USDA Forest Service, the New Orleans facility was one of several such research stations scattered across the South. Winters had joined the research division of the Forest Service in 1930 as an assistant silviculturist and was noted for taking the photos used in one of the organization's early publications, John Putnam and Henry Bull's *The Trees of the Bottomlands of the Mississippi River Delta Region* (1932). Tanner was most interested in ways of determining how long a tree had been dead. On both that subject and the history of logging Winters was a fountain of information. He also confirmed what Jim had already discovered: the extreme rarity of virgin forests across the south. If ivory-bills depended on such habitat, there were few places they could live.

At the history museum on Royal Street, he learned the names of two people who had reported seeing ghost birds recently. One sighting was near Vancleave, Mississippi, and the other was along the Pearl River on the Louisana-Mississippi border. Because it was closer, Jim drove to the latter area the next day but discovered that it had recently been cut over. He located no accounts of ivory-bills, and a local logging superintendent offered little hope that the bird was in the region. (In 1999 an LSU forestry student reported seeing an ivory-bill in the Pearl River Wildlife Management Area; his account was so richly detailed that it ignited renewed hope for the species. However, extensive investigations—including 4,146 hours of audio data recorded by sound-activated devices the Cornell Lab of Ornithology had installed—turned up nothing.)

In Gulfport, Mississippi, Tanner located Tom Burleigh, a forest wildlife biologist with the USDA's Bureau of Biological Survey. Burleigh was headquartered at Harrison National Forest (now part of the De Soto National Forest) near Saucier, doing research on the role birds played in the reseeding of longleaf pines. Like Tanner, Burleigh had been interested in birds most of his life, having first published a report on cowbird eggs in a yellow warbler nest in the *Oologist* in 1910, when he was only fifteen years old. A Pennsylvania native, Burleigh had heard of no reports or even rumors of ivory-bills in the area. Road-weary, Tanner decided to remain in Gulfport for the weekend, staying in a local tourist camp. He visited the local beaches and did some bird-watching along the shore.

Finally, he attended to the one last piece of unfinished business: the report of an ivory-bill near the small town of Vancleave, Mississippi. Jim met with J. J. Carter, a game warden who had lived in that part of the state a long time. He knew the bottomland and swamps associated with the Pascagoula River well and had never heard of ivory-bills in the vicinity. Nor had anyone else Jim was able to locate. The historical record has one report of the ghost bird in the region.

Concluding that the dense vegetation, silent birds, and depressing heat made work in the summer "practically a waste of time," Tanner drove north to Montgomery to begin the long trip back to New York. If he was getting homesick, he didn't mention it in his notes. However, he had been on the road, living out of his car, since early February—a total of 193 days. What more could he do?

On Monday morning, October 24, at the American Museum of Natural History in New York City, Tanner gave a twenty-minute presentation before the thirty-fourth annual convention of the National Association of Audubon Societies. It had been a year of highs and lows that saw Jim banding and photographing a nestling ivory-bill while also chasing many tips that led nowhere. The Santee region in South Carolina remained a big mystery. Reports were favorable, so it seemed to merit another search.

Chapter 16

From the Santee to the Sunshine State

In the Santee region the birds had been seen by several observers, most frequently by Alexander Sprunt Jr., but very little was known about their numbers and distribution there.

—James T. Tanner

Late in 1938 the gathering storm in Europe continued to gain momentum. Beginning on the night of November 9, an anti-Semitic rampage exploded throughout Germany and Austria. In what many consider the beginning of the Holocaust, Nazis destroyed or damaged thousands of Jewish-owned businesses and more than two hundred synagogues. Countless storefront windows were broken, and the shards of glass scattered on the sidewalks gave rise to the name *Kristallnacht*—the "Crystal Night," or "Night of Broken Glass." By the end of the bloody riots, some ninety people had been killed at random, almost all of them Jews.

That same month in the United States, which was still struggling through the Great Depression, President Roosevelt saw a number of his Democratic Party allies in Congress go down to defeat in the midterm elections. This setback was but one of several obstacles that were thwarting FDR's efforts to implement his New Deal agenda during his second term. Meanwhile, on the foreign-policy front, Roosevelt was engaged in secret talks with the French to sell them military aircraft in the face of the growing Nazi threat.

Back in western New York, Jim Tanner knew that winter was working its way to the South. The forests would be dropping their leaves, making it easier to find woodpeckers. Having one year left in his Audubon fellowship, he was anxious to get back on the road. On November 16, he drove east to New York City and met with his benefactor, John Baker, at the Audubon headquarters. After almost two years of searching, the big question on their minds must have been this: were there any ivory-bills left in the South outside of the Singer Tract? At that moment, the most promising place was the Santee bottomlands in South Carolina. Alexander Sprunt Jr. and Lester Walsh, Baker's personal assistant, had confirmed a sighting. The men had found an ivory-bill and possibly heard two more. Yet, Jim had visited the Santee region twice in 1937 but found nothing of note. Clearly, a third visit was in order.

That evening Jim stayed in the YMCA and took in a popular play on Broadway, *Tobacco Road*. Jack Kirkland's drama was based on Erskine Caldwell's 1932 novel about a family of poor white sharecroppers in Georgia—a family desperate to hang on to their small homestead while all around them other farms are being gobbled up and mechanized. The story about the Lester family probably resonated with Tanner more than with anyone else in attendance that evening. He had spent almost two years driving across the southern states, passing hundreds of tenant farms. Jim knew the "croppers" to be hardworking people, struggling to raise enough cotton and garden produce—potatoes, beans, onions, winter turnips—to keep their land and feed their families. Tanner had spoken to them, eaten with them. On more than one occasion, they had helped him find his way, loaned him a mule or a horse, talked to him about "kents," and assisted him by pulling his car out of the mud. They were good folks, not like the buffoons in the play.

After leaving the Big Apple, Tanner spent three days driving to Columbia, South Carolina, with overnight stays in Washington, D.C., and Raleigh, North Carolina. The route along U.S. Highway 1 mirrored the drive he had made with Allen and Kellogg almost four years before. In the state capital, Jim met the head of South Carolina's forestry commission as well as a state forester who gave him information about Hell Hole Swamp and the new Francis Marion National Forest established in July 1936. The Santee River formed the northern border for that woodland.

On Tuesday, November 22, Tanner traveled to the town of St. Stephens. Located just south of the Santee River and west of the new national forest, it had a population almost too small to count. He spent two days exploring the bottomland, interviewing outdoorsmen who might be familiar with ivory-bills. Several described them as being very rare; none could report a recent sighting. One afternoon, Tanner ate lunch on the porch of an abandoned plantation with a line of live oaks in front of the empty antebellum mansion. The ghost house was a vivid reminder of the change that had swept through coastal Carolina and other parts of the Southeast. Margaret Mitchell's 1936 novel *Gone with the Wind*, set in neighboring Georgia, had recently won the Pulitzer Prize; the premier of the epic movie was only a few months away. The end of the Civil War had ushered in a time of cheap land. Lumber companies flooded the vanquished South to harvest the timber, buying forests for as little as a dollar an acre. Thus, almost everywhere Jim traveled, the logging companies had already been there. What would things have been like if he had been able to do his ivory-bill search thirty or even twenty years earlier?

North of the Santee, Jim located a stretch of still-virgin timber, a low-lying black gum swamp but found little sign of woodpeckers of any kind. Interviews with locals suggested that the most likely place to look for ivory-bills was in the Wadmacon Creek section. The day after Thanksgiving, Tanner drove to the home of Hollie Shokes, a game warden hired by the National Association of Audubon Societies. He was tasked with watching over the section of Santee swamp the organization had leased to protect because of recent ivory-bill sightings. Jim hired Shokes as a guide, for which he paid him twenty-eight dollars. The Santee native had welcome news: he had recently seen an ivory-bill. The men got permission to use a cabin on Steward's Neck, a high ridge Jim had visited the year before near Wadmacon Island, but bad weather delayed their trip into the swamp.

Tuesday, November 29: "A cold day," Tanner began. "We paddled up Wadmacon Creek to the Cut-off, thru that into the big Santee, then paddled and floated down that and thru Push-and-go back to Wadmacon. The current thru the Cut-off was strong, and we had to paddle hard, taking occasional rests to get thru. The boat surged thru the water, but crept past the banks. Wadmacon Creek twists and turns, with many ox-bows, and the water frequently boils and ripples past snags; the big Santee is straighter, and tho faster, follows more placidly."

Woodpecker-wise, Tanner and Shokes saw little of interest all day. The pair spent the next eleven days exploring the lower section of the Santee bottoms "by boat and by foot." Together or separately they covered the entire area from Sand Creek to within a few miles of Lenude's Ferry. They paid particular attention to Wadmacon Island, where Shokes had recently seen ivory-bills several times. They found nothing. Tanner also spoke with local residents; most had never seen an ivory-bill. However, one man had encountered a giant woodpecker "with a white back" in the lower swamp on Wadmacon Island—but that had been over a year ago.

"I was sorry to be leaving," Jim wrote, "but felt some days ago that ivory-bills were not in the region, and that I should be trying other areas." Hopes had been high for Tanner's finding the ghost birds somewhere along the Santee after the recent sightings, but that was not to be, at least not on this trip. "Nowhere did I find any fresh sign similar to that normally found in the Singer Tract. And nowhere did I see any nest or roost holes likely to be dug by ivory-bills," he recorded. "Wadmacon Island had the biggest pileated population of any place visited. The ridge timber there is like that in the Singer, but is younger and healthier, showing very few dead tops. I believe the ivory-bills are gone from, or are not visiting this section of the Santee."

Tanner's two-week stay reinforced his belief that ivory-bills did not reside along the Santee but probably visited it from time to time in search of food. He noted:

> Hollie, Sprunt, and Bob Allen describe them as being mast-feeders. 1936, when the crowd was on the Neck, was a good mast year; 1937 was fair; 1938, the poorest in many years.
>
> In hunting through that area I found no signs that would indicate that ivory-bills had ever resided steadily there, nothing such as roost holes or extensive feeding sign. The years that ivory-bills were observed in the Wadmacon Island section were good mast and berry years, and the birds were seen feeding upon gum berries.

This also brought to light that the species ate something other than insects. Gum berries are considered soft-mast. (Acorns, hickory nuts, and beechnuts are hard mast.) But if they were not permanent residents on the Santee, where did they live? One logical place to look was only a few miles north along the Pee Dee River. Tanner ended the Santee ivory-bill search by writing, "Here's hoping I find them in the next 10 days."

The Great Pee Dee watershed is massive; its headwaters can be traced all the way upstream to the Yadkin River and beyond to the Appalachian Mountains of North Carolina. In the early 1900s, the world's largest lumber company was located near the river's mouth at Georgetown. The virgin pine forests of the region were cut over, and the logs floated in rafts downriver to the mill. There they were sawn into lumber and exported to the northern United States and Europe. This extensive logging didn't bode well for Tanner or ivory-bills, but one lumberman had told Jim in November that there was still some old timber left in the lower swamplands.

Tanner spent the next four days interviewing people and exploring the bottomlands from Georgetown north to Myrtle Beach, including a visit to Brookgreen Greens, where he met with Percy L. Hovey, who oversaw the park's wildlife. When Tanner learned that Hovey was originally from Ithaca, their meeting was like a homecoming. He learned that most of the area was cut over except for a small isolated section on the upper end of Bull Island. Much of the bottomland around the Pee Dee, Waccamaw, and Black rivers consisted now of abandoned rice fields, the timber having long since been harvested.

Perhaps dogged by frustration over the Santee reports, Tanner once gain drove south and spent two more days searching a section he had not visited: the Wee Tee Lake area roughly twenty miles upstream from Wadmacon Island. He walked into the swamp on the roadbed of a new railroad tram being built deeper into the forest to move cut timber out; skidders mounted on railroad flatbeds were dragging out the cut logs. Jim felt the woods were suitable habitat, but he found no evidence: "There was plenty of sweet gum, but I saw no sign, little encouraging for ivory-bills. I was not in there long enough to really judge the abundance of pileateds."

Late in his planned stay in the Santee, Tanner received word from E. Burnham Chamberlain, curator at the Charleston Museum, of a recent ivory-bill sighting. "On or about Oct. 19, 1938, Mr. Moultrie Ball had seen three ivory-bills on Black Oak Island, saying that he was within thirty feet of one bird, and that he also saw a large number of pileateds," wrote Jim. Black Oak Island is on the Santee River upstream from Wee Tee Lake. Tanner visited the location on December 23, the second full day of winter. He found the island to be a wide swamp—dominated by mixed hardwood, sweet gum, and laurel oak—and encountered a game warden and a local man who knew of ivory-bills in the area but had not seen one in four or five years. However, the man admitted he had not been in the swamp that often in recent years.

Could the ivory-bills seen by so many observers on Wadmacon Island actually live upstream on Black Oak Island? Would they fly that far to forage on soft mast? The two locations were roughly forty-five miles apart. Jim knew he would be back for an answer, but that would have to wait. A letter he received from Robert Porter Allen, director of sanctuaries for the Audubon Society, about recent ivory-bill sightings in Florida needed to be investigated. Quickly.

Allen became the sanctuary director in 1934, but he would go on to become one of this country's most passionate advocates for endangered species. Alexander Sprunt IV (the son of the man Tanner first met in January 1937) writes, "Bob Allen was the epitome of the field biologist. . . . [He] was an ecologist in the best sense of the word but was actually much more than that. He believed that in order to help an endangered species you must first know as much about it as possible, and then having gained this knowledge, you must *do something* about it." Although Allen was nine years older than Tanner, to a degree he followed in Jim's footsteps. After Tanner completed his research on the ivory-bill—the first in-depth study of a vanishing species for Audubon—Allen gave up the sanctuary directorship and completed two similar studies of his own: one on the roseate spoonbill and another on the vanishing whooping crane, America's tallest bird. His research kept him in the field for years, a place where he excelled.

But before all that, in the fall of 1938, Allen's letter to Tanner relayed two recent reports of ivory-bills in Florida that were "quite reliable, due to the character of both observers." One report came from a game warden at Highland Hammock and the other from the Big Cypress in the region between Deep Lake and Immokalee. Big Cypress was on Jim's list to revisit, having spent only a week of reconnaissance there in 1937. But it was a long drive from South Carolina.

Tanner spent Christmas with Herbert Stoddard at his Sherwood Plantation in south Georgia. A native of Chuluota, Florida, northeast of Orlando, Stoddard himself had seen his first ivory-bill in 1896 "on the trunk of a cypress growing in a swamp inlet on Lake Mills, less than a mile from home."

Soon enough Tanner was back on the road and into Florida just as the old year was yielding to the new. After a visit with his ninety-year-old grandfather, Edward Tanner, in Winter Park, Jim continued his search in the Sunshine State. He had not given up on Florida. After all, it was the only state located entirely within the bird's known range. There were historical records of the ghost bird all the way from the Okefenokee Swamp in the north to Lostman's River near the keys in the south. To the west, the bottomland and swamps along the Florida Panhandle were rife with accounts of the giant woodpecker. As Tanner noted: "More ivory-bill records and specimens have come from the state of Florida than from all the other states put together; this is partly due to the large number of collectors and observers that have worked in Florida, but it indicates that the ivory-bill was probably more abundant and widespread in that region than elsewhere." However, searches in 1935 by Allen, Kellogg, and Tanner and in 1937 by Jim alone had turned up nothing. Had curiosity seekers and specimen collectors found, killed, and tagged all that were left? Not necessarily.

Tanner spent the last days of 1938 with game warden Oscar E. Baynard at Hillsborough River State Park, only a few miles northeast of Tampa. A respected ornithologist, Baynard had been hired by Audubon to protect heron, egret, and ibis rookeries; he also served as superintendent of the state park from 1936 to 1942. "During the latter months of 1937," wrote Tanner, "Baynard frequently saw ivory-bills near Highlands Hammock State Park. He saw them in a small swamp near the park where many cypress trees had been killed, apparently by fire, and the woodpeckers were feeding in the deadening." Baynard reported seeing "one female ivory-bill occasionally from August to late November 1937, and one pair from then to the year's end. The birds had not been seen since."

Baynard had another remarkable bird sighting to report, telling Tanner that he had been observing a flock of six to ten colorful Carolina parakeets, although he did not tell Jim exactly where he had been watching the now-extinct species. "Oscar Baynard," according to Dr. Noel Snyder, "was possibly the last ornithologist to see wild Carolina parakeets. His sightings of the species may have continued into the 1940s, but he refused to reveal the location of his observation." Probably to protect the remnant flock from collectors, Baynard remained mute on the topic. (Baynard went on to become Florida's State Park Commissioner and died in 1971. The location of his parakeet sightings is still a mystery.)

Highlands Hammock is located in south Florida, east of Sarasota and northwest of Lake Okeechobee. One of the Sunshine State's oldest parks, Highland Hammock opened to the public in 1931. During the Great Depression, the Civilian Conservation Corps had developed many of the park's facilities, including the beginnings of a botanical garden. According to Baynard, ivory-bill sightings occurred in two separate locations near the hammock: along Charley Bowlegs Creek and in a swamp northwest of Polk City. The former was a perfect place for Jim to begin his 1939 quest.

On New Year's Day Tanner investigated the location: "Within a half mile of the park boundary are some cypress deadenings . . . now the bark has fallen, the sapwood is quite rotten, and there are not many woodpeckers working on them." Jim would spend a frustrating day and a half thoroughly searching the dead cypresses along the creek. He found no sign of ivory-bills, although he did see a few pileateds. Had he just missed the ghost birds again? Jim subsequently drove farther south to Fort Myers on the Gulf Coast and then inland to Immokalee.

Tanner had visited the Big Cypress in February 1937 during the early days of his field studies, spending a week exploring the region and conversing with local outdoorsmen in and around Immokalee. He had concluded then that he needed to return when he had more time. That time had come.

Located in Collier and Hendry countries, the Big Cypress Swamp is a nearly flat, mostly forested region with a greater variety of plant communities than the low-lying Everglades to the east and south. To the north, the high ground has a maximum elevation of twenty-two feet; to the south, roughly thirty-five miles away, the terrain slopes to almost sea level. "The result," writes Thomas E. Lodge in *The Everglades Handbook*, "is a range of plant communities from deep sloughs dotted with open ponds to cypress swamps, to regions of countless cypress domes, to open marshes, pinelands, and hammocks. Variations in forest cover often make the region appear to have hills, in contrast to the flatness of the Everglades." Of the same terrain, Tanner noted,

> The differences in timber and cover are caused by differences in elevation of but a foot or so. The higher ground is usually sandy, although limestone rock occasionally outcrops on the surface. In some places it is timbered with slash pine, usually called pine islands. Much of the drier ground is prairie, covered either with grass or saw palmetto and dotted here and there with ponds, small cypress heads, or hammocks."
>
> The Main Strand is on the Okaloacoochee Slough, which starts somewhere northeast of Immokalee and extends south and

> a little east. The slough itself is a broken series of marshes, some of them a mile across. In some parts, the marsh is bordered by a heavy cypress swamp, in others by prairie, and in others, especially towards its southern end, the slough is entirely a cypress swamp. Along the main runs of the swamp the bald cypress grows biggest. There the water is deepest, about thigh-deep when I was there.

On his first day back in 1939, Jim revisited some of the people he had met two years before, soon stumbling across a hot lead from a man named Ernest Douglas. "While talking with Douglas," Jim recorded, "he suddenly remembered seeing ten days before a big woodpecker which he thought was partly albino, near the Kissimmee Billy Strand. He pointed immediately to the picture of the ivory-bill when I showed it."

In 1937 Dewey Brown, another local backwoodsman, had mentioned the same location as a good place to search. The isolated swampy place lies only a few miles east of Main Strand and north of the Tamiami Trail. Several old unimproved roads, little more than muddy trails, led into the watery wilderness on what little high ground was available. That afternoon Tanner drove into the region, finding an old woodsy path off Deep Lake Road, but he misjudged its firmness: "While turning around, the car bogged, and I got a good introduction to that deceptive soil, firm on top, soupy below. I worked about four hours before I got out." Afterward, he discovered that the car's rear spring was broken and would need to be replaced.

On Friday, January 6, with the car fixed, a local woodsman named Tom Conyer, who knew the wetland and the best ways in and out, agreed to go with Tanner to Kissimmee Billy Strand. Tanner wrote,

> We were out there about three hours. The strand there was custard apple and pop ash, small and crooked trees. There were a fair number of pileateds around, and the trees showed some woodpecker work, but I saw nothing that looked like ivory-bill. In the swamp were quite a few ibises and herons, deer and turkey sign.
>
> Here and there are cypress trees. As the swamp extends to the south, from a quarter of a mile to two miles wide, cypress becomes more common and it greatly resembles the Main Strand although the runs are never as prominent.

That evening they returned to Conyer's house. Jim camped nearby, feeling comfortable with the local woodsman. That weekend, they searched two locations at the southern end of Main Strand, following tips that ivory-bills had been seen there in 1938 and 1939. Jim found the area to be mostly a cypress swamp with a lot of dead cypresses, although many appeared to be long dead and dried out, thus of little use to an ivory-bill. He also commented that Conyer, "an uncommonly keen man in the wood," had never seen an ivory-bill to know them.

"About ten years ago, the Big Cypress was very dry," Tanner wrote. "Fire burned into almost all the strands and did a huge amount of damage. The muck soil was completely burned away in many places to a depth of a foot or more; the small broad-leaved trees like maples and ashes were completely killed; almost all the cypress was killed in these burned areas." The fire-damaged places were now desolate, covered with water about a foot deep. Only a few tall trees were still living.

"Where the water is not covering the ground, a dense growth of willows has sprung up, surrounding the dead and dry cypress," Jim lamented. "The fires that burned those swamps were a great catastrophe to the Big Cypress. Such burned places are hard as can be to get thru, thick with either willows or marsh plants, the ground wet and covered with a litter of slippery poles. Only a few kinds of birds are found in those places." Off and on, droughts and the draining of the Everglades and surrounding wetlands had increased the likelihood of wildfire.

After returning to Immokalee late on a Sunday evening, Tanner looked up Dewey Brown, a local hunter and trapper he had met in 1937. Among the places Brown identified as the best possibilities for finding ivory-bills was Thickahatchie Swamp, which extended southward from a branch off the Main Strand. Having never visited that area, Tanner went there with Brown. It turned out to be, in Jim's view, the most unusual and interesting of all the strands. The plants were more tropical with many royal and silver palms. The timber was also bigger and heavier. "The swamp there looked quite good for woodpeckers, but there seemed to be few pileateds, no sign of ivory-bills," Tanner wrote after the morning visit.

Thursday, January 12: Back in Immokalee, Tanner spent the day interviewing locals with knowledge of the swamps. His results were mixed: some claimed to have seen ivory-bills; some had not. The hottest lead came at a camp near Ochopee. A lumberman there claimed to have seen an ivory-bill only a few days before along Turner River. Ochopee is a small town located southwest of the Big Cypress; the river flows nearby, emptying into the gulf south of Everglades City. Tanner spent most of the following day searching along a trail south of the river. He found no sign of ivory-bills and few pileateds. "Much of the country there is covered with low pond cypress; bald cypress seem to be confined to the river edge," Jim recorded. When it started to rain, he drove back to Immokalee to interview more people. There he encountered about thirty Seminoles who come from the nearby reservation "to get their pay and groceries." The Seminole reservation is on the northeast section of the Big Cypress.

The Second Seminole War (1835–42) was fought to drive the Native Americans from the state. Ultimately some four thousand Seminoles were banished to a reservation in Oklahoma, but a small group hid out in the Everglades, eventually settling at Big Cypress. During the 1930s, roughly 650 Seminoles still lived in the area. To earn a modest livelihood, the Native Americans had also built small villages of palm-thatched huts along the Tamiami Trail where they sold alligator hides and exhibited gators, wildcats, raccoons, and snakes in cages to passing tourists. Tanner was fascinated by their vivid, patchwork clothing made up of bright colors, intricate patterns, woven yarn, and beadwork. It was not, surprisingly, their traditional dress but actually quite modern, a blending of cultures that reached its zenith in the 1920s. "All the young men wore store trousers and bright, fancy shirts, loose fitting, and free, and most had big, wide-brimmed hats, some with bright, beaded hat bands," Jim observed. "The few women that were there wore loose, flowing dresses with wide skirts that reached the ground, long sleeves. Some of them had fancy hair-dresses, which Stanley Hanson said was an innovation."

Tanner spent most of the week camping at various locations in Kissimmee Billy Strand along the border of the Big Cypress Seminole Reservation. Many of the observers had mentioned the site. It contained mixed forest: pop ash and custard apple over part of it, with various oak, palm, and cypress stands elsewhere. The country east and north of Kissimmee Billy was thick with cypress heads intermingled with pine islands or prairie. Like much of the rest of the Big Cypress wooded environs, this section seemed ideally suited for ivory-bills: other woodpeckers, including pileateds, were common.

In all, Tanner spent almost five days searching every part of Kissimmee Billie Strand, undeterred by the cold weather that set in on Friday, January 20. Jim found a dead palmetto stub "with three big holes, looking very much like those of an ivory-bill, and the lower one looking as tho it were being used. I looked around but saw no other sign, and that evening and the next I returned and watched the holes until quite late, but saw nothing." On Sunday, January 22, Jim met a local named Frank Summerall, who added his own eyewitness account of seeing ivory-bills in the area. He knew exactly what the bird looked like from having seen several stuffed specimens.

Because he was running out of cash, Jim left the swamp and drove west to Fort Myers. During his entire three-year journey through the South, he had his Audubon grant money wired to him periodically as he traveled from place to place, staying in touch with an Ithaca bank about his projected itinerary. On this occasion, however, the money had not arrived at Fort Myers, and Tanner found himself almost broke. He took a part-time job helping refurbish a motor yacht. For four days he worked at sanding, painting, and scraping away barnacles. Enjoying the company of the vessel's three-man crew, Jim found it pleasant work. The Audubon stipend finally arrived, and with that and his earnings in hand, Tanner returned to Big Cypress. He searched the section where Summerall had reported seeing an ivory-bill, but to Jim, the country did not look at all good for them. There was no sign, and woodpeckers of all kinds were scarce.

Discouraged, Tanner drove on to the Seminole Reservation and a diversion: he spent the evening playing "Chinese Checkers" with Stanley Hanson, the reservation's personable superintendent, whom he had first met in 1937. The star-shaped board game, played with colored marbles, was actually of German origin and was introduced in the United States by J. Pressman & Co. in 1928. To capitalize on the American fascination with the Far East, the Pressman company first dubbed it the "Hop Ching Checker Game" before simplifying the name. The marketing ploy worked, and sales boomed to such an extent that by the late 1930s it had even found its way into remote southern swamps.

On the first Sunday in February, Tanner returned to East Hanson and the camp of local woodsman Dempsey Whiden, who had been his guide in Kissimmee Billy Strand. Together they visited a lake at East Crossing to investigate yet another reported ivory-bill sighting. On the second day of their search, they found some good woodpecker country. While pileateds were common, however, Tanner found nothing that looked like ivory-bill sign. "The most interesting thing that we saw during the day was panther tracks," he wrote. (Today, the Florida panther is listed as critically endangered, its numbers estimated to be less than one hundred.)

Tanner spent his last day in the Big Cypress alone. He drove north of Bear Island and hiked into the swamp. The border had been burned over recently, killing many trees: "Many of these deadened cypress had bark knocked off near the base of the tree, usually only on one side and for but a few feet of the lower trunk. It certainly looked like ivory-bill work. But coming thru there late in the afternoon, I came up to a pair of pileateds, and watching them, I saw them feed by knocking off the bark. They did not do it in the business-like manner of an ivory-bill but they did knock off some, leaving sign just like what I had seen."

By Thursday, February 9, it was time to move on. Although Jim had found no ivory-bills in his month-long stay, he felt confident they were there. Too many reliable people had seen them. Of the area's terrain and teeming birdlife, Tanner observed:

> The Big Cypress region has a varied charm, hard to describe. There is the open prairie of broad views, interrupted only by the hammocks of palm and oak, arched by a blue sky with a great variety of clouds, and there is the green swamp of luxuriant growth, big cypress growing upward into the sun and small trees bending over the dark water. Life is abundant in the swamp. Red-shouldered Hawks scream almost continually during late winter and spring. Egrets, herons, and ibis feed in the shallow runs and ponds. The small lakes have swimmers such as coots, gallinules, and grebes, while water turkeys [anhinga] perch in the trees bordering the water.

Tanner had seen many small songbirds in the openings and shrub borders, while the edges of the swamps teemed with deer, wild turkey, and quail. In all, Jim took note of eighty-nine species of birds and thirteen species of mammals he had found during this visit to the Big Cypress. "Swamps in the Big Cypress were good for woodpeckers," he concluded, "and pileateds were common. The occasional reports of ivory-bills being seen and the size and primitive conditions of the area are the best indications that the birds are still present. In my opinion ivory-bills very probably are there."

Not finding a ghost bird himself must have been disappointing, considering the effort he put into the search. Still, there was plenty of good habitat, and Jim concluded that "my failure to find any birds does not eliminate the possibility of them being there."

Tanner found that Thickahatchie Swamp lying west of the road that linked Immokalee to Deep Lake was the largest uncut wetland in the area. It had the richest and most tropical vegetation and a number of birds and much game—but no reports of recent ivory-bill sightings. The most timely accounts in the region came from East Hanson, East Crossing, and the Kissimmee Billy Strand. Tanner had searched each unsuccessfully. Still, Jim must have left the Big Cypress feeling somewhat relieved. There seemed to be enough proper habitat in extreme southern Florida for ivory-bills to survive. He believed there could be as many as eight in the region, even though none presented themselves to him. But what about the rest of the state?

After spending the night once again in Fort Myers, he drove east to Lake Okeechobee, the largest freshwater lake in the state and the second largest located solely within the country. At Cornwell, north of the lake on the Kissimmee River, Jim met up with Marvin Chandler to discuss the birds of his region. Since early 1936, Chandler had been one of six uniformed game wardens hired by the NAS to protect the birds of the region. Thus, in effect, he and Tanner were coworkers. Described as "a devoted guardian of the birdlife of central Florida" by Dr. Noel Snyder, Chandler worked mightily to protect the major glossy ibis colony on Lake Okeechobee from egg collectors. As Snyder writes, "His low regard for the ethics of egg collectors was no secret."

An Audubon game warden was equal parts conservation biologist, teacher, field guide, goodwill ambassador, and law-enforcement officer. Much of the land they protected was wilderness where existing environmental laws had been lightly regarded. In 1939 all the wardens began wearing standard uniforms: matching olive-drab trousers and shirt, the latter sporting a round, red patch on the left shoulder with the word *Audubon* and a silhouette of a heron. The native-born Chandler was lean and wiry. In one of a series of articles written for the *New York Herald Tribune* in the late 1930s, naturalist-reporter John O'Reilly characterized Chandler this way: "His face is tanned the color of dead palmetto. He is stingy with words, but his mouth is bordered by grin wrinkles. He patrols a wide area and knows it like a housewife knows her kitchen floor." During a typical month, Chandler might patrol three thousand miles and oversee thousands of birds.

Unfortunately, Chandler had no accounts of ivory-bills, and largely on the strength of Oscar Baynard's recent sightings, he believed that Highlands Hammock and farther north were the best places for Jim to search after Big Cypress.

Saturday, February 11: Tanner returned to Highlands Hammock near Sebring. It was his second visit in as many months. He spent the early morning hours walking around in a small swamp north of the park—the place where Baynard had reported seeing the evanescent woodpeckers during the closing months of 1937. "Mr. Baynard," Tanner wrote, "saw the woodpeckers in some cypress deadenings in this swamp. At the time of my visit, these dead cypress were beginning to rot, and very few woodpeckers were feeding upon them. The ivory-bills probably moved off to better feeding grounds, wherever that might have been."

But Jim found no sign of ivory-bills in any nearby area that was even suitable. He spent that night at the state park, sleeping on a cot in Baynard's office. As with the sightings on Wadmacon Island in the Santee, the question presenting itself had to do with an ivory-bill's range. "Many species of woodpecker are considered sedentary," Tanner would write in his 1942 book on the ivory-bill, "but it is well known that they will move into areas where a large amount of timber has been killed, affording abundant food for them, and they will leave when that supply diminishes." He ultimately decided that ivory-bills were not sedentary and probably moved often and farther than other species. They were strong, fast fliers, well adapted for traveling long distances. Usually the mated pairs traveled closely together. But how far could they fly to forage?

Following a tip from Baynard, Tanner next investigated a spot in Green Swamp roughly ninety miles to the north in the northeast section of Polk County. Most of the cypress heads there covered an acre or two. But Jim discovered that the entire area had been recently cut over. He found neither any suitable habitat left nor anyone who would profess to having seen an ivory-bill. Another lead, which Tanner picked up in Dade City, led him to nearby Loughman. A storekeeper told Jim that he hadn't heard of an ivory-bill in the vicinity for at least twenty years.

After a day of driving with several stops and interviews that yielded little new information, Tanner drove to Fort Christmas in Orange County. Jim had visited the area with Allen and Kellogg in March 1935 and once again on his first solo trip to the state in February 1937. The historic fort—with an eighty-by-eighty-foot stockade and two twenty-by-twenty-foot blockhouses—was built in three days beginning on Christmas 1837, hence the name. It was part of a chain of roughly two hundred forts built by the U.S. government during the Second Seminole War.

The name of the accompanying community was changed from Fort Christmas to just Christmas when a post office was opened there in 1892. The region is rife with small creek swamps, mostly cypress and mixed timber that flow into the St. Johns River. There had been reports of ivory-bill sightings as recently as 1934, but Jim found that the swampland was now almost completely cut over.

Monday, February 20: After a return trip to Winter Park, Tanner drove on to Leesburg and Wildwood, where he encountered the Withlacoochee River once again. The area west of Wildwood is a patchwork of lakes, creeks, and wetlands. The Withlacoochee originates in Green Swamp in west central Florida, twists and turns through sandhills as it flows northwest into flatter swampland, and finally empties into the Gulf of Mexico at Yankeetown. Jim camped out in the woods near the river, renting a boat the next morning to explore.

"This area must have been very beautiful once," he reported. "Cypress swamps are extensive along the river, especially between the river and Panasoffkee Lake. . . . Most of the woods have been cut over, but parts still are very pretty." Tanner found the river populated by many ducks, coots, herons, and even limpkins. Migrating spring warblers, parulas, and yellowthroats sang from the woods along the shoreline.

By late afternoon of Wednesday, February 22, Tanner reached the University of Florida in Gainesville, where he dined in the student cafeteria. The next morning he met with Dr. Thompson H. Van Hyning, director of the Florida Museum of Natural History. Formerly known as the Florida State Museum, it got its start in 1891 when Frank Pickel, a professor of natural science at Florida Agriculture College, purchased research collections of fossils, minerals, and human anatomy models to aid in teaching biology and agricultural sciences. Over the years, the collections grew steadily. When the agriculture college closed in 1905, the museum became a part of the newly created University of Florida, and the collections were moved to Gainesville. Van Hyning had been the museum's director since 1914. Originally housed in a dormitory, the museum had, by the 1930s, acquired nearly a half-million specimens and was running out of space on campus. When Tanner visited, the museum's collections had recently moved to the Seagle Building in downtown Gainesville. Jim wanted to photograph the museum's set of ivory-bill eggs. Van Hyning was agreeable but warned, "Yes, if we can find them in this new place."

Locating ivory-bill eggs in the museum's vast collections proved to be as difficult as finding them in the wild. Tanner, Van Hyning, and an assistant searched all afternoon with no success. Van Hyning was distressed but believed that the eggs had just been misplaced in the move. (Today, with more than 20 million specimens of amphibians, birds, butterflies, fish, mammals, mollusks, reptiles, plus plant, vertebrate and invertebrate fossils, the Florida Museum of Natural History is the largest such museum in the Southeast.)

Tanner left Gainesville, driving west on old Highway 13. It was the coldest day Jim had experienced in Florida. Camping out wasn't very appealing, so at Cedar Keys in Waccasassa Bay on the gulf, he spent the night in the aged Island Hotel. Built in 1859, it was constructed from seashell tabby with oak supports. It remains a landmark in the region, having withstood hurricanes for almost 150 years.

From the gulf, Tanner drove north to Vista in the Suwannee River basin. A local named Charlie Hudson gave him a tour and advice on the condition of the swampland. Because the weather had warmed, Jim drove down an old logging road and camped out on a raised pine island in the wetland. He spent the next day exploring the Suwannee and Gopher river environs on foot and in his car whenever possible. There was no sign of ivory-bills, although pileateds were common. The milder weather brought a threat of rain so serious that Jim decided it wasn't safe to continue driving the old logging roads. He had gotten stuck far too many times to risk it yet again. That evening he left the area, spending the night at Cross City.

Stephen Foster's song had made the Suwannee the most famous waterway in Florida, even though the songwriter never saw the river and actually misspelled its name as "Swanee." The real Suwannee is a wild, rambling stream that begins in South Georgia's Okefenokee Swamp and flows 266 miles to the Gulf of Mexico. Along its meandering course, the waterway is fed by three major tributaries and no less than seventy-one large springs. So much pristine water enters the river that the black water leaving the Okefenokee clears by the time the Suwannee reaches the gulf. The early American naturalist William Bartram, who traveled through Florida in 1774, described the river as being "pellucid"—that is, clear and limpid. The remote backwater forests were also one of the last reported bastions of the now-extinct Carolina parakeet. Covering hundreds of largely uninhabited square miles, the Suwannee bottomlands in northern Florida were one of the largest undeveloped wetland regions Tanner visited, but that is not to say the area was untouched.

Almost 165 years after Bartram's visit, Tanner spent the last five days of February exploring the region, but unlike his predecessor, Jim found much of it had been logged over: "There are small areas of hammock and swamp timber still uncut and occasional rumors of birds seen, which is possible even though I found no sign of them."

Only on the last day did Jim find anything remotely suggesting the presence of ivory-bills. "In one area many pines were scaled" he wrote. "At first I considered it likely ivory-bill work, but I walked the territory quite thoroughly, found scaling on only one hardwood, no ivory-bill holes. Closer examination of the pines showed that the woodpeckers responsible had skipped the heavy bark near the base of the tree, even tho grubs were present, and some of the scaling showed small bill marks." Jim thus concluded that it was not the work of the ghost birds.

Wednesday, March 1, came in like the proverbial lion. "My plans and activities today were as changeable as the weather, which did all but snow," noted Tanner. He elected to avoid the sogginess of backcountry roads and drive inland to Gainesville. Along the way, he visited Old Town and Shamrock, looking for anyone who might know of ivory-bills, but those who were familiar with the bird hadn't seen one in years. In Gainesville, Tanner met with Charles Doe, curator of birds at the University of Florida. Among the most colorful and controversial figures in ornithology this country has produced, he was a zealous egg collector. "By all accounts," writes Dr. Noel Snyder, "Charles Doe, may he rest in peace, was a thoroughly reclusive and single-minded man. Bridging the late nineteenth and early twentieth centuries in his lifespan, he pursued the passion of his life—collecting birds' eggs—with devotion and skill, and by middle age he had amassed a huge assemblage of specimens."

By the late 1920s, Doe had accumulated forty thousand items, mostly bird eggs but also about a thousand skins and mounted birds. Once you accumulate such bounty, what do you do with it? In 1931 Frank Parson, a wealthy patron, arranged through a substantial donation for Doe's collection to be housed at the Florida Museum of Natural History; Doe was hired as the collection's curator. It was a collection within a collection. Doe had no authority over Van Hyning, the museum director, and apparently, Van Hyning had little say over Doe. The two men did not get along, perhaps partly because of Doe's spotty reputation. Over the years, the validity and authenticity of some of his specimens have been questioned. Even Tanner had doubts about one particular grouping: "He showed me the set of eggs labeled ivory-bill in his collection, but did not want me to photograph them, did not have the measurements, and for a good reason—they are nice looking pileated eggs, labeled ivory-bill from Texas."

Doe also had two pairs of ivory-bill specimens that were simply labeled "Baker County, Florida, 1914." But Doe gave Tanner little more information than that. He also knew of no ivory-bills left in the Sunshine State and had only recently heard of one sighting by a man in the state forest service. However, Doe would not divulge the observer's name. Tanner looked over the rest of Doe's glassed-in displays and thanked him for his time. Afterward, he stopped by Van Hyning's office, only to learn that the museum's misplaced set of ivory-bill eggs (not under Doe's authority) was still missing.

Probably frustrated, Tanner left Gainesville and drove west to Chiefland to meet James Turner, a local who had reported seeing an ivory-bill. Jim spent the evening with Turner and his wife playing Chinese Checkers. The next morning, Jim, Turner, and Turner's father went to Suwannee Hammock. Though he had decided the night before that Turner had probably seen a pileated, Jim still enjoyed the man's company. Turner's father, a local doctor, remembered seeing ivory-bills twelve to fifteen years earlier in the Suwannee Swamp below Vista and farther southeast along the Wekiva River in Gulf Hammock. In all, Tanner spent roughly a week—except for his rainy trip into Gainesville to look at Doe's egg collection—exploring the Suwannee Swamp and Gulf Hammock region.

"From Gulf Hammock westward along the coast there is a largely uninhabited, swampy country covering hundreds of square miles," Tanner noted. "Formerly ivory-bills were recorded more commonly in this region than elsewhere; now almost all of it has been logged over and there are few really good woods left for the birds." Still, he was optimistic about the bird's presence: "In the areas I hunted I found no signs of ivory-bills, but several natives reported seeing them within recent years, and it is probable that some ivory-bills are still present. The territory is very large and there are some small tracts of virgin and nearly inaccessible timber still standing." Jim estimated that because of the size of the available habitat, two pairs of ivory-bills could survive in the most remote stretches of the hammock and go largely undetected.

Tanner returned to Winter Park on Saturday, March 4, for a meeting of the Florida Audubon Society, where he gave a short talk on the food habits of ivory-billed woodpeckers. The following day, he rode with Dick Kuerzi and other Audubon members to Sanford for a boat trip up the St. Johns River to Lake Harney. Like Tanner, Kuerzi was a New Yorker visiting Florida. Cofounder of the Bronx County Bird Club in New York City—a group of Bronx kids just "nuts over birds"—he had published his observations several times in *The Auk*, the esteemed journal of the American Ornithologists' Union.

At 310 miles, the St. Johns River is the longest river in Florida. It winds through or borders twelve counties, flowing roughly parallel to the Atlantic Ocean along the eastern edge of the state. But the river's elevation-drop from the headwaters to the mouth is less than thirty feet, which gives the St. Johns a very slow flow rate: a third of a mile per hour. It is also one of the few waterways in North America that flows north. As Tanner observed, "The river wound thru open country, mostly dry pasture but with many ponds and sloughs, bordered by cabbage or hammock woods. . . . It was a fine day for a trip, clear and with a slight breeze. We saw about 60 species of birds, including some Black-necked Stilts. The country was too dry for many things."

From Sanford, Tanner drove north to Foley. It was his twenty-fifth birthday, and the one-year anniversary of the day he had banded the ivory-bill nestling in John's Bayou. Was the young bird still alive? Tanner would soon find out, but he wasn't quite finished with Florida. At Foley, Jim interviewed J. B. Royalls, a onetime game commissioner for the state. As Royalls was friendly and knowledgeable he and Jim had a long talk about ivory-bills. "Birds used to be west of the Wacissa River, between the river and the pine country in Wakulla County," Tanner wrote. "He [Royalls] last saw them about late winter of 1937, has not been able to find them since. The woods have been logged clean since then. He believes there used to be five pairs there." Royalls also told Jim that the only place he remembered seeing Carolina parakeets was in the Big Cypress around 1895.

On the gulf side of the state, the rivers west of the Suwannee are all located on the two-hundred-mile-long panhandle. Their waters eventually empty into the Gulf of Mexico. As Jim drove west, the Aucilla and its tributary, the Wacissa, would be the first system he encountered. Both rivers flow through karst limestone topography, which is filled with sinkholes, springs, and caves. Tanner had heard that the inland stretches of the Wacissa—a clear, spring-fed stream east of Tallahassee, just where the crook of the Florida panhandle begins—were the best places to look.

The morning of Tuesday, March 7, was bright and clear. The date marked a first for Tanner: he became airborne. Jim had arranged to fly from Tallahassee

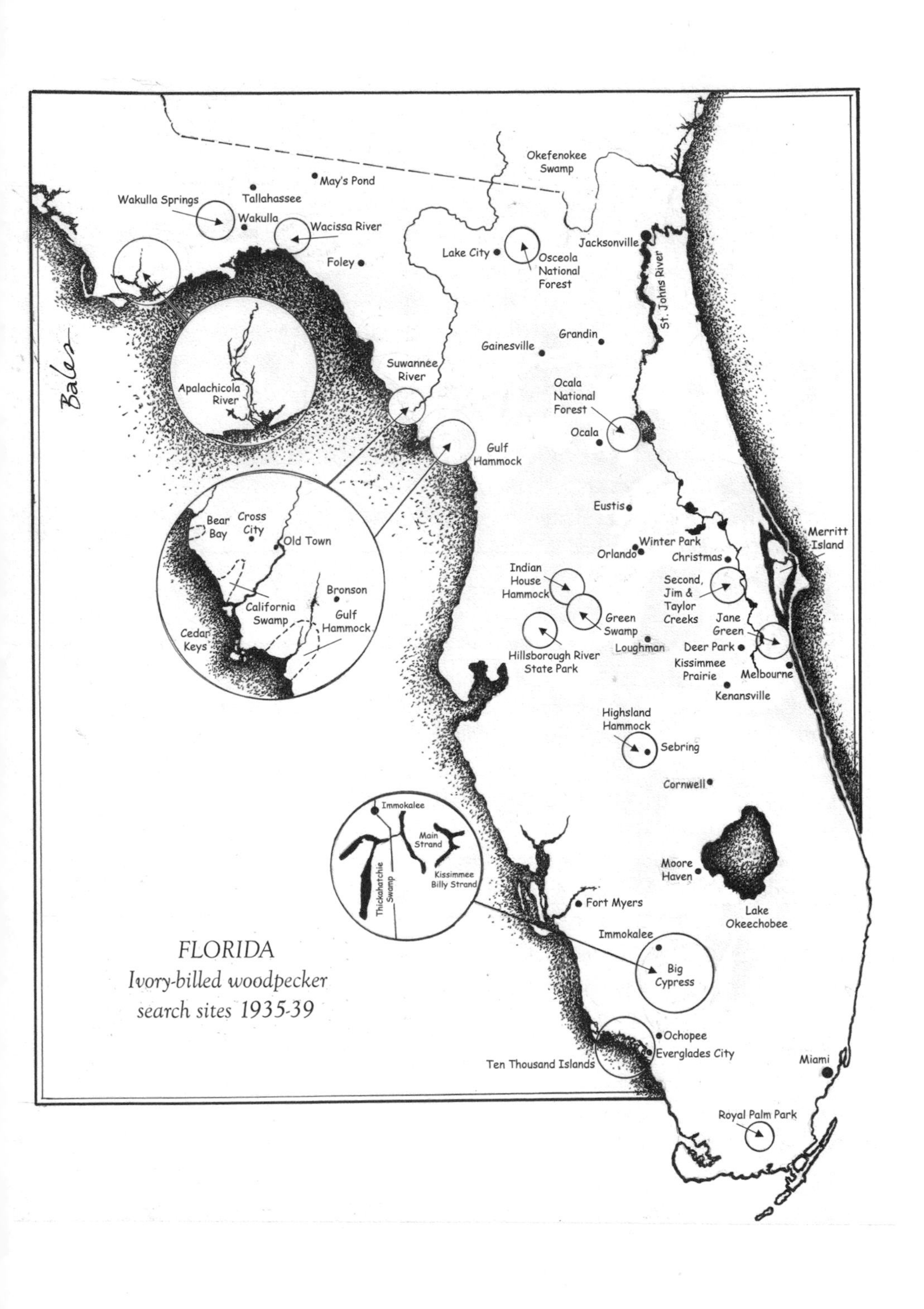

FLORIDA
Ivory-billed woodpecker search sites 1935-39

over Wacissa River bottomland to do reconnaissance from the air. "Objects and distances on the ground were easily recognizable," he recalled. "We hit the head of the Wacissa and turned down it. I quickly found I could recognize pine, cypress, hardwood, and from straight overhead—cabbage. Cut over timber could be recognized from overhead by logs, old tramlines. The best country unquestionably was from one to two miles west of the western sloughs, a country of heavy hammock and pines interlaced with sloughs." Tanner was even allowed to fly the plane on their way back to the airport: "It handled quite easily, although I hardly got used to the controls."

The trip cost Jim nine dollars—the equivalent, he noted, of two days' pay. But he considered it money well spent: "In a little over an hour, I had located the best area on the Wacissa, had an understanding of the surrounding region, had spotted a way to get into the place I wanted." Afterward, Tanner drove to Monticello, where he investigated reported ivory-bill sightings along the Pinhook River, a short distance west of the Wacissa River. With the aid of a local guide and the use of a "kicker"— a small boat with an underwater propeller to "kick" it through shallow water—Tanner entered the western sloughs of the Wacissa and later the Pinhook. The twelve-mile-long, slow-moving Wacissa is well-known for its large concentration of aquatic birds. In Jim's day, it was a paradise.

As Tanner explored the waters with his guide, ducks, mostly baldpates and widgeons, flocked in the wide places of the river, while turtles splashed into the water from their sunning places on logs. Interviews with locals along the way turned up no recent sightings of ivory-bills. The next day, hiking around the Wacissa's western sloughs, Tanner found that the big trees had already been removed. He concluded that there was "no likelihood of ivory-bills still being around that area."

Monday, March 13: Having gotten a good view of the Wacissa River from the air, Tanner elected to do the same over the Apalachicola Bottoms west of Tallahassee. Afterward, a visit to a nearby lumber company revealed that a section known as the "Texas Tract," on the west side of Brothers River, was one of the few remaining areas of old swamp timber. Located south of Willis Landing, it was known locally as Willis Swamp. When Jim attempted to investigate it, however, he encountered high water: the river completely covered the road. There was no getting into the swamp on foot, and the locals informed Tanner that it was "too thick to go in by boat." One man spoke of two giant woodpeckers in the area, one of them scarce.

Tanner had found drought conditions in south Florida, but here in the panhandle, the opposite prevailed. So Jim retreated and returned the next day to the lumber company, where he learned of another parcel of old woods, the Ben May Tract, that was still intact east of the river and accessible by car. Gathering more information about the area, he got encouraging news about some nearby ivory-bill sightings and was soon paddling through the flooded woodland in a borrowed boat. Two days of searching, however, produced no sign of ivory-bills, although the habitat looked right. High water made any sort of journey by foot impossible throughout the Apalachicola region, so Jim decided to move on and return in June.

Tanner spent the next few days tying up loose ends in Florida. He revisited Wakulla Springs, where he had spent so much time with Allen and Kellogg on his first trip to Florida in 1935, and then drove to Panama City, where he met with outdoorsman Roy Hallman, who spoke of a recent ivory-bill sighting in Apalachicola. (Years later, in July 1952, Hallman and photographer Sam Grimes would report seeing an ivory-bill in Wakulla County.)

With this, it was time to hit the road again. Jim had been in the Sunshine State for eleven weeks, and although he had not seen an ivory-bill, several places did look promising. To say that Florida was frustrating is perhaps an understatement. But science, especially field research, does not always yield positive results; sometimes all that one finds are tantalizing clues. Tanner still believed there were probably ghost birds in the state, but after three extensive searches—in 1935, 1937, and 1939—he never saw one.

As with the Santee swamps in South Carolina, Jim had spoken to many trustworthy, expert observers in Florida. The state also had places sufficiently untouched and remote to hide the woodpeckers. While he still hoped to find them here, that would have to wait. Growing anxious, he knew that 360 miles to the west, the Singer Tract ivory-bills should be beginning their nesting season. But two years of research had told him that their Tensas population was declining. Would they still be there? Jim had to find out.

Chapter 17

Finding Sonny Boy

The ivory-bill has frequently been described as a dweller of dark and gloomy swamps, has been associated with muck and murk, has been called a melancholy bird, but it is not that at all—the ivory-bill is a dweller of the tree tops and sunshine; it lives in the sun . . . in surroundings as bright as its own plumage.

—James T. Tanner

In mid-March 1939 much of what had once been the Czechoslovak Republic fell to Hitler's Germany. Moving with startling efficiency and meeting little resistance, German troops marched into Prague and unfurled the swastika from the onetime castle of the Bohemian kings. Crowds of Czech citizens filled the streets, watching their conquerors take over the public buildings and banks; a curfew was imposed on the city.

As the larger world became an increasingly dangerous place, Jim Tanner headed back to Louisiana. Starting in Pensacola, Florida, he made the drive to New Orleans in one day, passing through Pascagoula, Biloxi, and Gulfport on old Highway 90. It was Monday, March 21, the first day of spring. After a good night's sleep, Jim dropped by the office of Armand Daspit, director of Louisiana's Fur and Wildlife Division, to obtain a new permit to reenter the Singer Tract. He also learned that the permits would be curtailed because of demands that visitors were placing on the wardens. The word was getting out. Articles by Albert Brand in *Natural History* in 1936 and Arthur Allen in *National Geographic* in 1937 had alerted the world to where ivory-billed woodpeckers could be found. Both accounts detailed Cornell's rediscovery of the lost species, and the expedition's team, including Tanner, had achieved a certain amount of notoriety. After having lunch with state biologist James Gowanloch, Jim drove to Baton Rouge and once again looked up George Lowery at LSU. The question to both men was the same: Had either of them heard any recent news of ivory-bills? Unfortunately, nothing new had been reported since Jim had left the state.

The following day, Tanner drove north to Tallulah, finding that the small town hadn't changed since the previous summer: "The same people [were] doing the same things." One exception, however, was J. J. Kuhn. The able backwoodsman was in good health and spirits but would be unable to assist Jim this year. He was no longer a game warden. This loss must have disappointed Tanner, for the two men had become very close.

Kuhn was a man of integrity whose word was his bond. Explaining the circumstances that cost J.J. his job, Kuhn's daughter, Edith Whitehead, recalled that her father "had nothing but contempt for people who believed they were privileged above others." As she remembered,

> Mason Spencer came to my father and told him to "get lost" from a particular area, because Governor [Richard] Leche wanted to bring a big hunting party into the Tensas because of its abundant game.
>
> My father informed him he'd do no such thing. He was wearing the badge as officer of the law in the state and that Spencer should inform the governor that if he came that he'd be arrested just like anyone else breaking the law. Spencer was outraged but he delivered the message.

The governor shelved his plans for a hunting trip in the Tensas, but he did order the state to cut Kuhn's salary. Unable to support his family, Kuhn was forced to resign and later found a job as a pecan plantation manager. (The next year, Governor Leche's life also changed. In 1940 a mail-fraud conviction made him the first Louisiana governor to be sentenced to prison.)

Kuhn had also lost his son, J.J. Jr., to a freak mishap in which he was accidentally shot by a friend handling a loaded revolver. The loss of both his son and his job as game warden had profoundly affected him. He must have been deeply disappointed that he could no longer assist Jim in his research. "Tanner was totally at home in the woods and extremely able to take care of himself," declared Whitehead. "My father greatly respected his integrity. It was obvious to Dad that this young man truly loved the woods and was a dedicated scientific researcher. He loved him like a son."

Jim soon spoke with three new game wardens assigned to the region—Jim Parker, Gus Willet, and Sam Denton—who reported that ivory-bills, two males and one female, had been seen off and on all winter in John's Bayou. Could this be the same three that Jim had watched for months the year before? He was anxious to find out. The next day, after buying groceries and driving into a new camp off Sharkey Road, he confirmed that it was, spotting the woodpeckers off what he called the "old Tank Road" near John's Bayou. The young male traveling with the older pair was "still sporting quite conspicuously his band," the same one Tanner had placed on him a little over a year before. For the first time in his notes, Tanner referred to the bird as "Sonny Boy." The young ivory-bill's flight drew his attention: "Once during the time I noticed a swooping, pileated-like flight."

Jim continued, "He chased one pair of pileateds away from their workings several times, flying at them when they were pecking, then pecking himself a little in the same place. The pileateds gave way silently, but called and scolded some later." This observation is of note because normally the two species coexist, working on separate trees. Later in the afternoon, Jim staked out the old ash tree roost and waited until it was quite late. But the ivory-bills did not appear. Where were they now spending the night?

"Observing birds in their natural habitats," writes animal behavior professor Tim Birkhead, "is time-consuming and involves considerable patience, for often there are long hours in which nothing much happens." Jim certainly knew the meaning of long hours, for he had put in a lot of them during the past two years. That evening he stayed at the new camp, which consisted of two cabins, one much larger than the other. Wardens Parker, Willet, and Denton occupied one, along with Jesse Laird, a local woodsman. Jim moved into the smaller of the two. The camp would be his home for the next two months.

On Saturday, March 25, Tanner woke up early and walked down the old Tank Road, looping around to Methiglum Lake. He saw no ivory-bills. Tanner was in familiar territory. It was his fourth visit in five years. Mid-morning, he hiked the high ground to John's Bayou and located Sonny Boy almost immediately south of the old ash tree roost holes. Jim also found quite a bit of sign in the vicinity of the 1938 nest site. If ivory-bills were hard to find throughout their known range—and after weeks and weeks of searching, Tanner had proved they were—in John's Bayou they were like manna from heaven, there for anyone to see.

In the 1930s another bird species had also become somewhat difficult to find. The wild turkey was gone from most of its historic range, a victim of overhunting. The last reported observation of America's premier game bird in Connecticut came in 1813, in Vermont in 1842, in Massachusetts in 1851, in Ohio in 1878, and in Michigan in 1897. As settlers moved west, the flocks that once numbered in the thousands had disappeared.

They were still in Louisiana, however. "About two o'clock it started to thunder in the southwest," Jim noted in his account of March 25. "I sat down beside a big gum for a rest and to listen, when I heard a turkey gobbling a little ways behind me, gobbling apparently in answer to the thunder. I had a piece of cane in my pocket, so I took it out and yelped to the gobbler. He gobbled four or five times in the same place, and I answered each time. He was a big heavy bird, with a blue head and a deep chestnut tail."

After an all-night rain that filled the woods with new water, Tanner left his borrowed cabin before daylight to revisit the 1938 nest tree. As he approached, he heard ivory-bills; then he saw them—a male and a female. Thinking it was a mated pair, he watched the two birds go through their morning routine, in time noticing that the male had a shiny metallic leg band. It was Sonny Boy. The young bird was still apparently following his mother. The pair's demeanor surprised him:

> The female led most of the time. Twice when near Sonny Boy she tried to fight him and drive him off, but he would just move a little bit and then sulk. Once they were feeding on the trunk of a long dead striped oak. The female dug both circular and oblong holes in the semi-punky sapwood, apparently following the mines of borers and with some success. The young bird moved around more, pecking and poking into old diggings.
>
> Sonny Boy's plumage seems to be exactly that of an adult male, except that there is one primary tipped with white. His actions and voice are like those of an adult, except for his trying to feed in old workings of both ivory-bills and pileateds.

Sam Denton had seen three birds in the area just two weeks before. But where was the senior male? Was he tucked away incubating eggs? Or feeding a nestling?

The rain the night before had added fresh water to the bayou, but it was drier than Tanner had ever seen it at that time of the year. Only the deepest slashes held water, and all of the small bayous were virtually dry. It was early spring; trees were beginning to leaf out. The haw had finished blooming, and the sweet gums and oaks were about half green. After spending the morning in the woods, Jim walked to Tallulah. That night it rained heavily once again; perhaps, he noted, it was making up for lost time.

The next day, Tanner located three ivory-bills feeding together east of John's Bayou, very near the same location where he had found the two birds the day before. At one point the adult male flew away quickly, and twice Jim saw the adult female trying to chase Sonny Boy away, indicating that she was perhaps getting ready to raise a new family. Or had they already started to nest, and if so, where?

The following day, Tanner got his answer. About one o'clock in the afternoon, he located the mated pair together. The male held a big grub in its bill: "With some hesitation and calling he went to a tall, dead oak stub, disappeared around the other side, and when he reappeared he had no grub." Not wanting to alarm the adult bird, Jim waited. When things settled down, he moved slowly to the other side of the oak and found the nest hole. "The male then came to the tree, one young called and stuck out its head," he noted. A short time later, the female flew into the tree and fed the nestling as well. At three o'clock, both parents were near the nest tree; Sonny Boy flew in and "kiented," dodging as the female tried once again to chase him away. For the rest of the afternoon, Tanner watched the comings and goings of the pair: "The nest is in a dead stripped oak stub, branchless, somewhat punky, two feet at the base and ten inches at the top. Hole is egg-shaped, faces south and is about 65 feet up. Top of the stub has small hole and several diggings, much like red-belly work, which frequently lights there. Nest is located about three-quarters mile north of Sharkey Road, 200 yards east of John's Bayou." (Today, stripped oak is known as Nuttall's oak.)

In terms of ivory-bill research, John's Bayou was like the mythical El Dorado, the Lost City of Gold. Nest sites were located there four out of four years. Without the information collected by the Cornell team in 1935 and by Jim Tanner in the years from 1937 through 1939, very little would be known about the species' day-to-day nesting behavior. The immense value of John's Bayou was not lost on one dedicated birder.

Many amateur bird enthusiasts have a singular passion: to see all the species they possibly can. They keep "life lists": the sum total of all the different birds they have located in the wild. In the 1930s Jerome Kessler was one of those "life-listers," but to add to his list, he had to travel widely on a small budget from his home base in Philadelphia. Kessler spent considerable time hitchhiking and riding buses around the country looking for new birds. The three rarest birds he hoped to find were the California condor, trumpeter swan, and ivory-billed woodpecker. By 1938 only the last remained unseen. When word of the rediscovery of the ivory-bill began to appear in nature magazines—Kessler read about the Singer Tract in *Bird Lore*—he decided to head for Louisiana. After all, now that he knew where to look for the ghost bird, how hard could it be?

His first trip to the Singer Tract ended in failure, Kessler reported, because of "the damp sweltering heat, innumerable ticks and mosquitoes." Summer is not the best time to visit the swamp. In late March 1939, Kessler made another attempt to search for "the rarest, the most elusive of them all." He learned in Tallulah that the ivory-bill expert Jim Tanner was in the vicinity, and he got directions on where he might be found. "Sharkey Road cuts a wide swath through a dense hardwood forest," Kessler wrote about his trek into camp. "Being unpaved, it is almost impossible to drive over after a rain. It also makes walking very hard. The earth turns to a thick, sticky gumbo mud, which has a tendency to accumulate on one's shoes. Muck accumulates until each shoe weighs three or four pounds."

Not finding Tanner or even the camp on his first day and with threatening skies and fierce swarms of mosquitoes surrounding him, Kessler was forced to sleep in the open on the ground. After an overnight soaking rain, he continued his search the following day. Rain remained in the area, but in the clear light of morning, Jim was easier to locate, still at home in the small cabin.

"After breakfast," Kessler wrote, "Tanner led me along an obscure trail through the dense thicket-infested wilderness. We covered about a mile or so when suddenly Tanner's hand shot up, signaling silence. Somewhere from the dense maze of woods, brush and thickets came a peculiar sound, a sound that might have emanated from a small cheap New Year's Eve horn, but no great music ever sounded better to me. It was a sound somewhat similar to that of the call of a red-breasted nuthatch but more metallic and much louder—not at all like the pileated woodpecker."

The duo found all four birds were in the area. The adult male and female were bringing food to the nestling, while Sonny Boy tagged along nearby. During the intervals they were away, Jim began to drive spikes into a neighboring tree to set up a blind high off the ground, but he injured himself, driving a locust thorn deep into his left knee. By afternoon, it was too swollen and stiff for him to continue climbing so he limped back to the cabin. It was the only real injury Tanner received during his entire three-year search.

Kessler spent the next few days with Tanner. The weather was beautiful: blue skies and no rain. After a day of rest, Tanner's knee had improved enough for him and Kessler to return to the nest site. The mated pair soon came in, bringing food to their young one. Sonny Boy was still in tow. During the older birds' absences, Jim returned to work on the blind similar to the one the Cornell team had constructed in 1935. By late afternoon he had spikes two-thirds of the way up the tree.

Returning to the nest tree the following day, Tanner continued his work. Both men noted the agitation the ivory-bills displayed when a Cooper's hawk flew into a neighboring tree. After the adults chased the *Accipiter* away, they settled back into their feeding routine. Jim finished the blind in the early afternoon. "It is in a stripped oak about 15 feet from the nest tree," Tanner recorded later. "I had planned to put the blind on the same level as the nest, but when I got near the top I found that the wood was a little punky there, so I contented myself with it about 15 feet below the level of the nest." In this case, "punky" means spongy—wood too long dead to hold a spike. His labor aroused the curiosity of the nestling: "It spends much of its time looking out the hole; it watched me most of the time I was working on the blind. It looks like the other young I have seen, except that there is a small white spot on the forehead."

Having accomplished his mission, Jerome Kessler left the Singer Tract to pursue other birds. Meanwhile, rain returned, keeping Jim in camp.

Wednesday, April 5: Although it was cloudy, with rain still a threat, Tanner returned to the nest site and climbed the dead oak to the blind. He spent much of the morning literally up a tree, ignored by the parents as they came and went. The nestling called loudly and continuously when its parents were in the vicinity. In addition to food calls, it made vocalizations that resembled those of the adults. It would not be in the hole much longer. To be this close again to a young ivory-bill, closer than most other people had ever been, must have thrilled Tanner, especially after weeks on the road. The parent woodpeckers came and went, paying little attention to Jim's camouflaged viewing perch. When he climbed down the tree at mid-day, they scolded him as he walked away. That afternoon Tanner searched the area south of Sharkey Road, hoping to find signs of other ivory-bills. He found none.

Now that Jim had located a nesting pair for the third year in a row, it was time to fan out and search as much of the Singer Tract as he could in the next three weeks. Since Kuhn was unable to help, Tanner contracted with Jesse Laird, who had worked several years in the tract working for local cattlemen. That evening Laird joined Jim at the cabin. A good woodsman who knew the lay of the land, he quickly learned enough about ivory-bills and their roosting, nesting, and feeding sign to assist Tanner.

At daybreak Tanner and Laird went to the nest site, and Jim showed his new acolyte what he should look for in other parts of the tract. When the tutelage ended, Jim hiked to Alligator Bayou to investigate some areas he had not searched before. Finding nothing of note, he returned to the cabin late in the day. At about three o'clock, warden Willet and Martin Curtler, a birding friend of Alexander Sprunt, showed up. Curtler had published an article on lark sparrows in *The Auk* a few years before. As with Kessler the previous week, he was there to see an ivory-bill, and Tanner wasted little time in obliging him. They went immediately through the woods to John's Bayou, where they found both parents in the area. "Curtler got a good look at both birds and quite a thrill," noted Tanner, whose reputation was beginning to spread. If you wanted to see an ivory-bill, you had to find Jim Tanner. That evening the pair walked to Mason Spenser's cabin, where they spent the night with several others.

In the annals of ivory-bill lore, Friday, April 7, 1939, was a memorable day, although it began rather plainly. It was a cold, cloudy morning. Leaving Spenser's cabin early, Tanner and Curtler searched Greenlea Bend between Turkey and Rainey brakes, finding nothing of note. Kuhn had seen a lone ivory-bill in the vicinity in July 1937. Afterward, Tanner and Curtler parted, with Jim returning to Sharkey Road and camp. Something about not finding ivory-bills in one place made actually seeing them in another more alluring, an affirmation that the species did still exist. It was early afternoon by the time Jim reached the nest site at John's Bayou. The skies were beginning to clear. The adult female yapped at Jim until he climbed the tree and disappeared into the blind. Then she settled down. For the next several hours, the parent woodpeckers came and went at regular intervals—sometimes together, sometimes separately—feeding the nestling while Tanner finished a roll of color film he had in his camera. (This is the third mention in Tanner's notes of color photos of an ivory-bill, but only one session—apparently this one—survives.) The parents' behavior changed late in the afternoon. The male had been away for a while. The female was perched and stayed that way for quite some time when she began to call and pound single raps. At half past four, the male flew in with no food and landed high up in the nest tree. He also began to pound.

"A few minutes later," Jim recorded, "I suddenly heard a whistle of wings and the young bird passed the blind, flew on a downward slant to a tree about 20 yards from the nest, where it lit against the trunk. It had left the nest without any warning or preliminary climbing around." Jim was fully aware that he had just witnessed the nestling fledge: "The adults flew to the same tree, and then the male went to the nest, looked in, went in and stayed a minute or more, then came out and flew to the tree the young was in. Female went to the young and apparently fed it."

But the excitement wasn't over.

"Sonny Boy suddenly came in, the first time I had seen him in several days," Tanner wrote. With this, Jim knew that the blind was useless. The young bird would never return to the nest hole. As he started to dismantle the blind and climb down, Tanner was suddenly uncovered, fully visible to the ivory-bill family. The woodpeckers quickly showed their agitation. With the new fledgling exposed, its parents were on a heightened state of alert: "The three old birds came around me, yapping, scolding, pounding, making short flights from tree to tree. Male went twice to the nest hole. Young made its second flight." The canopy around the blind became charged with excited, downright fussy ghost birds, except these weren't apparitions.

Tanner vividly recalled the moment in an article he wrote years later: "In their short, excited flights they occasionally came to perches within a few yards of mine. It was too much to have three adult ivory-billed woodpeckers shouting and knocking so nearby, glaring at me from their yellow-irised eyes, while I straddled the crotch of a tree some 40 feet from the ground; for the first and only time in my life there were too many ivory-bills too near."

Jim once more concealed himself in the blind, thus quieting the birds. The adults soon rejoined the youngster, which moved into the small branches of an ash tree. "The adults first tried to entice him away from there, but he only sat and thinly yapped," Jim recorded in his notes. "Female came once and offered food, but he had trouble handling himself among the twigs and small branches and would not feed."

The parent birds spent the next several minutes trying to entice the fledging to follow them. As Tanner observed, "Sonny Boy and the adults went to the tree with the young, all chorused a loud 'kient-kient . . .' and then Sonny Boy left going north." The parent birds followed, stopping to call, but the alarmed fledging seemed to want to remain, unsure of its next move. Flight can be a hard thing to master, especially when it's all so new. With the entire winged family obviously distracted, Jim climbed down the dead oak to leave the bayou in the gathering darkness. It had been a good day.

On Saturday, April 8, Tanner elected not to disturb the John's Bayou family, giving them a day of peace to adjust to their new roles. Jim and Jesse went south to the Titepaper region, inspecting it thoroughly. The pair found some fresh ivory-bill sign and a fair amount of old on the eastern part of the ridges from Alligator Flat to below Boggy Slough.

The next morning was bright and sunny. Tanner and Laird returned to John's Bayou, and while Jesse cut down the nest tree, Jim went to look for the birds, locating them roughly a quarter-mile to the north. The parent ivory-bills and Sonny Boy yapped at him quite a bit. "The three started to move away, I followed, then the young yapped and I found him, alive and active," Jim recorded.

Afterward, Tanner returned to the cut nest tree, which now lay on the forest floor. An examination of the hole revealed about two quarts of sawdust and small chips, a few insect fragments, feather sheaths, one wing, and two body feathers. Tanner then measured the size of the opening, along with the depth and width of the cavity.

Late in the day, Tanner and Laird went into town for supplies. Tanner tried to drive the car back into camp but twice got bogged down in deep ruts along the way. And more rain was coming. The best time to search for ivory-bills was during the first four months of the year. The trees were without leaves, and the birds nested, remaining loyal to one site. In the swamp, however, these months were usually rainy. The more it rained, the harder it was to get around—a continuing source of frustration.

The Titepaper ridges posed a mystery to Jim. Tanner and Laird visited the region several times during the next few days as the weather allowed, finding some feeding sign but no roost or nest holes. Tanner wrote, "The situation is puzzling: Where are the birds that were apparently there last year? And where are the birds that have been making the sign?" In the previous two years, Tanner felt that a least one pair of ivory-bills lived somewhere in the Titepaper–Mack's Bayou region. In 1938 he found evidence and heard enough reports to indicate that one mated pair, two young, and an unmated male lived in that general area. The unattached male became known as Mack's Bayou Pete. On Saturday, Tanner borrowed Charlie—the same four-dollar horse he once owned—from Sam Denton, so that he and Jesse could travel on horseback to Mack's, a little farther south than Titepaper. Once there, they separated. Late in the morning, Tanner got lucky.

"I was riding along the white line, I heard a bird call," he noted. "I went to it and found a single male bird with some of the longer primaries tipped with white, certainly making it look to be Mack's Bayou Pete. The voice did not sound like Pete used to sound. He made two flights southwest and then another one and got away from me." Tanner continued in the same direction as Pete's last flight, and he found the solitary ivory-bill a short time later west of Largent's Bayou and east of what he called "the blue line" (the property line, perhaps, of the old Sharkey Plantation).

"He called quite a bit, did much rapping and pounding as he had done in the morning, sat and preened himself some," Tanner wrote. Pete flew again, and Tanner followed but had little luck finding him until he returned to the original location—a quarter-mile north of the old Foster Road and a quarter-mile west of the white line—where Jim watched him until he flew away again. Once an ivory-bill decides to leave an area, they are gone in swift direct flights that may cover miles. At the end of day, Tanner and Laird reunited. Jesse had found nothing in the country towards Hamilton's Bayou.

Sunday, April 16: After a week of beginning their days at 4:00 AM and dodging the rain as best they could, Tanner and Laird slept in, not rising until six. Spring was advancing rapidly: most of the trees had completely leafed out and migrants were arriving daily. Some even had started to nest. The rush to reproduce was on, and with the change of seasons, the ticks and mosquitoes were also plentiful. Both men left the swamp by way of John's Bayou, where they were unable to locate the ivory-bill family. The next day they returned to camp, and by late afternoon Tanner and Laird were back at the old ash roost trees. Sonny Boy was the first to arrive, followed in time by the rest of the family.

Tanner's frustration over Titepaper and Mack's Bayou continued. Outside of John's Bayou, this area had emerged as the best place to find nesting ivory-bills in the Singer Tract. Tanner and Laird spent the next two weeks thoroughly searching the region as Tanner had done with Kuhn the year before. They found fresh feeding sign but nothing else. One day, Jesse came across Pete flying across Mack's Bayou near what was known as the old Block Trail. The lone male made a few short hops that Laird could follow before he disappeared on a long flight to the south. But where was Pete spending the night? Where were the roost holes? By the end of the week, Tanner felt that the bird, or birds unknown, were coming into the area from another location, but if so, from where?

One day, Tanner rode as far south as Mills Bayou all the way to the river, but as with the year before, he decided that the habitat just wasn't right. At one point the understory became so thick that he had to dismount and lead the horse through the dense tangle of vines and bushes. "Nothing looked good anywhere in that area," he recorded.

On Sunday, April 23, Tanner and Laird left camp at 4:00 AM to go to town but not before a visit with the John's Bayou family. Jim located the entire family—both parents, Sonny Boy, and the young fledging, which he had nicknamed Baby Bunting—after each had left its separate roost hole. They were all together on a recently dead pecan just as the sun hit the tops of the trees. "The young bird is growing rapidly and flies strongly," Tanner observed. "His crest has lengthened from his head, is still blunted; tail is getting pointed; eye in certain light appears light. His voice is almost like the adults, but still is weak, and he gives the same food call when approached by parents. He pecks some himself now."

By the end of the month, Jim had decided that no pair of ivory-bills now lived in the Titepaper–Mack's Bayou region. In 1938 Tanner and Kuhn had found freshly excavated holes and a lot of recent feeding sign. And then on June 15 of that year, Kuhn had found a pair of ivory-bills in the region with two juveniles. At the time the fledglings appeared to be younger than Sonny Boy. But those four birds now seemed to be gone. Pete the bachelor was still there, but he wasn't always easy to find and may have been roosting in another sector. Their loss did not bode well for the ghost birds' future in the Singer Tract. Perhaps the highly mobile woodpeckers had moved somewhere else. This again posed the question of range: how far do ivory-bills roam? Or perhaps they had been shot. The steadfast Kuhn was no longer on duty guarding their domain. Tanner's pace quickened. In his search for answers, he was in a race against time in more ways than one.

On May 1, Jim began the new month by focusing on the other sections of the Singer Tract to the west. Recent mornings had been cool, but afternoon temperatures moderated. It was pleasant and hadn't rained for several days. The woods were drying out, becoming lush. Mosquitoes and ticks were everywhere.

And as the canopy leafed out, the ivory-bills became harder and harder to locate. In the afternoon, Tanner and Laird crossed the river to Hunter's Bend. They planned to stay two days. After a good night's sleep, Jim and Jesse got an early start.

"In the morning we walked over Hunter's Bend," Tanner wrote, "going pretty well over it as the new log roads made traveling faster. We found no recent sign. Altho there was a little sign of borers in the trees in the newer cutover, woodpeckers were still quite common there. In the older cutover, done about 18 months ago, woodpeckers were practically absent. It certainly did not look like the same place." In 1937 Tanner had believed that one pair of ivory-bills lived on Hunter's Bend. After the logging that began a short time later, however, none appeared to be left.

In the afternoon they crossed the river and scrutinized Dishroom Bend farther south: "The only sign was good and quite recent, a gum tree well peeled, on the second blue line a little north of Eagle Brake. There were a lot of it on that tree, but I could find nothing else." Tanner had found scattered feeding sign the year before on the bend west of the old Sharkey Plantation; Drew Denton had reported seeing an ivory-bill there in 1938. But this year the peeled gum was the only promising field marking.

Over the next two weeks, Tanner and Laird investigated the other western sections of the Singer Tract, including Greenlea and Andrew's bends. They found bits of scattered bark peeled from trees, the most promising south of Rainey Lake on Greenlea. It was the only location with quite a bit of concentrated feeding sign; Tanner thus concluded that the single male living there the previous year was probably still working the area. The other random sign sprinkled here and there perhaps had come from any one of the remaining birds traveling out of its home range. At least that's what Tanner conjectured. During these two weeks, he kept his field notes concise, reflecting the lack of anything positive to report. He was putting in the time but with diminishing returns. In 1937 Tanner believed that five mated pairs inhabited the region, but by 1938 that number had dropped to only three pairs. And now after six weeks, he had found evidence of only one pair: the reliable John's Bayou birds. Most alarming was the possibility that only one reproducing female remained. All the other birds seemed to be males. Knowledge can be bittersweet. By this time Jim had become the leading authority on the ivory-bill, but he knew that his expertise was, as poet Robert Frost might say, of "a diminished thing."

On Sunday, May 14, Tanner and Laird left the cabin a little before 4:00 AM and arrived at the John's Bayou ash roosting trees about forty-five minutes later. On this cool morning, Jesse positioned himself near the old roost hole, while

Jim moved farther east. One by one, the ivory-bill family stirred, calling from separate locations, and began to move in a loose group toward the southeast and Sharkey Road. The parent birds and Baby Bunting landed on a sweet gum with several dead limbs. In time, Sonny Boy joined them, and all four birds fed continually for half an hour. Completing the remarkable natural moment, a pileated woodpecker landed in the same tree and drummed.

As Jim observed, "The young bird is almost full size; its tail is a little bit short and stubby crest a bit short and blunt, all black; bill is pale ivory; eye is getting light. It gives a subdued food call when near an adult, and I saw the male feed it several times. It pecked some at the edges of scalings." The stubby black crest could mean that Baby Bunting was a much-needed female, but Tanner wasn't comfortable drawing conclusions about its sex until it had developed a bit more.

Tanner's time in Louisiana was almost over. There was little more to be learned and other places he needed to investigate. Before he could leave, he repaired the cabin (he actually called it a shack) that he had been staying in since March. Being handy, Tanner had promised to fix the floor and roof in lieu of paying rent. Late one day, he rode down to the trees he had girdled as part of a dying tree survey begun the year before. Some of the trees already showed signs of beetle damage but little woodpecker work. Not enough time had passed. After an unproductive trip south to D'Arbonne Swamp in Ouachita Parish, he returned to Sharkey Road, but recent rains had turned it into its old mushy self. He decided to walk into camp for one last look. Late in the day, he borrowed Laird's horse and rode to the roost holes, where he waited for the ivory-bills. To the southeast at about six o'clock, he heard one bird pound and three call: two in one tree, one in another.

"I located the tree the one was in, heard it pounding," Tanner noted, "but try as I might, I could not see the bird thru the thick foliage. They must have left there and flown off silently, for I heard nothing else. It was a poor observation for what may be my last one of an ivory-bill, but the leaves are so thick and the birds so quiet that not much else can be expected."

He had difficulty letting go, in part because he knew his findings were so troubling. The ivory-billed woodpeckers rediscovered by the Cornell team in 1935 barely existed only four years later. Instead of leaving the Tensas, he remained another day, walking down to Titepaper by way of Alligator Ridge one more time. Tanner still hoped to discover some evidence of the missing mated pair from that sector. But after hours of looking, he found nothing. It was time to move on.

Chapter 18

I Go Pogo

It was not until many years later, after the swamps had been reduced to shambles, that appreciation grew for the trees. By then the snorting steam skidders had literally torn the swamps to pieces.

—Herbert L. Stoddard

On Friday, May 26, Jim Tanner left Tallulah—and the John's Bayou ivory-bill family—for what he believed was the last time. His hope of seeing another *Campephilus principalis* now lay elsewhere. And after almost three years of searching, he knew just how difficult they were to find. Having been away from home on this trip since November 16, he was ready to return. But first he had to do a little backtracking and tie up a few loose ends

Tanner was most curious about the Pascagoula Swamp in Jackson County, Mississippi, but learned from biologist Tom Burleigh that the last reported sightings there were made by J. D. Corrington in 1921. The friendly Burleigh also gave Jim the name of an old "riverman" who knew the swamp and might have some anecdotal information.

It rained off and on the next morning. Tanner traveled to Vancleave, Mississippi, and down an old road into the swampy bottomlands of the lower Pascagoula River, eventually reaching the fishing camp of Burleigh's riverman, an old-timer named Goff, who had trapped and hunted in the region for over forty years. He had never seen an ivory-bill despite pointedly looking for them ever since Corrington's 1921 report had sparked his interest. Tanner also learned that just about all of the forests had since been cut over. Jim pressed on, arriving back at Apalachicola on Florida's panhandle on May 30. The water levels were much lower than they had been earlier, and the summer heat had arrived. The trees were lush and green, the canopies full.

"To view the Apalachicola's forested floodplain and high bluffs merely from a highway crossing is to forego great opportunities to observe its rich wildlife and rare plants. Reptiles and amphibians alone account for 108 species," writes naturalist John V. Dennis, who also notes that it was one of the last strongholds for both the Carolina parakeet and the ivory-bill. But in 1939, could the elusive woodpecker still be in the region?

At Willis Landing, on the east side of the bottomland, Tanner met Jack Tillman, a woods foreman who offered to take him into the swamp in his motorboat. It was a pleasant trip that turned up no signs of ivory-bills. That night, Tanner stayed at Wewahitchka, due south of Dead Lakes. Jim ultimately spent a week in the area, interviewing everyone he could and taking long walks and boat trips whenever possible. He returned several times to Willis Landing for good reason. All the ivory-bill reports he had received were from the uncut hammock of Willis Swamp and nearby locations.

Exploring Willis Swamp (also known as the Texas Tract) took up much of his time: "It was about one and a half miles wide at the northern end, narrows southward until about three miles south where it is only a margin between the pineland and the river swamp. While I saw no birds, I did find some holes and feeding sign, characteristic of ivory-bill work. Birds could easily have been missed because of the lateness of the season, hot weather, and thick foliage."

With a local who owned a motorboat, Tanner also spent two days exploring the Brothers River section from its mouth to Hooper Lake and Brickyard Landing. Jim ranked the Apalachicola region just below the Santee in the amount of old bottomland forest still standing at the time. Some of its virgin timber, he wrote, "present good habitat for woodpeckers." He further noted, "The lower part of the Apalachicola swamp has been almost completely neglected by competent naturalists and ornithologists and very little is known about it. Several natives and hunters in that region have reported seeing ivory-bills, some of them knowing the birds and some satisfactorily describing them."

In the end, Tanner concluded, "I do not feel that an adequate search of the area has yet been made; for at the time I visited, it was a poor season to hunt for ivory-bills." Still he remained optimistic about the possibility of the birds' presence: "There is adequate range for two pairs, or four individuals." But this could very soon change: "The Texas tract, which includes the virgin part of the Willis Swamp, is being cut over now, although they have not yet reached the swamp or hammock. This is not as serious a threat to the existence of whatever ivory-bills are there as it may seem; three of the places where ivory-bills have been reported are cut-over, showing that the birds can find a living somewhere in the large swamp area there." Though Tanner would have loved to spend more time in Florida's panhandle, he now had to investigate rumors of an ivory-bill sighting in Georgia's Okefenokee Swamp.

The swampy forestlands of south Georgia had been logged for decades. Before the advent of more modern railroad technologies, however, the trees had only been cut along the Savannah, Altamaha, St. Mary's, and Satilla rivers in the southeast portion of the Peach State. Logs were cut, dragged to the river by mules or oxen, tied together, and floated to mills in the coastal cities. It was arduous work and the operations small.

The vast Okefenokee is roughly the size of Rhode Island. The forested swamp covers 438,000 acres, and 370,000 acres of that are considered open wetlands. Principally, it's a huge peat-filled bog formed in a natural depression that was once part of the ocean floor. Its bottom is sand-covered, with organic peat beds up to fifteen feet deep. Masses of peat create floating islands that can be unstable. Consequently, the Native American Timucuan people called the watery region *Okefenoka,* meaning "Land of the Trembling Earth." Within the Okefenokee are islands, lakes, prairies, small hammocks, and forests. An average of fifty inches of rainfall replenishes the swamps each year.

In 1891 the Suwannee Canal Company purchased 238,120 acres of the Okefenokee Swamp from the state of Georgia. The goal was to build a canal and drain the swamp to create sugar cane, rice, and cotton plantations. Captain Henry Jackson and his crews spent three years digging the Suwannee Canal 11.5 miles into the swamp, but the economic recession of 1893–96 led to the company's bankruptcy and eventual sale of the land to Charles Hebard in 1901.

The Hebard family of Philadelphia had made a fortune cutting white pine in the forests of upper Michigan, but by the late 1890s work there had begun to slow, as most of the big trees had been cut. Like other timber barons, Charles Hebard looked to the South. Expanding rail lines and innovative logging equipment like narrow-gauge engines and "skidders" (steam-powered cable and winch devices built on rail cars) made logging inaccessible regions more feasible. The skidders could be sent on "dummy lines," or dead-end spur lines, deep into the forests. The powerful winches dragged or skidded downed logs over great distances to waiting rail cars.

This new technology made the inland forests of the Okefenokee accessible to logging, and there was money to be made. After buying a significant portion of the Okefenokee for $175,000, the Hebards employed an average of three hundred men a year to harvest the big trees within their holdings. More than 431 million board feet of timber were removed. By the 1930s, two outside forces began to eye the Okefenokee: one wanted to develop it, while the other wished to protect the swampland as a wildlife preserve. Ultimately, the latter group won, and the Hebards sold their 292,979 acres for $400,000 to the federal government, which placed the swampland under the control of the U.S. Biological Survey. A onetime lawyer named John M. Hopkins, who had helped survey the region for the Heberds, was named as its first game manager. He knew the swamp and its inhabitants well.

Historically, there were several accounts of ivory-billed woodpeckers in the Okefenokee Swamp. The oldest was a specimen collected by S. C. Dinwiddie in 1860. Having heard rumors that the ghost birds might still be in the area, Tanner was told to seek out Hopkins as well as Sam Mizell, who had acted as a local guide during the Okefenokee survey and who now helped patrol the protected area.

On Friday, June 9, after an overnight trip to Herbert Stoddard's, Tanner located Hopkins at his office in Waycross. Hopkins had not sighted an ivory-bill in the area since about 1915. Nevertheless, he gave Tanner directions and permission to travel into the swamp. He also told Jim where to find Sam Mizell, and Tanner wasted no time locating the Okefenokee patrolman at his cabin in the swamp. Like Hopkins, Mizell had not seen an ivory-bill in the region since between 1910 and 1915. In 1912, in fact, Mizell had accidentally shot and crippled a male ivory-bill on Craven's Hammock and had given the injured bird to one of the Hebards, who kept it alive for a time. After it died, it was mounted and eventually became part of the permanent collection of the Academy of Natural Sciences of Philadelphia, the Hebards' hometown. It is apparently the only ivory-bill specimen ever collected in the Okefenokee.

On Saturday, June 10, Tanner borrowed a boat and rowed through Billy's Lake to Billy's Island. Both were named for Chief Billy Bowlegs, who had led a group of Seminoles into the area to hide from Federal troops that had been sent to remove them from the South. "Almost all of the north end of the island was cut-over pineland, now mostly supporting a good young growth," Tanner wrote. "There are the remains of a fairly sizeable town still evident, occupied when the island and surrounding swamp was cut over. Around the island is a swamp of pond cypress, small trees. The cut over swamp, where there had been big trees, was now almost treeless, and further scarred by fire."

The ghost town Tanner encountered had been a settlement built by the Hebard Lumber Company in 1909. It served as their headquarters while they harvested the timber in the swampland. At its height, the company town contained a school, church, general store, baseball diamond, smithy, movie house, and a boardinghouse. In those days, it was home to roughly six hundred people, but all that ended in 1927, when the timber ran out. "The company tore down the small buildings and shipped the large ones elsewhere by rail, leaving behind only the rusting relics that are now lying about the island," writes Okefenokee chronicler Franklin Russell. "Pines, sycamores, wax myrtles, and various kinds of tall grasses have shot up everywhere around the ironmongery, and detritus left by man is disintegrating and blending into the landscape." If anything, such scraps of civilization epitomized the transitory nature of the logging industry

Tanner encountered throughout the South. The timber companies came and went. And where they had been, ivory-bills could no longer be found.

North of the island is Billy's Lake, a long, narrow body of water connected to the smaller Minnie's Lake by a watery canoe path known as Minnie's Run, often described as the most beautiful section of swamp in the country. "The run was a ribbon of dark water twisting among the trees, barely wide enough for a boat to pass," noted Tanner. "Here and there were small ponds, open and ringed by slender cypress. Some of the ponds were partially covered with bonnet-lilies. It was a pretty place, but there was very little bird life around."

Beginning on Monday, June 12, Mizell and Tanner explored the region for two days. The experienced woodsman gave the younger Tanner a grand tour of all the old ivory-bill haunts, but as Jim wrote, "Nothing looked good for woodpeckers." On the second day of their search, Tanner and Mizell paddled up the Suwannee River, exploring a couple of hammocks on foot. One was where Mizell had shot the ivory-bill in 1912 before logging had progressed that deeply into the swamp.

Tanner left the area the next day. From his own observations and his conversations with Mizell (whose knowledge of the swamp was encyclopedic), he concluded that no ivory-bills were left in the South Georgia swamp. (Three years after Tanner visited the Okefenokee, cartoonist Walt Kelly went there as well. Inspired by the wetland's uniqueness, Kelly later created a newspaper comic strip centered around an opossum named Pogo. The marsupial's adventures ran for twenty-seven years.)

From Waycross Jim drove through rain to Brunswick on the Georgia coast and then north to Darien at the mouth of the Altamaha River. He discovered that there wasn't enough suitable habitat left in on the lower Altamaha—the Boyle Swamp—for ivory-bills. He had already explored the upper swampy section of the river in 1937.

At the Savannah River Wildlife Refuge, Jim located Manny Carter, a refuge patrolman who had recently reported seeing an ivory-bill on the Canoochee River in Bryan County. He acted as Jim's guide to the area. As Tanner noted, however, "The tree that Manny pointed out to me as the one he first saw the birds on had some old woodpecker sign on it that looked like the work of pileateds." Of the pair's further explorations, Jim commented, "We stopped here and there to inquire about woodpeckers, and from the way Manny talked and described the bird to others, I began seriously to doubt if he really did know the birds." The two-day search was another dead end.

With this, Tanner returned to a nagging question: were there ivory-bills still living in the Santee bottomlands of South Carolina? His three previous visits

Logging operations in the Santee swamp and the main-line logging road near the center line of Santee Dam, July 26, 1939, one week after Tanner's fourth visit. (Photo by Harry Tinker Poe Jr. Special Collections, Clemson University Libraries, Clemson, SC.)

to the region had yielded no significant sign of the birds, but recent eyewitness accounts by several men he respected, including Alexander Sprunt, led him to search there once again. The sightings had generally occurred in the vicinity of Wadmacon Island, but Jim had found nothing on repeated trips, causing him to theorize that the birds only foraged there but lived elsewhere. But where? Late in the waning days of 1938, a reported sighting on Black Oak Island had surfaced. Moultrie Ball, a native of the area, had allegedly seen three ivory-bills together on the island upstream from Wadmacon the previous October, only eight months before. Tanner went there in late December but could only stay one day. He had found nothing, but it was time to go back.

Monday, June 19: After an overnight stay in Charleston, where he received a telegram and money from his father, Tanner drove on to Kingstree and stocked up on groceries. That night, he camped out at the construction site of a dam being built on the river. A WPA project, the eight-mile long Santee Dam would be completed in November 1941.

Before sunrise the next morning, Jim walked over to Black Oak Island, crossing Little River on a new tramline railroad trestle that was being built to allow logging access to the island. For once, Jim was able to visit a woodland before it was cut—but just barely. Trees were coming down all around the island.

Of the island, he wrote, "The timber is good there, of gum and oak ridges with few tupelo-cypress sloughs, some very large trees. Saw what looked like some old ivory-bill sign." Jim spent the entire day on the island, returning to his camp hot and sweaty around four in the afternoon. In all, Tanner spent three days searching the area but found nothing specific. However, the habitat looked right: at least the original forest was intact.

"Decided to call it quits," he concluded. "Temperature the last few days had been at or above 95. In the swamp little breeze stirred and the air was very damp. Very few birds sang at sunrise. The leaves were too thick to see the tops of the trees or any sign if it was there."

Although ivory-billed woodpeckers could well have been there, the conditions were not right to find them. Jim knew he needed to return in the fall after the leaves fell. He drove north to Washington, D.C., where he spent five days searching the libraries for historic accounts of ivory-bills. After that, it was back to New York. Jim had been away from home since the previous November—a total of seven months, or 225 days.

Chapter 19

The Fellowship Concludes

The Audubon Association is not prepared at this time to broadcast information about the locations of ivory-bills in this country, for the obvious reason that publicity will do most of them no good.

—James T. Tanner

Jim Tanner knew what he knew. The few remaining ivory-billed woodpeckers left in the wild were in trouble. In July 1939 he typed his final report to Audubon. His three-year study had come to an end, almost.

In October, the National Association of Audubon Societies held its thirty-fifth annual convention in New York City. Tanner was one of the presenters, revealing his findings with a short slide show—just twelve photographs—and a brief discussion about his research on the ivory-bill. He began by paying tribute to the one partner he had for the entire journey: his 1931 Model A Ford. "An excellent car for woods and muddy roads," he commented. "It has been the first car to break a way over many a muddy road, has had several springs broken, mufflers knocked off and running-boards knocked loose, bumpers broken on trees, and the front axle bent, but it still runs. In the three seasons of fieldwork it has traveled about 40,000 miles. In the rear of this car I carried a complete, although light, camping outfit, and could carry enough there to be self-sufficient and comfortable for a week or more." (Tanner had bought the car used in August 1936 for $175 and ultimately sold it in December 1939 for $45.)

Tanner also acknowledged that the car was intrinsically better in the dry season than in the wet, but even then it could only take him to the edges of the swamps. After that he needed a boat, canoe, horse, or mule—or he simply hiked as far as he could. "Legwork was needed and a pair of webbed feet would have been useful," he joked. Tanner couldn't even guess how many miles he had covered but knew he had worn out fifty dollars' worth of boots. (In 1938 a pair of Chippewa-brand calf-high outdoorsman boots from Sears and Roebuck sold for $8.98.)

He ended his slide presentation with a magnificent—even regal—photo of a protective male ivory-bill at its nest hole. The gentle humor that began the talk gave way to the somber truth of his findings. "The ivory-bill has frequently been associated with muck, has been called a melancholy bird, but it is not that at all," he reflected. "As you can see from this picture, it lives in the sun, not the shade, in surroundings as bright as its own plumage. It is true that the man trying to watch and follow these birds is probably in the shade and mud, among the fallen trees and running vines, but that does not affect the ivory-bill in the least. He stays above all that, and is a handsome, vigorous, graceful bird."

For centuries, the ivory-bills had survived by being somewhat removed from any perils beneath them. A hunter could only pursue them so far, for they were creatures of the canopy. But Jim knew the species was in dire straits; perhaps it was already too late:

> When this ivory-bill study started, almost three years ago, no one had a definite idea as to how many ivory-bills there were in this country nor where they were. As the work of finding the numbers and distribution of the birds progressed, the importance of knowing just how many ivory-bills there were and the locations of the birds became evident, for I found that the birds are now so few and in so few localities that conservation measures will have to be aimed at these localities and the conditions peculiar to each. The imperative first step will be the saving of the small ivory-bill populations still extant by knowing where they are and what to do for them.

Tanner also knew that keeping at least part of what he had learned a secret was also imperative:

> The Audubon Association is not prepared at this time to broadcast information about the locations of ivory-bills in this country, for the obvious reason that publicity will do most of them no good. As for the numbers of ivory-bills still living, the number is probably around twenty-five individuals. [Tanner later revised that down to twenty-two birds.] About a quarter of these are in the tract in Louisiana—there has already been considerable said and written about that area, and the remaining individuals are broken into smaller or larger groups in four or five scattered localities.

Why were the ivory-billed woodpeckers disappearing? One idea that emerged after the 1935 Cornell trip was this: perhaps the ivory-bill population had become so small, so inbred, that the species was having trouble reproducing. After all, two failed nests had been discovered that year alone in the Singer Tract. But the three nests that Tanner had closely monitored had all been successful. Also, he and J. J. Kuhn had observed other young ivory-bills in the region. Tanner estimated that by combining his own observations with reliable reports from others, the Singer Tract had probably produced "fifteen to twenty young" during the last eight years, a total that would certainly maintain a healthy population along the Tensas River bottomland. Yet, a careful review of the numbers indicated that the area's ivory-bill population was in sharp decline—from an estimated fourteen birds in 1934 to only six in 1939. That was a drop of 71 percent in five years. "Part of this decrease can be ascribed to reductions in the size of the forest thru lumbering operations," Tanner began his summation. "But I know that some birds have disappeared from areas which have not been touched by the saw."

He added, "In the area where dead wood was most abundant, and thus where there was more woodpecker food, a pair of ivory-bills had lived and nested for several years; in another area with less dead wood and dead trees per acre, the numbers of ivory-bills had decreased; and in a third area which had the poorest woodpecker food conditions, ivory-bills had stopped nesting." In short: "Where the amount of dead wood had decreased, ivory-bills had also decreased."

It seemed blindingly obvious: ivory-bills needed a large number of recently dead or dying trees whose decaying wood was full of insect borer larvae. The species had carved out a slim, precarious niche for itself. It was able to utilize recently dead wood because it was the only woodpecker big and strong enough to pry away the tight-fitting bark and get at the beetle grubs inside. The woodborers that live between the bark and sapwood—*Scolytids, Buprestids* (jewel beetles), and *Cerambycids* (long-horned beetles)—were the first to attack a tree or branch after it dies. Once the tree had been dead for longer than two years, other woodpeckers could take over.

Tanner's recommendation: the isolated old swampy forests he had identified as good ivory-bill habitat must be saved and protected. After all of his road miles gathering first-hand accounts and researching the availability of proper habitat, Jim believed that ivory-bills were probably still located in at least five places. In addition to the Singer Tract in northeast Louisiana, the ghost birds likely remained in only the Apalachicola River bottomlands, Big Cypress, Gulf Hammock, and near Highland Hammock in Florida. However, Tanner's estimate of no more than two dozen individual birds meant that only minimal numbers could be living in each location, perhaps a few breeding pairs or solitary individuals. Each group stranded on a wooded island miles and miles apart were lost to the others.

What next? At this point, perhaps the biggest mystery that remained was the Santee in South Carolina. Jim had made four trips there, finding little to nothing to back up the reported sightings. Had the birds just been passing through or were they dying out? And there, as in most places, logging was advancing from all directions. With that in mind, Jim believed that number one on the to-do list was preserving the Singer Tract along the Tensas River. And with the population decline he had already documented, that should happen sooner rather than later: "This tract is not only a habitat for ivory-bills, but also for every other wild animal native to the Louisiana country, deer, turkey, bear, wolf, and panther." Everything could still be found there except the extinct Carolina parakeet. "I believe that I have seen almost every bit of virgin timber in the South and unreservedly, the Singer Tract has the finest stand of virgin swamp forest," Jim declared. "The Singer Tract should be preserved, as an example of that forest with all its birds and mammals—a true bit of the north American wilderness."

With this, Jim ended his report: "The main part of the study is completed, and the necessary facts have been found for the beginning of a conservation program for the ivory-billed Woodpecker." If the species was in fact dying, James T. Tanner had been there to hear its deathbed rattle.

Submitting his report brought Jim's fellowship to a close—almost. There was still one nagging loose end that needed to be tied up: Black Oak Island in the Santee. On Wednesday, November 29, for a fifth time, Jim drove to South Carolina and his old campsite at the proposed dam site he had left in late June. Since he had been away, roughly a quarter-mile of timber had been cut. The loggers had advanced deeper into the woods. Tanner once again walked the tramline and crossed the new trestle onto the island. It was a warm day, partly cloudy; conditions were right for finding ivory-bill sign, if it was there. He soon discovered that parts of the island were already being cut. Jim spent a week searching the various sections of Black Oak Island, approaching it from different directions. He also made a return trip with game warden Hollie Shokes to Stewards Neck and downstream to Wadmacon Island.

"The most suitable woods for ivory-bills that I have seen in the Santee are on and adjacent to Black Oak Island," Tanner wrote. "The timber at the east end of the island is probably biggest, but I saw no sign there. At the west end there was some quite good looking sign, but old and nothing that I could be at all positive about. If the present rate of cutting continues, the island will probably be completely cutover in about 12 to 15 months." And thus he ended his 1939 field notes.

In a year-end report to Audubon, Tanner concluded, "The Santee swamp has been cut over from Black Oak Island to about eight miles below St. Stephens and the U.S. 52 bridge. They are cutting now at the lower edge of this area and are extending the main tramline, I understand, to within four or five miles of Lenude's Ferry. They are cutting clean, and in a few years the swamp there will be of no use to wildlife. The proposed Santee-Cooper diversion dam will cross the lower end of Black Oak Island, and what part of that swamp is not flooded will probably be cut over." He speculated that whatever ivory-bills that might be left in the region would be forced elsewhere, and with this he seemed to give up on the Santee.

Tanner had one last pressing piece of business that would complete both his ivory-bill study and his time at Cornell: his doctoral dissertation. He worked on it through the winter, presenting it to the faculty of the graduate school in February 1940. Titled "The Life History and Ecology of the Ivory-billed Woodpecker," it is a hefty tome: 311 typed pages, plus 43 separate pages of black and white photographs, graphs, charts, and maps inserted at appropriate places in the text. To hold it in your hands, to feel its weight, you get some sense of the relief the young graduate student must have felt. Just a couple weeks shy of his twenty-sixth birthday and having now earned his PhD—a requirement for a career as a university professor or researcher in most fields—James Taylor Tanner was now on his way to begin the next phase of his life. Ironically, he would once again find himself on a train headed to the South.

Chapter 20

At Home in Tennessee

I was in love with him. I would have followed Jim anywhere.

—Nancy Burnham Sheedy

Created by an act of legislation in 1909, East Tennessee State Normal School was founded in the northeast corner of the Volunteer State. Its location had been hotly contested, as several cities vied for the honor. On December 2, the *Johnson City Comet,* a local newspaper, reported, "The joyful news reached Johnson City by wire immediately and every whistle in the city was dampened with steam and the lusty throated songsters conveyed the glad tidings to the community and the rejoicing was 'above Normal.'" The pun was intended.

The term "normal school" derives from the French *école normale,* which dates back to the early 1800s; the name indicated that it was intended to serve as a model, and it was usually applied to two-year schools that trained teachers for the early grades.

Located on 141 acres within the corporate limits of Johnson City, the new campus was described as wonderfully beautiful. Indeed, nestled in the foothills of the Appalachian Mountains, with the Buffalo and Cherokee mountains due south of the area, it was a picturesque setting. Holston Mountain could be seen from the front steps of the new administration building. The school officially became a college in 1925, changing its name to East Tennessee State Teachers College and subsequently gaining accreditation from the Southern Association of Colleges and Secondary Schools in 1927. It was an ideal place to begin a career in teaching and an ideal place for two transplanted New Yorkers to meet.

In August 1940 the twenty-three-year-old Nancy Burnham Sheedy arrived on campus to begin her new job as assistant professor. She had been interviewed and hired at Harvard by Lester Wheeler, the head of the Psychology Department at the Tennessee teachers college. Himself a graduate of the famed Ivy League school, Wheeler had gone back to his alma mater to recruit a new faculty member. He had ended his interview with Nancy by asking her, in an exaggerated Southern accent, "You all want to go down to work in the sticks?"

She did. Although well traveled, the young, effervescent Nancy had never been to the South. Born in Seattle, Washington, on June 14, 1917, she is quick to point out—with her characteristic chuckle—that she was blessed with the appropriate coloration for a Flag Day baby: red hair, white skin, and blue eyes. But the same palette works for the country where she spent eight of her formative years: Great Britain. Her father, Joseph Edward Sheedy, president of the United States Shipping Line, had been named by President Warren G. Harding as a special envoy tasked with encouraging trade with Europe. Consequently, Nancy's father relocated his family to London for a few years. When they returned to the states, they settled in New York City.

Equally blessed with a quick smile and a blazing wit, Nancy became one of the first women to graduate from Harvard University with a master's degree in education. "Everybody else was at Radcliff and got Radcliff degrees," she remembers. "There were plenty of graduate students at Radcliff. But, I got a full scholarship to Harvard and there was only one other woman, just two of us and hundreds of men. In those days a woman was not allowed on Harvard Yard. You could walk through it, but could not pause. But we did have wonderful access to the professors. Every afternoon at four o'clock in a great big room the professors would come and sit around and talk to you and have tea and you could ask them any kind of questions you wanted."

Nancy had completed her undergraduate work at Mount Holyoke College in South Hadley, Massachusetts. A highly selective women's liberal arts college, it was originally founded as Mount Holyoke Female Seminary in 1837. One century later, Nancy Sheedy graduated magna cum laude (and Phi Beta Kappa) in 1939.

Pursuing a first-rate education seemed natural to someone with Nancy's inquisitive mind. She had always been a constant, even voracious reader "I can't stop reading," she says. "As a child, I was a very slow dresser, because I'd be putting a sock on and reading a little and so forth while I dressed. And you're put to bed and you take your flashlight with your book and when everyone is sound asleep, you put the covers over your head and you read." She was (and still is) charming and articulate, with a well-bred accent that reflects her Seattle-to-England-to-New York upbringing. In 1940, after finishing grad school in one year, she was ready for her life's next adventure.

By the summer of 1940, with World War II well underway, the dark news from abroad had turned even more ominous. The Germans had met little resistance as they had marched across the continent, with countries falling like dominoes, and now Hitler was hell-bent on invading the United Kingdom. The English, however, were proving to be far scrappier adversaries. They possessed an early warning system not shared by their European neighbors. A sophisticated new network of radar along the English Channel could detect enemy aircraft seventy-five miles away, giving RAF pilots time to get airborne. In July, 359 British airplanes were downed, but the German Luftwaffe lost 653. On August 20, Prime Minister Winston Churchill, speaking before Parliament, declared, "Never in the field of human conflict was so much owed by so many to so few."

Could the country where Nancy Sheedy had spent part of her childhood hold out against such a monstrous adversary? And if Britain fell, who would be next? This was the international situation when she arrived in Johnson City by train. Her move to Tennessee was her first foray into the South. Little did she know at the time that it would become her home for the next seventy-plus years.

"Jobs were very scarce then," Nancy says. "I was lucky to find one even with a master's degree." At East Tennessee Teachers College, she served in the Psychology Department, where she taught general, child, and adolescent psychology plus remedial reading and a class designed to discover and diagnose a student's reading difficulties. At first, she lived just off campus in the home of a couple affectionately known as Ma and Pa Worley; she then moved to a nearby house and roomed with three other female faculty members: Margaret Madden, Mary Williams, and Ella Ross, the dean of women for the college.

Shortly after arriving in Johnson City, Nancy learned that one of the few eligible bachelors on the college faculty was also a novice instructor from New York. A certain James T. Tanner was set to be the new assistant professor in the Department of Biological Science, replacing Dr. Charles Quaintance, who had left to take a similar position in Oregon. Tanner's schedule for the next three quarters was loaded. He would be teaching general biology, entomology, vertebrate zoology and anatomy, genetics, and the history of biology, plus two classes of "science for the elementary grades." The school's objective, after all, was to prepare their students to be teachers themselves.

That first fall quarter, "he had a class and a lab," Nancy recalled. "So he ate at 1 PM, an hour later than I normally had my lunch." Nancy had not met Jim yet, but she did not let that stop her; she simply switched her own schedule. "I zoomed myself down to the cafeteria at once, and there he was and I said, 'Oh, you must be Dr. Tanner,' and he said, 'Miss Sheedy, I presume.' Somebody had told him that I was around. So we ate together."

To keep the conversation flowing, Nancy asked, "Do you play tennis?" She was a skilled player and had even played in the mixed doubles finals at Harvard. Jim answered, "No, but I play Ping-Pong." As it turned out, he *could* play tennis, and the two soon discovered that they had even more than their northern roots in common; they both were athletic. They played tennis, Ping-Pong, and even occasionally a round of golf on a nearby course in Jonesboro.

"He could beat me at everything—it was very annoying," says Nancy, who soon realized she was falling in love. They also spent a lot of time exploring the mountains around Johnson City, which to Jim looked remarkably like the mountains around the Cornell campus.

"I followed him everywhere when we were courting," Nancy recalls. "Once, I followed Jim into a cave and it was very close quarters. I had terrible claustrophobia. He wanted to go way into where it was completely dark to see if the animals, crayfish, and so forth, had any color, which you know they don't. Anyway I just tried to stay close to his feet. I kept thinking, 'I'm going to die. I'll never be able to get back out of here.' We finally got inside where it opened up and you could sit down and I thought, 'I'll never get back out of here. Why do I love this man?' The entrance was just gosh awful. But I chased him until he caught me. I even chased him into a dark, dark cave."

On September 16, President Roosevelt signed the Selective Service and Training Act, which required all male citizens between the ages of twenty-six and thirty-five to register for the military draft. Jim Tanner was twenty-six years old. Roosevelt considered reinstating conscription a prudent step. America had to be ready should it have to defend itself against the growing threat of the fascist and militarist regimes in Europe and across the Pacific in Japan.

FDR responded to British distress by selling the country more military equipment and providing humanitarian aid. But how long could America's involvement be kept to a minimum? After signing the Selective Service Act, Roosevelt warned, "America stands at the crossroads of its destiny. Time and distance have been shortened. A few weeks have seen great nations fall. We cannot remain indifferent to the philosophy of force now rampant in the world. We must and will marshal our great potential strength to fend off war from our shores. We must and will prevent our land from becoming a victim of aggression." But many Americans were still war weary. Hadn't World War I—the war to end all wars—just ended a generation ago?

For Jim Tanner and Nancy Sheedy, the growing threat seemed far away. The fall quarter passed quickly for the couple. And as it turned out, Tanner's ivory-bill curiosity had not yet been sated. After all, you cannot easily walk away from something that had so dominated your life. He couldn't help but wonder: how were the ones in the Singer Tract doing? The fall quarter ended in mid-December. The holiday break was a long one, giving Jim time for a quick trip to Louisiana. He arranged beforehand to stay with J. J. Kuhn. Nancy would accompany him and stay in a single room in the Montgomery Hotel. It was their first of a lifetime of road trips together.

"In those days, a dating couple would have never stayed in the same room," recalls Nancy, "but it was certainly okay for me to tag along. I was in love, I'd follow Jim anywhere, even into the swamp."

Nancy soon learned that following Jim Tanner meant starting the day long before dawn. On Friday, December 20, Jim arrived at her hotel at 4:00 AM, finding the ardent Nancy ready to go. A waning gibbous moon hung over the Singer Tract, providing a pale luminous light for the hike into the watery environs. "I'll tell you, plowing through a swamp in the dark is very difficult," said Nancy. "You sink in the mud; you have to push through briars and climb over fallen logs." Tanner knew the swamp's highs and lows; he had traversed it many times. "Jim never found the birds unless he heard them first," Nancy adds, "so we were in the woods very early in the morning." By 6:30, the pair was in position. As morning crept into the old swamp, they waited.

BAM-bam! Jim and Nancy heard the distinctive double rap of the ivory-bill. It was out of its roost hole and about to begin a new day. "The ivory-bill doesn't drum like other woodpeckers," Nancy says. "He has sort of a signature call, a loud BAM-bam! It's like an ax, whacking against a tree, followed by almost a quick echo. . . . And then he called, like a toy tin horn's toot, a nasal *kent, kent . . . kent, kent . . . kent.* We heard some more calling but we didn't see the birds."

With the leaves off the trees, the sound carried a long distance. That first outing, Jim and Nancy did not see the birds, only heard them. Jim spent the rest of the day looking for their likely roost holes, which he found after hours of searching. Now, he knew where to begin their day the following morning. "It was December 21," remembers Nancy. "The first time you see a bird somewhere, you sort of remember the date and the place." She continues,

> The second morning, we started again at about four o'clock and had to wade through bayous, and go through mud and get caught by vines; it was very difficult going. By 6:30 we were at the roost holes he had found the day before and heard all the other birds waking up. And finally about 7:15, when the sun was on the tops of the trees, out came the male ivory-billed woodpecker and he jerked and pulled himself up to the top of the tree. And he preened and stretched and he went *BAM-bam!*
>
> I remember that gorgeous red crimson crest and that white bill . . . what a striking creature. And then he called and the female came out of her roost hole and went over and joined him and they talked softly for awhile, a sort of *key-ennnt, keey-eennt*

> and then the pair took off flying fast. And Jim said, "Stay where you are," and he took off after them."

In a flash, Jim was gone. Nancy sat there patiently waiting for him to return. Tucked deep within an unknown swamp, surrounded by the sounds of early morning, the red-haired Harvard girl with a proper Kate Hepburnish accent was now sitting alone in the watery wilderness, thinking about snakes and wolves and beginning to wonder: would her escort ever be able to find her again? And if not: what should she do? But Tanner returned, and they spent the rest of the day in the woods moving about, watching the birds. "In 1940, we saw five birds, three males and two females," she says. That was one more female than Jim had found the spring before. Only a few months earlier, Nancy had never heard of a ivory-bill, but the woodpecker would, in effect, follow her the rest of her life.

Wanting to spend time with their families during the holiday break, Jim and Nancy kept their stay in Louisiana brief—though it was certainly memorable nonetheless. Back in Johnson City by Christmas Eve, they soon parted to visit their separate families in New York. But over the next seventy years, Nancy would tell and retell the story of that day in the Louisiana swamp and her first encounter with an ivory-billed woodpecker.

Chapter 21

Our Lives Changed Forever

> *The ivory-bill was never common, apparently because it had developed an ecological niche of its own as an exploiter of trees that had been killed or sickened by attacks of drought, fire or the flat-headed, wood-boring beetle. In its search for this insect, one of its favorite foods, the ivory-bill could strip nearly all the bark off a stricken tree. But the large-scale destruction of Southern forests wiped out the magnificent stands of hardwoods in which the bird thrived.*
>
> —Franklin Russell

As 1940 gave way to 1941, the war in Europe cast a long, dark shadow across the Atlantic. You could deny it, but inevitably, you couldn't escape it: talk was everywhere. Along with the weather and goldfish-swallowing—a fad sweeping across college campuses—the growing threat of war was the chief topic of conversation at local barbershops, diners, and courthouse benches. Foreboding hung over the entire country. A New Year's proclamation released by Adolf Hitler declared, "The year 1941 will bring consummation of the greatest victory in our history." The failed art student was getting cocky. German soldiers already occupied Poland, France, Belgium, and the Netherlands. Luftwaffe pilots were dropping bombs on London, and the British city was blacked out at night to hide itself from the bombers. The word *blitzkrieg*, meaning "lightning war," began to appear in newspapers around the world. It was a frightening time. Hitler's tone was caustic. In a separate proclamation, he announced to the world's democracies that it was "a dumb and infamous lie" to think that Germany and its ally Italy wanted to conquer the world. But as the New Year arrived, much of the country believed that was precisely his intent.

As early as 1904, New Year's revelers had been coming to the heart of the Big Apple to celebrate. The famous lighted New Year's Eve Ball made its first slow descent down the flagpole atop One Times Square in 1907. Decorated with one hundred twenty-five-watt lights, the original iron and wood globe weighed seven hundred pounds and was five feet in diameter. In 1920 a new ball made entirely of iron and weighing only four hundred pounds replaced the original.

Anybody who was anywhere near the city on New Year's Eve simply had to go to Times Square to celebrate, especially young couples.

With 1940 fading into history, bookings in the downtown hotels swelled, running 50 percent higher than they had the previous year. With the gloom of war enveloping the country, people wanted to escape the bad news. Nancy Sheedy and her mother, Ella, stayed in the Plaza Hotel. Jim Tanner joined them later for a New Year's Eve dinner after arriving by train from Cortland and renting a room at the YMCA. Afterward, the young couple walked to Times Square, joining the estimated one million people in town to celebrate. Thousands of lights lit their way.

The sky was clear and the temperature milder than the twenty-two degrees that had chilled celebrants the year before. The city had warmed to the low forties on the afternoon of December 31, and by 10:00 PM the thermometer hovered around thirty-nine degrees. Soldiers and sailors in uniform were everywhere throughout the crowd. The sidewalks soon became so congested that the overflow spilled into the streets. By 10:55 all traffic near the square was being rerouted. A temporary police headquarters was set up at Forty-sixth Street, with 1,489 uniformed policeman on duty in the area.

As midnight approached, the festivities escalated, building to a boisterous crescendo. During the most celebratory period—just after the ball dropped and 1941 began—a Mardi Gras–like atmosphere ran infectiously through the crowd. Many celebrants wore false noses and ears, the fad du jour, and an impromptu Conga line led by a man wearing an enormous red, white, and green headpiece sprang to life. It moved like a chunky millipede down the street. Side to side. Back and forth. Horns blared, flashbulbs popped, and paper streamers and chunks of confetti thrown from windows fluttered in the air like minnows in a stream. The atmosphere was a curious mix: part patriotic, part bacchanalian. A sign that read "God Bless America—the Bahaman Dancers" was carried through the clamorous mass. Because of the war in Europe, French champagne was in short supply, but that mattered little. Music wafted into the streets from the dance floors in the crowded hotels. A new tune, "Beat Me Daddy, Eight to the Bar," was requested and played time and time again. The atmosphere was more than the traditional New Year's Eve celebration. It was cathartic, fueled by an overwhelming desire to escape the gloomy news of war.

The patriotic fervor was evident throughout the celebration, indoors and out. An estimated five thousand people filled every room at the Waldorf-Astoria. The Persian Room at the Plaza had two dance floors set up with entertainment all through the night. The New Yorker was decorated in red, white, and blue, and bugles replaced the traditional horns. "God Bless America" and Sousa martial marches were interspersed with swing music. The Hotel Astor estimated that more than six thousand people ushered in the New Year at public and private gatherings inside its many rooms. In the hotel's grand ballroom, at the stroke of midnight, the lights were dimmed and a snowstorm was simulated: a single shaft of light pierced the make-believe swirling flakes and fell on a model of the U.S. Capitol, complete with a small fluttering flag. Everyone stood as the national anthem was played.

Across the Atlantic, the peaceful, reasonable world had broken down. That night in New York City, much or most of the crowd outside was made up of young adults, who knew that if they weren't in uniform then, they soon would be.

"The streets were jam-packed," recalls Nancy. "You could hardly move. Many had had too much to drink and were too amorous. In those days, couples did not show affection in public. You were more reserved. Jim and I had only been dating a short time. We usually greeted each other with a handshake." Needless to say, the celebration that ushered in 1941 was the biggest party that either had ever attended. "Or ever hoped to," says Nancy. "What I remember the most is how much my feet hurt. In those days a woman only traveled with one pair of shoes and I had taken dress shoes. But we could not have danced even if we had wanted to because we were so packed into the crowd."

Amid this sea of humanity, the going was slower than Jim's treks through the southern swamplands, and if his mind was on anything other than Nancy and the war, it was on his desire to get back to Johnson City before the students began to arrive, fresh from their winter break. Jim had only been a college professor for four months and took his responsibilities seriously. His loyalties were to his students. The masses that crowded the country's largest city would have been more of a curiosity to a cultural anthropologist than to a field biologist. Measured against the totality of their life together, the few hours they spent in the raucous crowd may merit little mention, but it was a memorable portal to a most remarkable year.

To some degree, January 1941 marked Tanner's entry onto the national stage with the appearance of his first published work on the ivory-bill. His benefactor, long known as the National Association of Audubon Societies for the Protection of Wild Birds and Animals, had only just updated its name to the much simpler "National Audubon Society." The group's monthly publication had also changed its moniker—from *Bird-Lore* to the *Audubon Magazine*—and it was in the January/February 1941 issue, the first under its new name, that Tanner's article, "Three Years with the Ivory-billed Woodpecker, America's Rarest Bird," appeared. The changes represented the growing clout of the name "Audubon" and the organization's increased scope of activities in the field of wildlife sanctuaries and conservation. Tanner's research was the first of several such projects. His thoroughness set the tone others had to follow.

Arthur Allen's article "Hunting the Voices of Vanishing Birds," published in *National Geographic* in 1937, had touched on the rediscovered ivory-bill. Allen and Paul Kellogg's article "Recent Observations on the Ivory-billed Woodpecker" appeared in *The Auk* the same year, but that was a publication for ornithologists. Tanner's in-depth *Audubon* article was the first produced for the general public—the first synthesis of his three-year research—and it included several black-and-white photographs he had taken. It was also the first time his name was so closely linked to the ghost bird in the national arena, apart from academia.

"Few living naturalists have ever seen a live Ivory-billed Woodpecker, the rarest bird on the North American continent today," Tanner began the piece. "In what might prove to be the twilight of the species, it has been my singular good fortune to spend three interesting years tracing its history and almost living with the scattered remnant of its vanishing clan."

"Living with the scattered remnant" was a tantalizing turn of phrase. The newsmagazine *Time* picked up on the story in its March 17, 1941, issue, running a short article about America's extinct or disappearing birds titled "Sad Birds." As the article reported, "The ivory-billed woodpecker, rarest of U.S. birds, was considered extinct about 1926. But in the latest issue of *Audubon* Magazine Ornithologist James Taylor Tanner of Cornell estimated that some four & twenty of these birds still live in the loneliest swamps of Louisiana, Florida and South Carolina. Biggest U.S. woodpecker, the ivory-bill once ranged the southern primeval forest, eating larvae from recently dead trees. As the forest dwindled, so did the ivory-bill, and Tanner gives it only a slim chance of surviving."

Getting mentioned in *Time* magazine was no small feat. The small college in northeast Tennessee now had a celebrity, and the modest Tanner would be forever conjoined with the ivory-bill. From this point on, it would be a rare article about the bird that did not also mention or quote James T. Tanner. But national spotlight aside, Jim and Nancy had a school year to complete, and a romance to nurture.

In late spring, Jim proposed four times. "You always turn down a proposal three times," says Nancy. They were sitting in the car and Jim was as persistent as he had been in pursuing the ivory-bill. Call him dogged. On his forth attempt, Nancy relented and said "yes."

"It wasn't a big surprise," she says. "He knew I was crazy about him."

After the school year ended in June, they drove north to New York. Nancy's mother, Ella, who had been down for a visit, rode with them. The trip was memorable because along the way, the trio experienced three flat tires. Tanner calmly dealt with each; he was used to car troubles after all. When Jim asked Mrs. Sheedy for permission to marry her daughter, Ella gladly gave it, knowing that he was one of the most unflappable men she had ever met, a good match for her spirited Nancy.

The young couple was married on August 15, 1941, at the Village of Saranac Lake in upstate New York. Ella was there caring for Nancy's brother, Burnham Sheedy, who was a patient at the Trudeau Sanitarium, convalescing from tuberculosis. The Saranac "Cure Cottages," with their large screened-in porches, were world renowned for the treatment of pulmonary infectious disease, also

Nancy Burnham Sheedy and Jim Tanner were married on August 15, 1941. (Photo courtesy of Nancy Tanner.)

known as "consumption" or simply TB. It had become an overwhelming public health concern, killing an estimated 100 million people worldwide, mostly in the first half of the century. At Trudeau, patients were exposed to as much cold fresh air as possible under conditions of complete bed rest, and by 1938 there were more than seven hundred sanatoriums throughout the United States that followed Trudeau's model. Nancy's brother slowly recovered but remained frail, having lost the use of one lung. (In November 1944 the antibiotic Streptomycin was administered for the first time to a critically ill tuberculosis patient, who recovered almost instantly. The disease could now be treated.)

After their wedding, Nancy and Jim honeymooned at nearby Elk Lake in the Adirondacks. Returning to Johnson City, Tanner had a draft notice waiting for him; but at this point the army wasn't inducting married men, so Jim was reclassified. The newlyweds moved into a second-floor apartment at 800 West Locust Street in Johnson City, only a few blocks from the biology building. (The house remains as a rental property for students and professors at what is now known as East Tennessee State University.) Many of the streets in this quiet neighborhood east of campus are named after trees—walnut, maple, chestnut, and so on—a fact surely not lost on Jim Tanner.

John H. Baker, executive director of the National Audubon Society, asked to publish Tanner's dissertation as the group's first research report. So, that fall, Jim began retyping and slightly reconfiguring his opus for a broader audience. He worked quietly at nights on a card table while Nancy tiptoed around the apartment. Published about a year later, the book had a plain gray cover and, for its frontispiece, a color painting of a pair of ivory-bills by George Miksch Sutton. In the preface, Arthur Allen praised Tanner for having "an ability to rough it and to get along with all kinds of people in all kinds of situations, a natural adaptability, ingenuity, initiative, originality, and a willingness to work. Above all, he had shown a clear mind and superior intelligence." (Today, the "profoundly hard-to-find" first editions of Tanner's book, *The Ivory-billed Woodpecker: Research Report No. 1 of the National Audubon Society*, sell for over four hundred dollars online.)

The book laid out a conservation plan for ivory-bills and called for the creation of refuges. "Studies of the ivory-bills in the Singer Tract," Tanner wrote, "indicate that the minimum area for one pair of birds should be two and a half to three square miles. They do not need all of that forest at any one time, but that much would be necessary to insure an adequate food supply from year to year." How to determine a good forest for ivory-bills? Oddly, look for pileateds. A parcel that already had five to six pairs of pileateds could support one pair of ivory-bills. Tanner knew that buying land was expensive and that the logging industry was tenacious and well funded. And unfortunately, two of the ivory-bill's favorite trees—sweet gums and Nuttall's oak—were also prized by the lumber companies. But perhaps the two could coexist. Was Jim being optimistic or realistic? He proposed a compromise whereby a refuge could be parceled into three basic usages: *reserve areas*, which would contain prime ivory-bill habitat with no logging; *partial cutting areas*, which would include habitat of secondary ivory-bill importance and could be selectively cut; and logging areas, which would encompass the poorest ivory-bill habitat and could be logged. Tanner's book featured a map that shows how the Singer Tract could be parceled out in this way. Jim also proposed that if enough dead or dying trees were not available in a given area, then selective girdling would in time create more feeding opportunities. An ivory-bill refuge would also have to be protected with armed game wardens. There were still plenty of people who would kill an ivory-bill for money.

The plight of the South's ghost bird was no closely held secret known only to university biologists and birdwatchers: it had become common knowledge in the popular press. In his 1941 book *How to Become Extinct*, noted journalist and humorist Will Cuppy included some sound advice for the "the fast-vanishing" ivory-billed woodpecker: "Keep away from bird lovers, fellows, or you'll be standing on a little wooden pedestal with a label containing your full name in Latin. . . . I don't want to alarm you fellows, but there are only about twenty of you alive as I write these lines, and there are more than 200 of you in American museums and in collections owned by ivory-billed Woodpecker enthusiasts. Get it?" Cuppy's admonition was spot-on.

Time magazine reviewed Cuppy's book in its December 8 issue—noting that the writer "made even footnotes funny"—but the review fell on a particularly humorless gray day. Many distracted readers probably did not even notice it. In all likelihood, they were glued to their radios, listening to President Roosevelt deliver his "a date which will live in infamy" address to the nation. He was referring to the Japanese attack on Pearl Harbor the day before.

It was 7:53 AM in Hawaii when the first assault wave struck the airfields and battleships anchored in the scenic harbor. The picture-postcard morning turned into Armageddon. The American military stationed in the mid-Pacific paradise was taken completely by surprise. In all, 2,403 died—close to two-thirds of those in the first fifteen minutes of the battle, when the U.S. Navy ships *Oklahoma*, *Utah*, and *Arizona* were bombed.

Back in the East, it was a typical Sunday afternoon when word reached the nation's capital. Like most in the country, Nancy and Jim Tanner first learned of the assault when bulletins began to interrupt regularly scheduled radio entertainment programs. They were on the sofa listening to a symphony on the Firestone Hour at around three o'clock. Word spread quickly across the campus and the quiet winter streets nearby where many of the faculty and staff lived. Nancy remembers her first words to Jim: "Please don't go on a submarine." She knew if her new husband got to choose, he would enlist in the U.S. Navy. He came from a family with a naval tradition. And indeed, according to Nancy, Jim shortly thereafter visited the local naval recruitment office to make his intentions known.

Across the country, the 1941 Christmas season was different: the holiday was not the topic foremost on everyone's mind. The Japanese bomb attack had changed all that. In Tallulah, Louisiana, there was still the annual cantata at the Methodist Church on the Sunday night prior to Christmas on Thursday. A local grocery had its usual selection of Christmas trees priced from 25 cents to $1.25, and Franklin Furniture on Depot Street stayed open until 9:00 PM throughout the week for late holiday shoppers. At the Bailey Theatre, *Charlie's Aunt,* starring Jack Benny, was playing on Monday and Tuesday night, while *Navy Blue and Gold,* with James Stewart and Robert Young, finished out the weeknights before Christmas. Both features included a comedy and a short featurette. But was anyone in the mood?

Of course, all of this had been put into place before Pearl Harbor. Events were happening fast. On December 8 the United States declared war on Japan; on December 10, Japanese troops invaded the Filipino island of Luzon; on December 11, America declared war on Germany and Italy; on December 19, the Japanese landed in Hong Kong and engaged the British; and on December 23, Japan captured Wake Island in the Pacific. Among Tallulah's three-thousand-plus residents, the war was the talk of the town, and emotions ran high. They had already lost one of their own. Navy Ensign Thomas Ray Jones, the twenty-three-year-old son of Mr. and Mrs. H. L. Jones, was listed as one of those "lost in the action in Hawaii."

"It will not only be a long war," President Roosevelt told radio listeners, "it will be a hard war . . . the sources of international brutality wherever they exist, must be absolutely and finally broken." The Tallulah newspaper, the *Madison Journal,* ran excerpts of FDR's speech on its front page, including such stirring words as these: "With confidence in our armed forces—with the unbending determination of our people—we will gain the inevitable triumph . . . We will win the war and we are going to win the peace that follows."

In New Orleans, the Mardi Gras set for February was cancelled. The Rose Bowl in Pasadena was at first cancelled and then moved to Durham, North Carolina, because California was regarded as more vulnerable to enemy attack than any other state, but few minds were on the holiday bowl games. As one local unnamed Tallulah writer wrote, "Americans love football, baseball—fun sports of any kinds—but they love their country more." Hungry for news, people stayed riveted to their radios, fearing that the U.S. mainland would be the next target.

The American Red Cross mobilized, announcing it needed to raise $50 million; Madison Parish was challenged to contribute $4,250 toward that goal. Most in the rural agricultural parish donated at least one dollar and their names were listed on the front page of the paper. The state quickly organized a Civil Defense program with an announced objective of registering everyone over eighteen years old—male or female, black or white. "There's a place for you in the ranks," Louisiana governor Sam Jones enthused. "You will be told how you can, how you must, become a warrior for victory in Louisiana. No matter what your age or sex, you have been drafted—not by any government—but by the rushing tide of circumstances. This is a war in which the rich and poor will suffer alike, but it is a war in which rich and poor must work alike." The publisher of Tallulah's weekly newspaper, W. L. Rooftree, served as the local Civil Defense organizer. The abandoned jail building on the corner of Green and North Chestnut housed the Tallulah USO to give aid and comfort to local servicemen. (The former jail courtyard is where the Cornell expedition moved their recording equipment from the truck to Ike Page's wagon in 1935, just six years before.)

Tallulah was still struggling to get back on its feet. "The Great Depression had not ended here," said Geneva Williams, Rooftree's daughter. "It may have ended in other places, but not here." In 1941 Williams was a sixteen-year-old senior in high school. "My graduating class had 72 people in it. There was a rush to graduate. Everybody wanted to finish school and go fight the war."

This was the heightened atmosphere that Jim Tanner found in Tallulah, arriving at about 2:30 PM on December 18. Over the past few years, the town had become like his second home. Knowing that his life would be changing soon, he had come back one last time to check on the ivory-bills at the request of John H. Baker. Nancy would join him soon, but Tanner had arrived early to visit J. J. Kuhn and meet with the local officials of Chicago Mill and Lumber—including S. C. Alexander, the head of the logging department—about their plans for the Singer Tract timber. At this point, conservation was low on everyone's priorities. There was a war to win. Woodpeckers, rare or otherwise, were just woodpeckers. The military needed lumber.

After his meeting at the lumber company, Jim drove to Sharkey Road and walked north as he had done on so many other occasions to John's Bayou. A lot had changed in only one year. "Logging was more thorough than I had thought," he wrote in his journal. "All sweet gum was cut, and from half to three-quarters of the total area was completely logged. Rather spotty job. I didn't recognize many places I had known." Luckily, Tanner did spot some new-looking ivory-bill sign. He borrowed a horse from Jim Parker and explored Methiglum Bayou to the lakes and west to Mason Spencer's cabin on Greenlea. Some additional sign turned up, and Jim spoke to several locals. A logger had recently seen an ivory-bill on Andrew's Bend; Parker reported one near Sharkey Road not far from Alligator Bayou; and another local said his father had seen a pair in John's Bayou about a month earlier. Armed with this evidence, Tanner set out early on Saturday, December 20, for the site of the old roost holes in John's Bayou—always the most reliable place for spotting ivory-bills—but heard nothing. Searching the area through out the day, he finally heard an ivory-bill call and rap once late in the afternoon. Not finding it, he made note of the spot so that he could return to it later.

Early the next morning, he hiked to the site—between Sharkey Road and John's Bayou—where he had heard the call the afternoon before. In the dim gray light of early morning, Jim arrived and waited. As daylight approached, a brown thrasher called, and two barred owls hooted. "At seven o'clock, a sapsucker whinnying cry came," Tanner noted. "Soon after a red-bellied woodpecker called, and another answered immediately. One flew to a dead stub . . . and drummed on the top. Suddenly, a female ivory-bill appeared on the side of the stub and climbed to the top, where she pounded a few times. Flying to another tree, she was joined by a second female, which came from I know not where." Two females where there had always been a mated pair—what could this mean? Jim continued, "The two soon flew, going northeast across the new cutting. They called and pounded a few times, but I could not keep up with them and they got away."

Spending the day searching more of the tract, Jim was back at the new roost tree by late afternoon. It was cloudy and slightly windy. Jim recorded,

> At 4:15 the two females suddenly flew in from the east, one landing on, the other near, the roost tree. Each rapped several times, called once or twice. One had an irregular crest, not well formed and up-curved, and looked immature. Could it be Baby Bunting?
>
> They flew one or two hundred yards north, fed a bit by scaling, rapped and double rapped a few times but scarcely called.
>
> At 4:45, one flew back towards the roost tree and disappeared. . . . The other had already disappeared, probably to roost nearby.

And that was it. Tanner waited a while, hoping to hear or see a third ivory-bill, but it didn't happen. The roost tree appeared to be a dead oak, with three large holes chiseled out near the top. With darkness approaching and several miles to walk, Jim left the site.

The next day it rained all day into the night. Tanner stayed in town. On Tuesday, December 23, unable to borrow a horse, he set out on foot to explore other sections: "Went down along Alligator to Mack's Bayou at the white line, crossed, and walked south along white line to old road. In woods along white line there was a little fresh feeding sign. I looked at some of the trees that I had deadened three years ago next to the line; some of them looked as tho some kind of woodpecker had fed on them." The fresh sign indicated that perhaps an ivory-bill was still in Mack's Bayou. Could it be Pete, the young male that had lived in that section? It was the only encouraging thing Jim found all day.

Nancy arrived by train early the next morning. It was Christmas Eve. After carrying her things to the hotel, she and Jim went to the woods, or rather, to a low ridge near what was left of John's Bayou. Shortly after noon, Jim heard an ivory-bill call, and they found the pair of females north of Sharkey Road. The birds called as Jim and Nancy approached, and then quieted. Locating the woodpeckers, the Tanners watched their activity until the birds flew away, not to be seen again.

Christmas: It was their first together as a married couple, and the first that Nancy had spent away from family. They exchanged modest Christmas presents in their hotel room. A heavy rain fell once again in the morning, and later on, they drove to Vicksburg for dinner. "What I remember most about the dinner was the roast pig in the center of the table with an apple in its mouth," says Nancy. "I'd never seen anything like it!"

After a day off to celebrate the holiday, the Tanners drove to Sharkey Road and borrowed two horses for the day from James Parker and a local named H. C. Sevier. Jim had planned to ride to Greenlea Bend, but the recent rains had raised the water level, making the river too deep to ford. They rode south instead, down through Alligator and Spring bayous all the way to the white line, then west along an old railroad bed to Sharkey Road. It was a clear, cold day, and the couple found very little.

On Saturday, December 27, Tanner again met S. C. Alexander at office of the Chicago Mill and Lumber Company. From this meeting, Tanner got a better sense of what areas were being logged: "He was able to go with me, so we drove to Sharkey Road and then walked into the woods. I showed him the kind of trees that ivory-bills fed on, and some old sign. He was interested and cooperative, but his most pointed comment was, 'They ought to learn to feed on something different.' He promised to do what he could, when he heard from the higher office."

In the afternoon, Jim and Nancy drove down Sharkey Road to Andrews Bend until they reached a wide path that had been cleared for a railroad spur to carry away the harvested timber. The timber activity seemed to encroach on the area from all sides, although most of the cutting was happening on the west side of the river. Still, it was only a matter of time until the loggers were finished there and moved to the east, the last stronghold of the ghost bird. Part of John's Bayou had been cut over because it was close to Sharkey Road. Trucks could be used to carry out the logs, but the rainy season had made this one thoroughfare too muddy for them. As Jim well knew, however, it would dry in the summer. And then all hell would break loose.

Sunday, December 28: At the time, Tanner didn't know the significance of the date. As was his habit, he got up early and drove to Sharkey Road. A starry night still hung overhead; the moon was 80 percent full. Tanner walked in the dark to the new roost tree he had found just eight days before. Two squirrels were already out and about eating acorns from a Nuttall's oak behind him. At 6:55 AM the adult female ivory-bill appeared. Jim wrote, "[It] came quietly from the lower hole, climbed to the top of the stub where it called and double-rapped. After a few moments, it flew to a nearby tree, where it called and rapped again, and then sat and preened itself."

Ten minutes after the older bird had presented herself, the other bird appeared: "The young female ivory-bill called from the north, then flew southeast over the cut-over. They fed about one half-hour or more in the big trees standing in the cut-over, not long in any one place. They called frequently, kept close together; flights were from 100 to 200 yards. I lost them about 7:45." A prophetic choice of words: "I lost them."

He watched silently as the two females worked the few big trees remaining near John's Bayou. He looked out over the ravaged landscape: a primeval wilderness that had stood for centuries was now gone. The wetland that had occupied so much of his time over the last few years had become unrecognizable. Yes, the world was changing.

That early-morning encounter in late December was the last time Jim Tanner would ever see a live ivory-billed woodpecker.

Chapter 22

Aftermath

We are just money grabbers. We are not concerned, as you folks, with ethical considerations.

—The chairman of Chicago Mill and Lumber Company

After watching the two female ivory-bills north of Sharkey Road, Tanner returned to Nancy in Tallulah. They quickly packed for the long drive back to Johnson City, a distance of roughly seven hundred miles. It would be forty-four years before Jim would return to the Tensas. A lot would happen in the interim.

Upon his return to Tennessee, Tanner was asked to file a report on what he found in the Singer Tract with the National Audubon Society. He composed it quickly: time was of the essence. Dated January 3, 1942, it's a matter-of-fact account, with an underlying sense of urgency. Even though he had only seen two live ivory-bills, he had found recent feeding sign of one in Mack's Bayou and heard reliable reports of others. He concluded that there was probably still the same number as in 1939. Probably. "The only significant change in the numbers of ivory-bills that has occurred recently is the apparent and unexplained disappearance of the male birds from the John's Bayou area," Tanner wrote. He only found the two females feeding along the edges of the recent cutting. Perhaps trying to put a hopeful spin on things, he speculated that the adult male and the banded Sonny Boy could have relocated because of the logging.

Jim noted that the war had sparked a new demand for timber. The Tallulah mill was working night and day, with Chicago Mill and Lumber hard pressed to supply enough logs. And even though Tanner had pointed out the kinds of trees that ivory-bills needed, S. C. Alexander, their logging department head, did not seem overly optimistic that they could be spared.

The good news: "Most of their cutting has been done on the west side of the Tensas River, away from most of the ivory-bill territories," Jim reported, estimating that it would take over two years to finish there. The bad news: "They have already done some cutting on the east side of the river, and unfortunately, right in the middle of what used to be the best ivory-bill range." Sharkey Road, the same primitive thoroughfare that had given Jim easier access to John's Bayou and other eastern sections, served the same purpose for the timbermen. Much logging had been done during the summer between his last two visits.

Tanner concluded his nine-page report with some recommendations, conceding that because of the increased demand for wood fueled by the new world war, preserving the entire Singer Tract was probably no longer an option. It was too late for that anyway. However, he hoped that a few prime sections could be spared. All were east of the river, but several had already been partially cut. His fallback position was something of an ecological Hail Mary: the recommendation that key trees be spared. Jim hoped that perhaps the trees in the lowlands could be left standing because these old trees were not that valuable: often they were defective, having spongy parts, dead tops, or dying branches. The best timber, the healthy living trees on the ridges, was not what the woodpeckers fed on anyway. Thus, Tanner was down to a plea to save certain trees and dead or dying ones at that. Even if the lumber company complied, could this possibly be enough?

The wartime demand for lumber was overwhelming. The War Department needed wooden crates of all sizes to ship tanks, guns, food, equipment, you name it. Chicago Mill could supply as many shipping boxes as it could possibly turn out. But a curious thing happened: so many able-bodied men left Madison Parish for the war effort that the lumber company had trouble finding a workforce. Without it, selling the land to become a wildlife refuge, principally to protect the ivory-billed woodpecker, began to look appealing. The lumbermen wanted to make their money while they could.

Responding to the recommendations and information Tanner had supplied, Audubon's John Baker had done his part to rally support. At first, untouched Greenlea Bend was on the table. Chicago Mill wanted $200,000 for the four thousand acres, and Governor Jones had the money. (The governors of Tennessee, Arkansas, and Mississippi, plus officials for the Roosevelt Administration, pitched in with an appeal to the Chicago-based consortium and the Singer Company to save the land.) By March 1942 a deal looked promising. Hopeful, Baker sent Richard Pough, now head of the Audubon's "Persecuted Species Department," on a top-secret mission to look for ivory-bills along the Tensas.

Here is where the tricky hand of irony played its card. British jails were being overrun with German POWs captured in North Africa. Hundreds of thousands of prisoners had to be housed somewhere. The POWs were marched onto flat-decked "Liberty Ships" and sent to the United States, where they were parceled out and transported under guard by railroad to prison camps across the country. As fate would have it, one of those makeshift jails was the fairground in Tallulah, Louisiana. The War Department dictated that the captives could be used as laborers as long as each received some small salary. It was a boon for Chicago Mill and Lumber. Cheap labor had dropped into their laps.

Now, the lumbermen were no longer interested in a refuge; after all, they could cut all the trees, harvest the timber, and sell the stripped Singer Tract parcels to local farmers. John Baker reported that Chicago Mill refused to cooperate and wouldn't deal unless forced to do so. "We are just money grabbers," said their chairman. "We are not concerned, as you folks, with ethical considerations." The ivory-bill be damned. The Singer company agreed. Fewer women were sewing, so they no longer needed to preserve the wood for future sewing machines. Ditto on the ivory-bill.

There was money to be made. Quickly. The War Department needed boxes. And here came the ultimate irony with an international twist. Part of the wood cut by the German prisoners went to the British. As author Phillip Hoose notes, "The Tallulah plant was so busy making tea chests for supplying the English army with its tea that they had a regular production line which ended in three box cars sitting side by side on the railroad siding tracks." And so went the ivory-bill's aged forest known as the Singer Tract. Trees for tea.

World War II had its share of near misses and direct hits. For the ivory-bills of the Singer Tract, it produced both. In war the innocent suffer, even if they are reclusive woodpeckers.

Epilogue

The crux of the matter—the extinction of . . . any species—is not who or what kills the last individual. That final death reflects only a proximate cause. The ultimate cause, or causes, may be quite different. By the time the death of the last individual becomes imminent, a species has already lost too many battles in the war of survival. It has been swept into a vortex of compounded woes. Its evolutionary adaptability is largely gone. Ecologically, it has become moribund. Sheer chance, among other factors, is working against it. The toilet of its destiny has been flushed.

—David Quammen

In the spring of 1942, Tanner's draft notice for the U.S. Army and commission in the U.S. Naval Reserve arrived by mail on the same day. He chose the latter, entering the navy as a lieutenant, junior grade, a junior officer who ranks above ensign and below lieutenant. He was now twenty-eight years old. A portrait of him in full-dress navy blue shows a very young man going off to war. But he was not alone. Nancy followed him to the Norfolk Naval Base in Virginia. She was now the wife of a naval radar officer.

Radar was new to the U.S. Navy. Most ships didn't have it, as their captains really didn't trust the new technology. They preferred to stand on the bridge, surveying the horizon with a good pair of binoculars. Because of Jim's education and experience as a teacher, the Naval Reserve assigned him to the CIC Group Training Center. He was to give instruction to ships' crews about the new radar systems being installed on their ships and how to integrate them into their Combat Information Centers, or CICs. The tactical center of a warship, the CIC was manned and equipped to collect and disseminate information to the ship's commanding officer. During World War II, the British were the first to fully exploit radar as a defense against aircraft attack, but the Americans would soon follow suit. For this assignment Tanner had to teach himself calculus and advanced math.

Tanner in his U.S. Navy uniform. He enlisted in the spring of 1942. (Photo courtesy of Nancy Tanner.)

Tanner spent most of the war on shakedown cruises, which test a ship's performance. But that is not to say he was out of harm's way. Most U.S. citizens were completely unaware of the amount of German U-boat activity off the Atlantic coast from Canada to the Gulf of Mexico. Numerous ships were sunk in and around Norfolk and the Chesapeake Bay. The navy kept it out of the newspapers for fear it would generate widespread panic. Nancy volunteered for the Red Cross at the hospital on the naval base and clearly remembers the night that scores of burn victims were brought in after a U.S. ship was struck, caught fire, and sank.

In early 1945 Tanner was assigned to the *U.S.S. Indianapolis* as their radar officer, but because Nancy was pregnant, Jim's commanding officer decided to let him stay stateside until his first child—a son named David—was born. The *Indianapolis* played a pivotal role in the war in the Pacific. Its top-secret mission was to deliver critical parts for the first atomic bomb to an air base on the Pacific island of Tinian. After making its delivery, the cruiser was sunk by a Japanese submarine on July 30, 1945. Only 317 of the 1,196-member crew survived; most died while adrift in the shark-infested waters. One week later, the atomic bomb dropped on Hiroshima hastened the end to the war on that side of the world.

In early 1946, with the war over, Tanner was discharged with the rank of lieutenant commander. He returned to East Tennessee State Teachers College in Johnson City, where he became an associate professor.

While Tanner was in the military, logging had continued in the Singer Tract. In May 1942 naturalist Roger Tory Peterson and his friend Bayard Christy (with guidance from J. J. Kuhn) found two female ivory-bills together near where Jim and Nancy had seen them on their last visit just six months earlier. "The question inevitably rises," Christy wrote, "will the further cutting away of the forest complete the extinction? The case of the ivory-bill seems hopeless. And I am not now intending to say that its case is not hopeless. I do, however, mean to say that we cannot be sure."

Over a year later, John Baker sent Richard Pough back to the parcel to determine how many ivory-bills remained. Although he searched for a month, he found only one lone female in a small stand of trees in John's Bayou, surrounded by devastation from logging. He also searched Mack's Bayou, which still was fairly intact, but found no ivory-bills. (Pough later went on to help found the Nature Conservancy.) In the spring of 1944, Ludlow Griscom, chair of the Audubon's board of directors and researcher at Harvard's Museum of Comparative Zoology, traveled to the Tensas. He found no ivory-bills and reported, "The whole area is full of portable sawmills. You can't get away from the sound of tractors hauling out logs. It is too late."

As something of a postmortem, wildlife artist Don Eckelberry was dispatched to document the last known ivory-bill—if possible. With Jesse Laird as a guide, Eckelberry spent nearly two weeks in the area, ultimately observing and sketching a lone bird. His watercolor of the female ivory-bill flying over a cut-over, ruined forest is haunting. (It appears in black and white in Jerome Jackson's book, *In Search of the Ivory-billed Woodpecker.*) After Eckelberry's visit, there were no more reported sightings of a *Campephilus principalis* in the Singer Tract. The ghost bird had become a true ghost in the eviscerated woodland.

In 1947 Tanner joined the faculty at the University of Tennessee in Knoxville, becoming an assistant professor of zoology. The move reunited him with an old friend. Joe Howell, who had assisted the original Cornell Expedition years before, had already been teaching in the Zoology Department at UT-Knoxville for a year.

Also in 1947 Jim joined the Knoxville Chapter of the Tennessee Ornithological Society, eventually becoming very active on the state level. He served as editor of the group's quarterly journal, *The Migrant,* from 1947 to 1955; president of the society from 1971 to 1973; and curator from 1974 to 1991. In 1953 Tanner was promoted to associate professor at the university and full professor in 1963. Very much like his mentor Arthur Allen, Tanner believed his top priority was to be a good teacher. Also like Allen, he was much loved by his students. He kept no scheduled office hours: his door was always open to whoever needed advice, either on an academic or a personal level. All of the former students with whom I spoke enthused—to the point of becoming teary-eyed—about Jim's skills as an instructor, advisor, and friend.

Although Tanner's life took him away from the ivory-billed woodpecker, he never forgot the ghost bird. Jim remained outdoorsy, taking numerous canoe trips with Nancy or son David along many of the same rivers he had explored during the 1930s: Altamaha (1965), Wakulla (1970 and '75), Suwannee (1973, re-creating with Nancy the historic 1890 trip of William Brewster and Frank Chapman), Wacissa (1975), St. Mark's (1977, '78, and '80), Satilla (1978), and Congaree (1980), as well as numerous trips to the Okefenokee Swamp between 1970 and 1989. He routinely searched the trees for any signs of ivory-bills, as old habits die hard. In June 1962 Tanner and David traveled to Mexico to hunt for the imperial woodpecker, an extinct and closely related species.

All through his life, Tanner routinely received letters and phone calls from people who sincerely believed they had just seen an ivory-bill. Tanner's dismissal of a highly publicized sighting in the Big Thicket was met with a charge that he was a "PhD snob." Yet, that suggests a professor hidden away in an ivory tower, far removed from his early fieldwork. Nothing could have been further from the truth. Any good scientist has to remain skeptical until proven wrong. In January 1968, after the report surfaced, Jim returned to Texas with Paul Sykes of the U.S. Fish and Wildlife Service. Almost thirty years after his initial visit, they found no feeding sign, no good habitat, nor any credible substantiating reports. Jim's belief that the species was not in the area remained unchanged.

In 1986 U.S. Fish and Wildlife appointed Tanner, Jerome Jackson of Mississippi State University, and Lester Short of the American Museum of Natural History to the Ivory-billed Woodpecker Advisory Committee to determine, once and for all, whether the bird was extinct or not. If the former, the bird was to be taken off the Endangered Species List. Tanner and Short were prepared to declare the ivory-bill extinct in this country, but Jackson believed that since a thorough search had not been conducted since Jim's in the 1930s, another one was needed. That task fell on Jackson.

In his 2004 book, *In Search of the Ivory-billed Woodpecker,* Jackson details his findings: "With continuing search efforts, and with the combined abilities of dozens of competent ornithologists and birders, why can we not say for certain that the ivory-bill woodpecker is gone forever? It is complex. The biology of the ivory-billed woodpecker, the attributes of its habitat, and human nature prevent a declaration of extinction from being scientifically defensible at this point. There just might be ivory-bills out there." As Jim Tanner proved, time and time again, the failure to actually find the bird in any given location does not prove that it isn't there.

In late summer 1990, doctors diagnosed Tanner with a malignant brain tumor. During a routine biopsy, a blood vessel was struck, leaving him paralyzed. He also could not speak or swallow. Jim died five months later on January 21, 1991, with Nancy and his family by his side.

On November 16, 2009, Nancy and I visited St. John's Cathedral in downtown Knoxville. It was a warm, cloudless day; a few trees still retained their fall colors. Jim's cremated remains are buried in an unmarked location in the Episcopal church's memorial garden on the southern edge of the courtyard labyrinth between the nave and great hall. Two sweetbay magnolias shade the site. At the northeast corner of the outdoor plaza is a trickling pool, a birdbath. A small bronze sign reads, "This fountain is dedicated to the glory of God and in loving memory of James T. Tanner." While we were there, a female cardinal worked her way through the ornamental shrubbery. Jim would have liked that.

Now, let us suppose for a moment that World War II had not happened and the Audubon Society had somehow been able to create five wildlife refuges in the places Jim Tanner believed the ivory-billed woodpecker was still living in the late 1930s. Could that have saved the species?

Throughout his later years, Jim Tanner was often asked: "Do you think that the ivory-bill is extinct?" His answer generally went something like, "Yes, I think they are, but I hope that I am wrong."

Thirty years after his days in the Singer Tract, Tanner turned his attention to the science of ecology. At the University of Tennessee in Knoxville, he organized the nation's first graduate-level program in ecology, serving as the its director from 1970 to 1974, eventually writing one of the field's early textbooks, *Guide to the Study of Animal Populations,* published in 1978 by UT Press. One anonymous reviewer noted, "The style is readable. In fact it is one of the few understandable texts in mathematical ecology."

As an ecologist, Tanner would have been aware of the groundbreaking work of Edward O. Wilson and Robert MacArthur. Their 1967 book, *The Theory of Island Biogeography,* changed the science and created a scientific revolution. The book presented their theory of equilibrium and the ability to predict mathematically how many species could be found on an island of a given size, the so-called species-area relationship. Simply put: size matters, and there were mathematical equations to prove it. For every tenfold increase in size, there is a twofold increase in the number of species. In time, any island reaches an equilibrium in the number of species it can support. Larger islands have a greater biodiversity. Species come to the island through immigration (floating, flying, or swimming) and leave through local extinction, but the overall number of species remains roughly the same. The theory was easy to test on isolated islands, particularly if they were small. After MacArthur's untimely death, Wilson (with the help of graduate student Dan Simberloff) proved that stripped of all fauna, an island would return, in time, to equilibrium, roughly the same number of species that it had in the beginning, although it might not be the same species.

Wilson and MacArthur's concept could be applied to more than just islands lost at sea. It could be used on islands created on the mainland under natural conditions, or as David Quammen writes, "As humanity chops the world's landscape into pieces, those pieces become islands too. A nature reserve, by definition, is an island of protection and relative stability in an ocean of jeopardy and change." The Singer Tract was a good example of this. Because of the clear-cutting going on around it, it had become an island, much smaller than the original, vast stretch of swampy forest it had been. And for every tenfold decrease in size, there was a twofold decrease in the number of species that could live there.

Tanner was also probably aware of the work of Frank Preston, who posited that if you carve out a refuge, it is not possible to create an exact replica with the same number of species as the larger ecosystem of which it had once been a part: smaller islands support fewer species than larger ones. Ecologist Jared Diamond calls this phenomenon "relaxation of equilibrium"; others call it "ecosystem decay." Quammen writes, "The relaxation is actually a loss of species, as the species number came to equilibrium again at a new, lower level commensurate with the new, smaller area of the insular patch."

Whether or not Diamond and Preston were correct was a matter of much debate in the late 1970s—the so-called SLOSS, or "single large or several small," question. Was a single large refuge vastly better than several small ones close together? In other words, if you could not create one large refuge, it wasn't worth the effort to create several small ones. It was an all-or-nothing approach. Ecologist Dan Simberloff balked at this notion, contending that we don't have enough information to rule out the importance of several small sanctuaries in our conservation planning.

If Preston is correct, however, the species that would lose out are the largest and most rare—in the case of the Singer Tract, the ivory-bill. So poof. There's actually a mathematical formula suggesting that the ghost bird had already lost the battle for survival.

Yes, ecologist Jim Tanner knew what he knew, sincerely believing that the birds were extinct. But he hoped he was wrong.

A modern-day postscript: despite the mathematical formulas, could the ivory-bill really still exist? Bayard Christy, who was one of the last to see the ivory-bills in the Singer Tract, pondered their extinction but wondered how we could be sure. As Scott Weidensaul asks in *The Ghost with Trembling Wings,* how do you demonstrate beyond any doubt that they are *not* here? How do you prove a negative? One whisper of hope comes from an observation Richard Pough made when he visited the Singer Tract at the end of 1943. Pough observed the one remaining female ivory-bill feeding on "relatively small Nuttall oaks," but he didn't see the bird stray into the adjacent cutover areas. It appeared to be trapped, isolated from the rest of the world. Tanner, on the other hand, had witnessed the birds feeding "quite a bit" in the cutover slashes. He also knew that they were capable of flying great distances.

Could the species be living in second- and third-growth forests, shuttling from place to place, always on the go, moving from one small swampland to another? Do such transients really exist, only to be observed every few years by someone lucky enough to be in the right place at the right time? Supposed sightings over the past three decades have raised that possibility. In August 2005 *Birder's World* magazine published a list of twenty-one reported noteworthy ivory-bill sightings from 1950 to 2004. The observations range from the Big Cypress in Florida to the Neches River Swamp in Texas. The list was compiled by ivory-bill expert Jerome Jackson. Four received considerable scrutiny and media attention. There were the photos, allegedly taken in the Atchafalaya Basin in 1971, that George Lowery received from an anonymous source. There was David Kulivan, who reported seeing an ivory-bill in the Pearl River Swamp in 1999. And, in 2004, there were the much-publicized sightings by kayaker Gene Sparling and several others in Arkansas's Big Woods—sightings that set off the most recent round of Cornell-backed searches, which were finally suspended in 2009.

To the above list, we add the most recent. In 2005 a group of well-experienced birders affectionately called "The Other Guys"—Brian Rolek, Geoffrey Hill, Dan Mennill, Tyler Hicks, and Kyle Swiston—announced that they had observed several ivory-billed woodpeckers along the Choctawhatchee River in the Florida panhandle. Hill is an ornithology professor at Auburn University. Like the Cornell group in 2004, he knows his birds. In May 2006 Hill and his coauthors published a paper on their findings in the online journal *Avian Conservation and Ecology.* As Jerome Jackson quipped, "The truth is out there." Finding it is the bugaboo.

Could it be possible? Could the species actually stay hidden from us, its persecutors? Hope really *is* the thing with feathers, because if we can find the bird and save it, it would perhaps prove that we are not quite as bad as we often think we are.

As poet Emily Dickinson wrote, "Sweet is the swamp with its secrets." And sweet are the secrets indeed.

Appendix

Jim Tanner's Itinerary, 1937–1939

1937

Jan. 14–17	Groton Plantation, SC
Jan. 18–19	Savannah River, SC
Jan. 20–25	Altamaha River, GA
Feb. 3–4	Royal Palm, FL
Feb. 6–13	Big Cypress, FL
Feb. 16–17	Fort Christmas, FL
Feb. 19–23	Ocklawaha River, Ocala, FL
Feb. 24–26	Gulf Hammock, FL
Feb. 26–27	Lower Suwannee, California Swamp, FL
Mar. 4–5	Indian House Hammock, FL
Mar. 8–9	Lower Suwannee, California Swamp, FL
Mar. 12–15	Wakulla, FL
Mar. 16	Panama City, FL
Mar. 21–July 15	Singer Tract, LA
June 15–16	Ayer's Tract, LA
June 29–30	Black Bear Bottoms, LA
July 3	Avery Island, LA
July 7–9	Ponchatoula cypress swamp, LA
July 19–24	Steward's Neck: Santee, SC
Dec. 1–11	Steward's Neck: Santee, SC
Dec. 12–22	Singer Tract, LA

1938

Feb. 14	Tombigbee River Bottoms, AL
Feb. 15–June 6	Singer Tract, LA
June 8–9	Tensas River Bottoms, LA
June 10–12, 16	Boeuf River Bottoms, AR & LA
June 13–15	Tensas River Bottoms, LA
June 17–18	White River Waterfowl Refuge, AR
June 20–22	Yazoo Delta, MS

June 24–29	Singer Tract, LA
June 30–July 1	Ayer's Tract, LA
July 1–2	Back Bear Bottoms, LA
July 4–8	Atchafalaya Basin, LA
July 9	West Feliciana Parish, LA
July 14–15	Big Thicket, TX
July 18–19	Bunn's Bluff, TX
July 23–26	Big Thicket, TX
July 29	Caddo Lake, TX
July 30	Sulphur River Bottoms, TX
Aug. 1–6	White River Waterfowl Refuge, AR
Aug. 8–16	Singer Tract, LA
Aug. 19	Pearl River Bottoms, MS & LA
Aug. 22	Pascagoula River swamp, MS
Aug. 23	Mobile Bay, AL
Nov. 27–Dec. 11	Steward's Neck: Santee, SC
Dec. 12–14	Pee Dee River Bottom, SC
Dec. 16–18	Santee Bottom, SC
Dec. 23	Black Oak Island: Santee, SC
Dec. 31	Highlands Hammock, FL

1939

Jan. 2	Highlands Hammock, FL
Jan. 3–Feb. 9	Big Cypress, FL
Feb. 11	Highlands Hammock, FL
Feb. 13–15	Green Swamp, FL
Feb. 17–18	Fort Christmas, FL
Feb. 19	Jane Green Swamp, FL
Feb. 23–28	Suwannee Swamp, FL
Mar. 2–3	Gulf Hammock, FL
Mar. 7–9	Wacissa River, FL
Mar. 10–11	Bear Bay, FL
Mar. 14–17	Apalachicola River Bottoms, FL
Mar. 23–May 25	Singer Tract, LA
May 22	D'Arbonne swamp, LA
May 30–June 7	Apalachicola River Bottoms, FL
June 15–16	Canoochee River, GA
June 15–16	Okefenokee, GA
June 17	Savannah River, SC
June 19–23	Black Oak Island, Santee, SC
Nov. 29–Dec. 7	Black Oak Island, Santee, SC

Author's Note and Acknowledgments

Thank you for reading this book about Jim Tanner and the ivory-billed woodpecker. I could have easily written five hundred or six hundred pages on the topic, but books have to be contained.

As with a two-and-a-half-hour "rough cut" of a movie that has to be trimmed down to two hours, the last two months of editing were all about nipping scenes and background information. So, in keeping with the movie analogy, I invite you to visit the "special features" section online. It contains deleted scenes and other background information that I collected but was unable to include in the final product. Here is the Web address: http://stephenlynbales.blogspot.com/2010/04/deleted-scenes.html.

Writing a book is a journey, an incredibly long journey. Its course is unpredictable, its obstacles unforeseen, its demands on your time unrelenting, but like any adventure it has a beginning, a middle, an end. And I have come to the end.

Along the way I met many people, who helped refine my peregrination. At the beginning of this book, I acknowledged Nancy Tanner, the wife of the late Jim Tanner. Without Nancy's help and encouragement, this book would not exist.

Many others also played a role. Additionally, I thank Eleanor Brown, curator for media and digital collections, and the other helpful archivists at the Carl A. Kroch Library, Cornell University, Ithaca, New York; Jennifer Smith, administrative assistant, communications and marketing, Cornell Lab of Ornithology, Ithaca; Judy Bolton, Leah Jewett, and Rebecca Miller at the Hill Memorial Library, Louisiana State University in Baton Rouge; Geneva Williams, Hermione Museum, Madison Historical Society, Tallulah, Louisiana; and Stan Howarter, Tensas River National Wildlife Refuge, Tallulah.

A nod of appreciation also goes to fellow ivory-bill scribes Christopher Cokinos, Tim Gallagher, and Dr. Noel Snyder for their words of support; friends Patty Ford, Janet Lee McKnight, Gordon and Judy Gibson; my Ijams Nature Center family, which includes Peg Beute, Paul James, Pam Pekto-Seus,

Sheila Goforth, Louise Conrad, Kara Jill Remington, Kimberly Womack, Sally Judiscak, Jennifer Moore, Paul Forsyth, Emily Boves, Sarah Brobst, Ed Yost, Ben Nanny, Sabrina DeVault, and Marielle Robertson; and my University of Tennessee Press family, which includes Scot Danforth, Kerry Webb, Stan Ivester, Thomas Wells, Lisa Davis, Cheryl Carson, Tom Post, Maryann Reissig, Barbara Karwhite, Stephanie Thompson, Chad Pelton, Kelsey Hicks, David Brill, and especially Gene Adair, the manuscript editor who patiently helped craft this work into its final form.

And, of course, my supportive family: mother Helen; sister Darlene and her family, David, Leighanna, Michael, and Logan Brett; and my two loving at-home bibliophiles, Karen Sue and Rachael, who patiently tiptoed around the house, watching me put that "woodpecker book" together.

Well, it's together. Bless your patience, but you're not the first to wait on a ghost bird.

Bibliography

PRINCIPAL SOURCES

Unpublished Materials

Howarter, Stan. Interview with the author, January 10, 2007. Mr. Howater is a wildlife biologist with the Tensas River National Wildlife Refuge, LA.

Tanner, James Taylor. Papers. #2665. Division of Rare and Manuscript Collections, Cornell University Library. Box 1, folders 1, 2, 3, 4, 5, and 8. This collection, which includes Tanner's 1935–39 field notes, reports, letters, and other personal papers, was the main source for this book.

———. "Sound Recording for a Natural History Museum." Master of science thesis, Cornell University, June 1936.

Tanner, Nancy. Interviews with the author, 2005–08.

Williams, Geneva. Interview with the author, January 9, 2007. Ms. Williams is director of the Hermione Museum, Madison Historical Society, Tallulah, LA.

Whitehead, Edith Kuhn, to Nancy Tanner. Personal handwritten letters about Ms. Whitehead's father, J. J. Kuhn. April 2007. Copies in possession of the author.

Published Works

Allen, Arthur A. "Hunting with a Microphone the Voices of Vanishing Birds." *National Geographic* 71, no. 6 (June 1937): 697–723.

———. "Vacationing with Birds." *Bird-Lore,* January–February 1924, 212–13.

Allen, Arthur A., and P. Paul Kellogg. "Recent Observations on the Ivory-billed Woodpecker," *The Auk* 54, no. 2 (April 1937): 164–84.

Tanner, James T. "A Forest Alive." *Living Bird* 24, no. 3 (Summer 2005): 37–41.

———. *The Ivory-billed Woodpecker.* 1942. Reprint, Mineola, NY: Dover Publications, 2003.

———. "A Postscript on Ivorybills," *Bird Watcher's Digest,* July–August 2000, 52–59.

———. "Three Years with the Ivory-billed Woodpecker, America's Rarest Bird," *Audubon Magazine,* January–February 1941, 5–14.

ADDITIONAL SOURCES

Al-Nassir, Wafa, Michelle V. Lisgaris, and Robert A Salata. "Brucellosis." *eMedicine* Web site: http://emedicine.medscape.com/article/213430-overview.

"The Audubon Research Fellowship Plan." *Bird-Lore* 38, no. 6. (November–December 1936): 444–46.

Banham, Russ. *The Ford Century.* New York: Tehabi Books, 2002.

Benét, William Rose. "A Remembrance of Will Cuppy." *Saturday Review of Literature,* October 15, 1949, 40.

Bent, Arthur Cleveland. *Life Histories of North American Woodpeckers.* New York: Dover Publications, 1964.

Beyer, George. "The Ivory-billed Woodpecker in Louisiana." *The Auk* 17, no. 2 (April 1900): 99.

Birkhead, Tim. *The Wisdom of Birds: An Illustrated History of Ornithology.* New York: Bloomsbury USA, 2008.

Brand, Albert R. "Bird Voices in the Southland." *Natural History,* February 1936, 127–38.

———. *Hunting with a Mike: The Voices of Vanishing Birds.* Self-published, 1935.

———. *More Songs of Wild Birds.* New York: Thomas Nelson and Sons, 1936.

Bransilver, Connie, and Larry W. Richardson. *Florida's Unsung Wilderness: The Swamps.* Englewood, CO: Westcliffe Publishers, 2000.

Brinkley, Douglas. *Wheels for the World.* New York: Viking Penguin, 2003.

Churchill, Winston. "Their Finest Hour." Speech before House of Commons, June 18, 1940. The Churchill Centre and Museum at the Cabinet War Rooms, London, Web site: http://www.winstonchurchill.org/learn/speeches/speeches-of-winston-churchhill/122-their-finest-hour.

Christy, Bayard. "The Vanishing Ivory-bill." *Audubon Magazine,* March–April 1943, 99–102.

Daniel, Clifford, ed. *Chronicle of the 20th Century.* Mount Kisco, NY: Chronicle Publications, 1982.

Dennis, John V. *The Great Cypress Swamps.* Baton Rouge: Louisiana State University Press, 1988.

Dickinson, Emily. "Poem 254" and "Poem 1740." In *The Complete Poems of Emily Dickinson,* edited by Thomas H. Johnson, 116, 705. Boston: Little, Brown and Co., 1951.

"East Tennessee State Normal School." *Johnson's Depot* (Web site devoted to Johnson City, Tennessee, history): http://www.johnsonsdepot.com/normal/normal.htm.

Fishman, Gail. *Journeys through Paradise: Pioneering Naturalists in the Southeast.* Gainesville: University Press of Florida, 2000.

Fitzpatrick, John W. "Ivory-bill Absent from Sounds of the Bayous." *Birdscope* 16, no. 3 (Summer 2002). Published by the Cornell Lab of Ornithology and available online: http://www.birds.cornell.edu/Publications/Birdscope/Summer2002/ivory_bill_absent.html.

Gallagher, Tim. *The Grail Bird.* New York: Houghton Mifflin Company, 2005.

Graham, Frank. *The Audubon Ark: A History of the National Audubon Society.* New York: Alfred A. Knopf, 1990.

Howell, Thomas R., and John P. O'Neill. "In Memoriam: George H. Lowery, Jr." *The Auk* 98, no. 1 (Jan. 1981): 159–58.

Hoose, Phillip. *The Race to Save the Lord God Bird.* New York: Melanie Kroupa Books, 2004.

Jackson, Jerome A. *In Search of the Ivory-billed Woodpecker.* Washington, D.C.: Smithsonian Books, 2004.

Johnson, Josephine W. *The Inland Island.* New York: Simon and Schuster, 1969.

Kessler, Jerome. "The Big Three." *Cassinia,* no. 31 (1938–41): 31–32.

Lodge, Thomas E. *The Everglades Handbook: Understanding the Ecosystem.* Boca Raton, FL: CRC Press, 2005.

Loughmiller, Campbell, and Lynn, comps. and eds. *Big Thicket Legacy.* 1977. Reprint, Denton: University of North Texas Press, 2002.

Lowery, George H. *Louisiana Birds.* Baton Rouge: Louisiana Wild Life and Fisheries Commission and Louisiana State University Press, 1955.

Nelson, Megan Kate. *Trembling Earth: A Cultural History of the Okefenokee Swamp.* Athens: University of Georgia Press, 2005.

Niedrach, Robert J., and Robert B. Rockwell. *Birds of Denver and Mountain Parks.* Denver, CO: Denver Museum of Natural History, 1939.

O'Reilly, John. "South Florida's Amazing Everglades." *National Geographic* 77, no. 1 (January 1940): 115–42.

Pearson, T. Gilbert. *Birds of America.* Garden City, NY: Doubleday & Company, 1917.

Peterson, Roger Troy. *All Things Reconsidered: My Birding Adventures.* Boston: Houghton Mifflin, 2007.

Pettingill, Olin Sewall. "In Memoriam: Arthur A. Allen." *The Auk* 85, no. 2 (April–June 1968): 192–202.

Pitts, T. David. "Dr. Joseph C. Howell, 1913–1998" *The Migrant* 69, no. 1 (1998): 27–28.

Quammen, David. *The Song of the Dodo: Island Biogeography in an Age of Extinctions.* New York: Scribner, 1996.

Rooney, Bill. "Once upon a Century: A Magazine for the Ages, History of *American Forests* Periodical," part 2, *American Forests,* March–April 1994. Available online at http://www.highbeam.com/doc/1G1-15295482.html.

Roosevelt, Franklin D. "Proclamation 2425—Selective Service Registration." *American Presidency Project* (Web site maintained by John Woolley and Gerhard Peters at the University of California, Santa Barbara): http://www.presidency.ucsb.edu/ws/index.php?pid=15858.

Rosen, Jonathan. *The Life of the Skies: Birding at the End of Nature*. New York: Picador, 2009.

Russell, Franklin. *The Okefenokee Swamp*. New York: Time-Life Books, 1973.

"Science: Sad Birds," *Time*, March 17, 1941. Available online at http://www.time.com/time/magazine/article/0,9171,765300,00.html.

Snyder, Noel F. R. *The Carolina Parakeet: Glimpses of a Vanished Bird*. Princeton, NJ: Princeton University Press. 2004.

Sprunt, Alexander, IV. "In Memoriam: Robert Porter Allen." *The Auk* 86 (January 1969): 26–34.

Steinbeck, John. *The Grapes of Wrath*. New York: Viking Press, 1939.

Stoddard, Herbert L. *Memoirs of a Naturalist*. Norman: University of Oklahoma Press, 1969.

Sutton, George Miksch. *Birds in the Wilderness*. New York: Macmillan Co., 1936.

Vonnegut, Kurt. *Galápagos*. New York: Delacorte Press, 1985.

Walters, Mark Jerome. *A Shadow and a Song: The Struggle to Save an Endangered Species*. Post Mills, VT: Chelsea Green Publishing Co., 1992.

Way, Albert G. "Burned to Be Wild: Herbert Stoddard and the Roots of Ecological Conservation in the Southern Longleaf Pine Forests." *Environmental History* 11, no. 3 (July 2006): 500–526.

Weidensaul, Scott. *The Ghost with Trembling Wings*. New York: North Point Press, 2002.

Williams, Frank B., Jr. "East Tennessee State University." In *The Tennessee Encyclopedia of History and Culture*, edited by Carroll Van West. Knoxville: University of Tennessee Press. Online edition: http://tennesseeencyclopedia.net/imagegallery.php?EntryID=E005.

Wordsworth, William. "The World Is Too Much with Us." In *Selected Poetry of William Wordsworth*, edited by Mark van Doren, 515–16. New York: The Modern Library, 2001.

Index

A

Adventures of Robin Hood, The, 166
Akeley 35mm ciné camera, 40, 45, 76, 84
Akeley, Carl Louis Gregory, 40
Alexander, S. C., 239, 241, 243
Allen, Dr. Allen A., ix, 3, 5, 7–12, 15–17, 22–25, 27, 29–31, 35, 36, 38–41, 43–45, 48, 49, 51, 53–58, 61–65, 67–71, 73–77, 79–86, 88, 92, 93, 97, 102, 107, 118, 176, 188, 197, 234, 236, 250
Allen, Elsa, 25
Alligator Bayou, Singer Tract, LA, 114, 154, 162, 163, 203, 240
Altamaha River, GA, 96, 215, 250
American dippers, 80, 81
American Forestry Association's Dixie Crusaders, 18
American Museum of Natural History, 7, 12, 24, 40, 174, 250
American Ornithologists' Union, AOU, 11, 24, 34, 64, 90, 166, 192
American Red Cross, 239, 248
Amonette, LA, 114
Andrew's Bend, Singer Tract, LA, 117, 126, 154, 157, 208, 240, 242
Apalachicola River, bottomland, FL, 97, 193–95, 211, 212, 221
anhinga, 30
Antler's Hotel, Colorado Springs, CO, 68
Atchafalaya Basin, Swamp, LA, 123, 124, 166, 167, 253
Audubon, John James, 3, 89, 120
Audubon magazine, 89, 233, 234
Audubon Research Fellowship Plan, 91–93
Auk, The, 64, 107, 125, 192, 203, 234
Avery Island, LA, 51–54, 124
avian botulism, 80
Avian Conservation and Ecology, online journal, 253
Ayer Tract, LA 122

B

Baby Bunting, 207, 209, 240
Bachman's warbler, 120
Bailey, Alfred M., 76, 77
Baker, John Hopkinson, 91, 92, 93, 95, 127, 175, 236, 239, 244, 245, 249
bald cypress, 30
Ball, Moultrie, 179, 216
Bang's Disease, brucellosis, undulant fever, 151
Bartram, William, 3, 190
Baynard, Oscar E., 180, 187, 188
Bayou de View, AR, 162
Bayou des Ourses, LA, 167
Bayou Petit Anse, LA, 51
Bear River Migratory Bird Refuge, UT, 80
Beard, A. M., 123, 165
beetles: ivory–bill food, 26, 44, 106, 120, 140, 221, 231
Beyer, Dr. George, 34, 125
Big Cypress, FL, 95, 100, 101, 179, 181–86, 221, 253
Big Thicket, TX, 169, 250
Big Woods, AR, 253
Billy's Lake, GA, 215
Bird City, 51, 52, 124
Birder's World magazine, 253
Birdlore magazine, 26, 91, 95, 201, 233

Birdsong Nature Center, 19
Birkhead, Tim, 7, 199
Black Bear Bottoms, LA, 166
Black Oak Island, SC, 179, 216, 222, 223
Black Sunday, 55
Blackwater Swamp, FL 99
Blickensderfer, Clark, 77
blue line, 115, 206, 208
Boeuf River, LA, 160, 161
Boggy Slough, Singer Tract, LA, 205
Bosco, 158
Bowlegs, Chief Billy, 214
Boyle Swamp, GA, 215
Brand, Albert, 7, 10–12, 15, 23–25, 28, 43, 197
Breaux, Kennedy, 125, 167
Breaux, Norman, 167, 186
Brewster, William, 250
Bristol Hotel, Oklahoma City, OK, 59
Bronx County Bird Club, 192
Brookgreen Gardens, 178
Brown, Belvin, 155, 159, 172
Brown, Dewey, 182, 183
Browne, W. E., 28, 29, 98
Bulter, Edward, 168
Burleigh, Tom, 173, 211
Burroughs, John, 85
burrowing owl, 57, 58

C

Cache River National Wildlife Refuge, AR, 162
California condor, 92
Camp Ephilus, 44, 48
Carolina parakeet, 180, 190, 192, 212, 222
Carter, J. J., 173
Carter, Mannie, 96, 215
Cash, Pete, 162
Catesby, Mark, 3
Chamberlain, E. Burnham, 179
Chandler, Marvin, 186, 187
Chapman, Frank, 7, 10, 250
Charley Bowlegs Creek, FL, 181
Charleston Museum, 95, 179
Charlie, the horse, 147–50, 155–59, 170, 172, 205; photo of, 147
Charlie's Aunt, 238
Chicago Mill and Lumber, 122, 123, 239, 241, 243–45
Chinese Checkers, 185, 191
Choctawhatchee River, FL, 253
Christmas Bird Count, 34, 132
Churchill, Prime Minster Winston, 227
Christy, Bayard, 249, 253
Civil Conservation Corps (CCC), 133, 181
Civil Defense, 239
Cochran, Ed, 47, 105, 130, 135
Cokinos, Christopher, 3
Colorado Museum of Natural History, 68
Colorado Rockies, 68
Congaree River, SC, 250
controlled burns, 18
Conyer, Tom, 182
Cooper's hawk, 102, 202
Cornell Expedition of 1935, 13, 15–88, 97, 124, 133, 221, 239, 249
Cornell University, Cornell Lab of Ornithology, ix, 4–13, 16, 23, 37, 79, 88, 92, 93, 144, 162, 173, 223
Cornell's Macaulay Library, 10
Corrington, J. D., 211
Cortland, New York, 12, 69
Cory, Charles B., 90
Craven's Hammock, GA, 214
Creature from the Black Lagoon, 21
crested caracara, Northern, 28
Crystal Night, 175
Cuppy, Will, 237
Curtler, Martin, 203, 204
cypress dome (definition), 98
cypress, bald, 98

D

D'Arbonne Swamp, LA, 209
Davidson, Verne, 49, 54, 56, 68
Davidson Ranch, 54, 55, 67
Daspit, Armand P., 34, 197
Dead Lakes, FL, 212

Dennis, John V., 97, 165, 212
Denton, Drew, 149, 152, 208
Denton, Sam, 106, 155, 198–200
Despair Bayou, Lake, Singer Tract, LA, 111, 131, 133, 157, 165
DeVry, Herman, 45
DeVry movie camera, 44
Diamond, Jared, 65, 252
Dickerson, Dr. L. M., 61, 62
Dickinson, Emily, 254
Dinwiddie, S. C., 214
Dishroom Bend, Singer Tract, LA, 149, 150, 1529
Doe, Charles, 190, 191
Douglas, Ernest, 182
Dufaycolor color film, 145
Dunne, Pete, 102
dusky seaside sparrow, 26
Dust Bowl, 54, 55, 56, 67
Dutcher, William, 91

E

East Crossing, Big Cypress, FL, 100, 185, 186
East Hanson, Big Cypress, FL, 186
East Tennessee State Normal School, 225
East Tennessee State Teachers College, 225, 227, 249
East Tennessee State University, 236
Eckelberry, Don, 249
Edgerton, Claude, 166
Endangered Species List, 250
Everglades National Park, FL, 99, 181
Eyemo, Bell & Howell camera, 28

F

Fakahatchee Strand, Big Cypress, FL, 100
Field and Stream magazine, 89
Florida Museum of Natural History, 189, 191
Ford, Model A: introduction of, 94, 95; photo of, 147; 152; cost of, 219
Fort Christmas, city of Christmas, FL, 24, 26, 27, 188
Fort Wilkinson, 17
Foster, Foster's Plantation, LA, 63, 64, 109, 117, 155, 172
Foster, Stephen, song "Swanee", 189
Fox-Case Movietone Corporation, 9
Francis Marion National Forest, SC, 176
Frederick, Charlie, 166
Frost, Robert, 208

G

golden eagle, 68–71, 73–76, 79, 140, 146
Golden Triangle, TX, 169
Gone with the Wind, Margaret Mitchell, 176
Gordon Hotel, Lafayette, LA, 49
Gowanloch, James, 197
Graflex camera, 45
Grapes of Wrath, The, 56
Great Depression, 55, 91, 133, 175, 239
Great Divide Basin, 79
great egret, 52, 53
Great Flood of 1927, 37, 167
Great Plains, 68, 86
Great Plume War, 52
Green, Ralph Waldo, 15
Green, Charlotte Hilton, 15
Green Swamp, FL, 188
Greenlaw Hotel, New Orleans, LA, 172
Greenlea Bend, Singer Tract, LA, 112, 114, 115, 118, 126, 159, 161, 171, 204, 208, 240, 244
Grey, John, 157, 158
Grimes, Sam, 28, 195
Grinnell, George Bird, 89
Griscom, Ludlow, 249
Groton Plantation, SC, 95
Gulf Hammock, FL, 95, 101, 191, 221

H

Haeckel, Ernst, 109
Hahn, Paul, 103
Hallman, Roy, 195
hammock, head, (definition), 96
Hanson, Stanley, 100, 184, 185

Harding, President Warren G., 226
Harvard University, 225, 226, 227
Hauptmann, Bruno Richard, 6
Hawks of North America, The, 91
heath hen, 56
Hebard, Charles, 213
Hebard Lumber Company, 214
Hell Hole Swamp, SC, 176
Hemenway, Harriet, 90
Henry's Lake, ID, 82
Hicks, Tyler, 253
High Plains, 69, 70
Highland Hammock, FL, 179, 180, 181, 187, 221
Hill, Geoffrey, 253
Hillsborough River State Park, FL, 180
Hilton, Charlotte, 15
Hitler, Adolf, 133, 197, 226, 231
Hollis, Avery, 62
Homer, NY, 12
Hoose, Phillip, 13, 245
Hopkins, John M., 213, 214
Horseshoe Lake, Singer Tract, LA, 156
Hovey, Percy L., 178
Howell, Joe, 23, 24, 102, 249
Hudson, Charles, 189
Hunter's Bend, Singer Tract, LA, 133, 147, 149, 150, 151, 152, 157, 165

I

Ijams Nature Center, 27, 141
Indian House Hammock, FL, 101
Island Hotel, Cedar Keys, FL, 189
Ithaca, NY, 6, 7, 10, 15, 23, 43, 63, 85, 88, 178, 184
ivory-billed woodpecker: discovery of 1935 nest, 38, 39; first recording of, 40–44; description of 1935 nest site, 41; specimen collecting, 103; 1937 nest site, 107; description of 1937 fledging, 109; description of 1937 nest hole, 113, 114; double–rap description, 132; 1938 nest, 136–38; banding nestling 1938, 140–44; color photos of 145, 147, 204; habitat requirements vs. pileated's, 156, 236; habitat requirements, 171; 1939 nest site, 201; beetles species preferred, 221; last seen at Singer Tract, 249
Ivory-billed Woodpecker Advisory Committee, 250

J

Jackson, Jerome, 249, 250, 253, 254
Jefferson, Levi, 122
Jim Creek, FL, 101
John's Bayou, Singer Tract, LA, 38, 39, 43, 47, 64, 106, 109, 115, 126, 130, 131–33, 136, 139, 140, 145, 146, 147, 148, 156, 158, 171, 172, 199, 200, 201, 203, 205, 206, 207, 208, 239, 240, 241, 243, 244, 249
Johnson, Josephine, 2
Johnson City, TN, 225, 227, 228, 230
Jones, Ensign Thomas Ray, 238
Jones, Governor Sam, 239, 244
Jungle Gardens, 52, 54

K

Keane, Peter, 11
Kellogg, Peter Paul, 4, 8, 9–12, 15, 16, 22, 24–27, 30, 31, 35, 40, 41, 43–45, 48, 49, 51, 53, 54–56, 61–63, 67, 68, 70, 73, 74, 76, 79, 80, 81, 83–86, 88, 92, 102, 176, 188, 234
Kelly, Walt, Pogo, 215
Kessler, Jerome, 201–3
Kissimmee Prairie, FL, 24
Kissimmee Billy Strand, Big Cypress, FL, 100, 182, 184, 186
Knoxville Chapter of the Tennessee Ornithological Society, 249
Kodachrome, 77
Komarek, Ed, 18
Kroodsma, Donald, 138
Kuerzi, Dick, 192
Kuhn, Joseph Jenkins, (J. J.) ix, 34, 36, 38–41, 43, 62–64, 105–7, 109, 112–15, 117–19, 124, 126, 129, 131, 132, 135,

140–60, 162, 163, 165, 166, 170, 198, 211, 221, 228, 239, 249
Kulivan, David, 253

L

Laird, Jesse, 199, 203, 205–9, 249
Lake Carters, LA, 111, 126, 154, 162
Lake Nick, LA, 117, 155
Lake Pontchartrain, Swamp, LA, 125
Lake Providence, LA, 160
Laughton, Blois, 152
Lavigne, Dan, 125
Leche, Governor Richard, 198
Leopold, Aldo, 18
lesser prairie chicken, 49, 56–58, 67
limpkin, 21, 22
Lindbergh, Charles, 6, 9, 94
Little Bear Lake, LA, 106, 115, 126
Lodge, Thomas E., 181
Logan Canyon, UT, 79, 80, 81
Lostman's Key, FL, 99
Louisiana State University, LSU, 34, 144, 145, 166, 173, 197
Lowery, George, 34, 166, 197, 253

M

MacArthur, Robert, 251, 252
Mack's Bayou, LA, 118, 133, 140, 146, 147, 148, 152, 153, 154, 155, 162, 172, 205, 207, 249
Mack's Bayou Pete, 153, 154, 157, 205, 241
Madison Parish, LA, 34, 64
Main Strand, Big Cypress, FL, 100, 181, 182, 183
Mammoth Hot Springs, 86
Manywings (Bird Sanctuary), 28, 98
Mardi Gras, 238
May, John B., 91
McCulloch, George, 101
McIlhenny, Edward Avery, 51, 90, 124, 126
Melamphy, George, 127
Mennill, Dan, 253
Merritt Island, FL, 26, 27, 97
Methiglum Bayou, Singer Tract, LA, 36, 105, 106, 110, 111, 112, 117, 118, 120, 123, 126, 130, 131, 135, 140, 147, 149, 150, 153, 155, 158, 159, 162, 170, 199, 240
Migrant, The, 249
Milledgeville, GA, 16
Mills Bayou, LA, 155, 207
Milner Hotel, Macon, GA, 127
Minnie's Lake, Minnie's Run, GA, 215
Mizell, Sam, 214, 215
Montana Gun Club, 83
Montgomery Hotel, Tallulah, LA, 33, 61, 105, 129, 228
Morgan, J. P., 106, 113, 126, 130
Mount Holyoke College, 226
mountain plover, 70–72, 74
Mullens, William, 7

N

National Association of Audubon Societies, 12, 64, 91, 127, 132, 159, 168, 174, 187, 219, 233
National Audubon Society, The, 35, 89, 236, 243, 251
National Geographic Magazine, 28, 77, 197, 234
National Geographic Society, 15,
Naughty Marietta, 59
Natural History magazine, 197
Navy Blue and Gold, 238
Nazi Germany, 105, 133, 175, 197, 226, 231, 248
Neches River, Swamp, TX, 253
New Years Eve, 1940–41: 231–33
New York State Audubon Plumage Law, 90
Niedrach, Robert J., 68–70, 73, 74, 76, 77, 81
normal school, 225

O

O'Conner, Flannery, 17
O'Reilly, John, 187
Oastler, Dr. Frank, 64
Ocala National Forest, FL, 101

Okefenokee Swamp, GA, 190, 212–15, 250
Oklahoma Dust Storm, 45, 55–58
Osceola, 99

P

Page, Ike, 36, 40, 41, 43; photo of, 37
Parker, Jim, 198, 199, 240
Parker, John, 168
Parson, Frank, 190
Pascagoula Swamp, River, MS, 211
Pearl Harbor, 237
Pearle River, LA, 125, 173, 173, 253
Pearson, T. Gilbert, 4, 64, 168
Pee Dee River, SC, 178
Peterson, Roger Tory, 127, 135, 249
Pettingill, Olin, 8
Pickle, Frank, 189
Piedmont Hotel, Atlanta, GA, 17
Pierre Part, LA, 167
Pike's Peak, 68
pileated woodpecker, 35, 37, 38, 65, 96, 99, 101, 109, 119, 125, 128, 131, 161, 165, 168, 170, 177, 181, 182, 184, 185, 189, 209
plume trade, plume hunters, 90, 168
Pough, Richard, 244, 249, 253
POWs, German, 244
prairie chicken, 68
prairie falcon, 68, 74, 76
Preston, Frank, 252

Q

quail, 18
Quaintance, Dr. Charles, 227
Quammen, David, 65, 247, 252
Quimby, LA, 63, 117, 135

R

Rainey Lake, LA, 114, 118, 120, 126, 131, 159
Red Rock Lake, Upper and Lower, MT, 82, 83
relaxation of equilibrium, theory of, 252
Rex Hotel, Eudora, AR, 161
Rockwell, Robert, 77
Rolek, Brian, 253
Rose Bowl, 238
roseate spoonbill, 168, 179
Rosen, Jonathan, vi, 2
Rooftree, W. L., 239
Roosevelt Lodge, 86
Roosevelt, President Franklin Delano, 133, 175, 228, 237, 238
Roosevelt, President Theodore, 90, 168
Royal Palm State Park, FL, 99
Royalls, J. B., 192
Russell, Frank, 214, 231

S

sandhill crane, 25, 27, 28
Santee-Cooper Dam, 216, 223
Santee River, swamp, bottomland, SC, 95, 127, 128, 129, 175, 215
Satilla River, GA, 250
Savannah River, GA, 95, 215
Savannah River Wildlife Refuge, 215
Sawyer, Edmund Joseph, 85
Sears & Roebuck, cost of boots, 219
Selective Service and Training Act, 228
Selous, Edmund, 7
Seminoles: 100; colorful dress, 183, 184; reservation, 184; Second Seminole War, 184; Tanner visit, 185, 188
Semple, John Bonner, 24, 25
Shakespeare's Romeo and Juliet, 92
Sharkey Road, Singer Tract, LA, 36, 38, 47, 63, 107, 109, 111, 120, 130, 131, 146, 148, 170, 172, 198, 201, 203, 204, 209, 239, 240, 241, 242
Sharkey Plantation, 47, 115, 147, 153, 208
Shannon, J. E., 101
Sheedy, Burnham, 235
Sheedy, Joseph Edward, 226
Sheedy, Ella, 232, 234, 235
Sherwood Plantation, 17, 19, 103, 180
shinnery, 56, 57, 58, 68
Shokes, Hollie, 127, 177, 222

Short, Lester, 250
Sibley, David Allen, 102
Simberloff, Dan, 252
Singer Manufacturing Company, 47
Singer Tract, LA: Cornell 1935 trip to, 36–49, 55, 59; second Cornell 1935 trip to, 61–65, 95; Tanner first 1937 trip to, 105–23; Tanner second 1937 trip to, 129–32; first 1938 trip to, 135–63; second 1838 trip to, 170–72; Tanner 1939 trip to, 197–209, 221, 222; Tanner 1940 trip to, 228–30; Tanner 1941 trip to, 239–42; 243, 249, 252, 253
Smith, Bud, 153
snowy egret, 51, 52, 53, 90
Snyder, Dr. Noel, 180, 187, 190
Song of the Dodo, The, 65
Songs of Wild Birds, 11
Sonny Boy; ix, first use of name, 199–202, 204, 205, 206, 207, 243
Southern Forest Experiment Station, 172
Sparling, Gene, 253
Speaker, Dr., 135, 147, 159, 163
Spencer, Mason, Mason Spencer cabin, 4, 35, 105, 117, 118, 125, 130, 159, 165, 198, 203, 204, 240
Spindletop oil strike, 169
Sprunt, Alexander, Jr., 95, 127, 129, 130, 175, 179, 216
St. John's River, 22, 23, 26, 101, 188, 192
St. John's Cathedral, 251
St. Mark's River, FL, 250
strand (definition), 100
Stanford, Professor J. S., 80
Stanley, Ed, 83
Stanolind Oil Company, 168
Steinbeck, John, 55, 56
Steward's Neck, SC, 127, 129, 177, 222
Stoddard, Herbert, 17, 18, 19, 21, 22, 33, 103, 180, 211, 214
Stresemann, Erwin, 7
Summerall, Frank, 184, 185
Sutton, Dr. George Miksch, 29, 31, 35, 36–41, 236
Suwannee River, FL, 97, 102, 189, 190, 191, 250
Suwannee Canal Company, 213
Swainson's warbler, 112
swamp (definition), 97, 98
Swiston, Kyle, 253
Sykes, Paul, 250

T

Tabasco Sauce, 51–54
Tall Timbers Research Station, 19
Tallulah, LA, 33, 35, 37, 49, 61, 63, 105, 107, 126, 129, 131, 135, 145, 149, 238
Tamiami Trail, FL, 99, 182
Tanner, Betsy, 1
Tanner, Clifford, 12
Tanner, David, 1, 248, 250
Tanner, Edward, 180
Tanner, James Taylor: birth, childhood, 12, 13; master's thesis 92; began Audubon fellowship, 93; PhD dissertation, 223; first teaching position, 227; marries Nancy, 235; book published, 236; military service, 247–248; ecologist, 251; publishes Guide to the Study of Animal Populations, 251; death, 251
Tanner, Jane, 1
Tanner, Nancy Burnham Sheedy, x, 1, 144, 225–38, 241, 242, 247–51
Taylor Creek, FL, 25, 26, 97, 99
Ten Thousand Islands, FL, 100
Tensas River, bottomland, LA, 33, 34, 106, 243
Tensas River National Wildlife Refuge, 144, 155
Theory of Island Biogeography, The, 251
Thickahatchie Swamp, Big Cypress, FL, 100, 183, 186
Thompson, Colonel L.S., 17
Thompson, Jack, 160
Thomson, Mark, 168
Tillman, Jack, 212
Time magazine, 234, 237
Times Square, New York City, 231

Titepaper section, Singer Tract, LA, 118, 133, 145, 146, 154, 155, 162, 163, 205–7, 209
Tobacco Road, Erskine Cardwell's novel, Jack Kirkland's play, 176
Tombigbee Bottoms, AL, 135
Tosohatchee Game Preserve, 101
Tosohatchee Creek, FL, 101
Trudeau Sanitarium, 235
trumpeter swan, 81–85
tuberculosis, 236

U

U.S. Navy, 238, 247
U.S.O., 239
U.S.S. Indianapolis, 248
University of California at Berkeley 92
University of Florida, 188, 189
University of Tennessee, 24, 249
Utah State Agricultural College, 80

V

Van Hyning, George, 103, 104
Van Hyning, Dr. Thompson H., 188, 189, 191
Village of Saranac Lake, NY, 235
Vonnegut, Kurt, 2

W

Wacissa River, bottomland, FL, 192, 193, 250
Wadmacon Island, SC, 127, 129, 177, 178, 216, 222
Wakulla National Forest, FL, 103
Wakulla Springs, River, FL, 21, 29, 195, 250
Walsh, Lester, 127, 175
Ward, Jesse, 161
Wayne, A. T., 103
Wee Tee Lake, SC, 178
Weidensaul, Scott, 253
Westover Plantation, 17
Wewahitchka, FL, 212
Wheeler, Lester, 225
Whiden, Dempsey, 185
white line, 115, 118, 123, 126, 131, 206, 241
White River, White River Waterfowl Refuge, AR, 161, 162, 170
Whitehead, Edith, ix, 34, 198
whooping crane, 179
wildlife management, 18
wildlife sanctuary, 91
wild turkey, 17, 30, 42, 109, 111, 127, 199
Willet, Gus, 198, 199, 203
Williams, Fred, 160, 161
Williams, Geneva, 239
Willis Swamp, Landing, FL, 193, 212
Wilson, Alexander, 3
Wilson, E. O., 251, 252
Winters, Dr. Robert, 172
World War II, 226, 245, 247, 251
Worley, Ma and Pa, 227
Works Progress Administration (WPA), 133, 216
wolf, 145, 146
wood duck: eggs, 112, 113

Y

Yellowstone National Park, 85, 86

6340224